SECONDARY DATA ANALYSIS

SECONDARY DATA ANALYSIS

An Introduction for Psychologists

Edited by
Kali H. Trzesniewski, M. Brent Donnellan,
and Richard E. Lucas

American Psychological Association • Washington, DC

Published by
American Psychological Association
750 First Street, NE
Washington, DC 20002
www.apa.org

To order
APA Order Department
P.O. Box 92984
Washington, DC 20090-2984
Tel: (800) 374-2721; Direct: (202) 336-5510
Fax: (202) 336-5502; TDD/TTY: (202) 336-6123
Online: www.apa.org/pubs/books/
E-mail: order@apa.org

In the U.K., Europe, Africa, and the Middle East, copies may be ordered from
American Psychological Association
3 Henrietta Street
Covent Garden, London
WC2E 8LU England

Typeset in Goudy by Circle Graphics, Inc., Columbia, MD

Printer: Maple-Vail Book Manufacturing Group, York, PA
Cover Designer: Mercury Publishing Services, Rockville, MD

The opinions and statements published are the responsibility of the authors, and such opinions and statements do not necessarily represent the policies of the American Psychological Association.

Library of Congress Cataloging-in-Publication Data

Secondary data analysis : an introduction for psychologists / edited by Kali H. Trzesniewski, M. Brent Donnellan, and Richard E. Lucas. — 1st ed.
 p. cm.
 Includes bibliographical references and index.
 ISBN-13: 978-1-4338-0876-0 (print)
 ISBN-10: 1-4338-0876-5 (print)
 ISBN-13: 978-1-4338-0877-7 (electronic)
 ISBN-10: 1-4338-0877-3 (electronic)
1. Psychology—Methodology. 2. Psychometrics. I. Trzesniewski, Kali H. II. Donnellan, M. Brent. III. Lucas, Richard E. (Richard Eric), 1971- IV. American Psychological Association.

 BF39.S39 2011
 150.72'1—dc22
                                        2010010687

British Library Cataloguing-in-Publication Data

A CIP record is available from the British Library.

Printed in the United States of America
First Edition

CONTENTS

CONTRIBUTORS

Matthew DeBell, Stanford University, Stanford, CA
M. Brent Donnellan, Michigan State University, East Lansing
Nicholas R. Eaton, Washington University, St. Louis, MO
Karen Fingerman, Purdue University, West Lafayette, IN
Melissa M. Franks, Purdue University, West Lafayette, IN
Kevin J. Grimm, University of California, Davis
Jon A. Krosnick, Stanford University, Stanford, CA
Robert F. Krueger, Washington University, St. Louis, MO
Todd D. Little, University of Kansas, Lawrence
Richard E. Lucas, Michigan State University, East Lansing
Eva Matthews, University of Arizona, Tucson
John J. McArdle, University of Southern California, Los Angeles
Katherine M. McKnight, Pearson Education, Fairfax, VA
Patrick E. McKnight, George Mason University, Fairfax, VA
Laura Miller, Messiah College, Grantham, PA
Daniel K. Mroczek, Purdue University, West Lafayette, IN
Jaime L. Napier, Yale University, New Haven, CT
Michelle B. Neiss, Oregon Health & Science University, Portland
JoAnne McFarland O'Rourke, University of Michigan, Ann Arbor

Amy M. Pienta, University of Michigan, Ann Arbor

Lindsay Pitzer, University of Notre Dame, Notre Dame, IN

Kristopher J. Preacher, University of Kansas, Lawrence

Stephen T. Russell, University of Arizona, Tucson

Gita M. Sawalani, University of Wisconsin—Eau Claire

Daniel Schneider, Stanford University, Stanford, CA

Jürgen Schupp, German Institute for Economic Research, Berlin, Germany

Constantine Sedikides, University of Southampton, Hampshire, England

Patrick E. Shrout, New York University, New York, NY

Thomas Siedler, German Institute for Economic Research, Berlin, Germany

Jim Stevenson, University of Southampton, Hampshire, England

Kali H. Trzesniewski, University of Western Ontario, London, Canada

Nick Turiano, Purdue University, West Lafayette, IN

Evert Van de Vliert, University of Groningen, Groningen, The Netherlands

Gert G. Wagner, German Institute for Economic Research, Berlin, Germany

Keith F. Widaman, University of California, Davis

J. Douglas Willms, University of New Brunswick, Fredericton, Canada

SECONDARY DATA ANALYSIS

INTRODUCTION

M. BRENT DONNELLAN, KALI H. TRZESNIEWSKI,
AND RICHARD E. LUCAS

We have sometimes joked that there is no good reason to collect new data, given the wealth of existing data sets that can be used to answer important research questions. These existing resources are often longitudinal and usually have sample sizes that are larger than most samples typically found in psychological research. Unfortunately, our enthusiasm for the analysis of secondary data sets such as the National Longitudinal Study of Adolescent Health (Add Health), the British Household Panel Study (BHPS), the General Social Survey (GSS), the German Socioeconomic Panel Study (GSEOP), and Monitoring the Future (MTF) is not always widely shared by our colleagues. We have even encountered a few psychologists who dismiss the importance of studies from these data sets. Nonetheless, the analysis of secondary data sets is common in allied fields such as sociology and economics, and the practice is gaining acceptance in psychology (see, e.g., the 1991 special section of *Developmental Psychology*; Brooks-Gunn & Chase-Lansdale, 1991). One potential barrier to greater acceptance of secondary data analysis, however, is that the methodological training of many psychologists does not introduce them to this approach.

Accordingly, the overarching purpose of this book is to fill this gap by providing an accessible introduction to secondary data analysis. We use the term *secondary data analysis* largely to refer to the existing national studies like Add Health, the BHPS, and MTF. However, we also use the term more loosely to refer to archives of existing data that are available to researchers who were not involved in the original data acquisition (see, e.g., Chapter 13, this volume). Specifically, we hope this volume provides readers with an introduction to the research possibilities that can be realized through the analysis of existing data and provides psychologists with a set of accessible methodological primers that can help them begin their own secondary data analyses. This book is designed to serve as a springboard for the further development of methodological skills and is not presented as an exhaustive compendium that covers all of the issues (Bulmer, Sturgis, & Allum, 2009). To facilitate further learning, the authors present a list of recommended readings at the end of each chapter.

WHY BOTHER LEARNING ABOUT SECONDARY DATA ANALYSIS?

We are extremely enthusiastic about the potential for secondary data analyses to advance psychological science. However, we recognize that there are several issues that researchers should consider when thinking about secondary data analysis. Indeed, it is reasonable to ask whether a researcher should take on the challenge of analyzing existing data. The effective analysis of existing resources is deceptively time consuming and requires some degree of quantitative sophistication. It is possible to underestimate the time, effort, and analytical acumen required to use existing data sets. And for this reason, we do not recommend secondary data analysis to researchers who are not well versed in multivariate analysis and basic issues of psychological measurement.

More broadly, we can identify several advantages and disadvantages of secondary data analysis, and we encourage readers to carefully consider these issues (see also Hofferth, 2005) before undertaking any secondary data analytic project. Researchers who undertake these analyses should do so with a clear sense of the pros and cons of this approach.

The most significant advantage is that the data have already been collected. This, of course, has the potential to save quite a bit of time in a research project because the primary investigator does not need to design a new study and collect a new set of data. But more important, the types of data that are typically archived tend to be higher quality than could be obtained by individual researchers. Many existing data sets (e.g., Add Health, BHPS, GSEOP) are often longitudinal, and they typically have large sample sizes obtained using elaborate sampling plans. Thus, these resources can be used to generate estimates that are representative of large populations of interest (e.g., high school seniors in the United States). Many of these resources are free or available at a very low cost to qualified researchers. Thus, learning how to analyze secondary data sets can provide individual researchers with the raw material to make important contributions to the scientific literature using data sets with impressive levels of external validity. This advantage is the primary reason we advocate secondary data analysis.

A second advantage is that the analysis of secondary data sets encourages an "open source" approach to science. Researchers using the same resource should be able to replicate findings using similar analyses. This fact encourages careful reporting of analysis and a reasoned justification for all analytic decisions (e.g., explaining why certain covariates are included in a given model). Moreover, researchers who might wish to test alternative explanations can use the same resources to evaluate competing models. Thus, we believe that the analysis of secondary data sets encourages transparency, which in turn helps facilitate scientific progress. It should certainly help researchers develop good habits such as fastidious record keeping and careful attention to detail.

Despite these notable advantages, there are also several disadvantages associated with secondary data analysis. The first, and primary, disadvantage is the flip side of the major advantage—the data have already been collected. The user of an existing resource may not have all of the information about data collection procedures or important details about problems that occurred during data collection. And more important, there is no guarantee that any existing data set will be useful for addressing the particular research question of primary interest to a given researcher. We want to stress the perspective that high-quality research should proceed first and foremost from an important (and, ideally, interesting) question that is informed by theoretical concerns or glaring gaps in knowledge. Good research is motivated by great questions, and this holds for all forms of research. The purpose of analyzing data is to refine the scientific understanding of the world and to develop theories by testing empirical hypotheses.

The second disadvantage is that there is a significant investment of time and energy required to learn any particular existing data set. These start-up costs become a central concern because of the risk that someone else will be pursuing answers to the same research questions. There is a real possibility that a new researcher might be "scooped" by someone using the same data set that the researcher has chosen to analyze.

A third disadvantage is one that is probably of most concern to psychologists. That is, the measures in these existing resources are often abbreviated because the projects themselves were designed to serve multiple purposes and to support a multidisciplinary team. Many of these data sets have impressive breadth (i.e., many constructs are measured) but with an associated cost in terms of the depth of measurement (i.e., constructs may be measured by only a few survey items). For example, at least two of us are very interested in global self-esteem, and it is exceedingly rare to find existing studies that have administered all 10 items of the widely used Rosenberg (1965) Self-Esteem Scale. Rather, it is quite common to find studies that administered a subset of the Rosenberg items (see, e.g., Trzesniewski & Donnellan, 2010; Trzesniewski, Donnellan, & Robins, 2003) or studies that administered alternative measures of self-esteem that are unique to that project (e.g., the Add Health data set; see Russell, Crockett, Shen, & Lee, 2008). This fact can create concern among psychologists who are used to evaluating studies based on the entire set of items associated with conventional measures.

Measurement concerns are therefore a major issue in secondary data analysis, and these issues frequently require some amount of defending in the peer-review process. For example, short forms tend to have lower levels of internal consistency than parent scales, given how the alpha coefficient is calculated (see Chapter 4). On the one hand, this reduction does not always mean that the predictive validity of a given scale will be dramatically impaired. On the other hand, short forms may have such reduced content that they end up assessing a much narrower construct than the original scale. Thus, basic issues of reliability and validity are of paramount concern when conducting secondary data analyses. Researchers who do not have a good grounding in psychometrics might be frustrated because they are not able to carefully evaluate trade-offs in reliability and validity (for a good summary of psychometric issues, see Clark & Watson, 1995). However, for those researchers with even basic quantitative training (or for those willing to acquire this training), the analysis of existing data is a useful skill to have in their tool kit.

A fourth disadvantage has to with the potential for "fishing" exercises (e.g., searching for significant correlations instead of testing hypotheses) that can be undertaken with existing resources. Different researchers will find this concern more or less compelling, given their views on statistical significance testing. We list this as a disadvantage because colleagues, tenure-review committees, and reviewers might be among those researchers who are extremely concerned about the potential for data exploitation. Our view is that all findings need to be replicated and that the actual risks associated with fishing are often overstated (see Rosenthal, 1994, p. 130). That is, there seems to be little reason to dismiss findings from secondary analyses simply because of concerns of increased Type I errors. The data have an important story to tell regardless of how many articles have been published from a project. The fact that resources are often publicly available also helps to counterbalance fishing concerns because others are able to verify the robustness of the results across different ways of operationalizing the variables and different ways of formulating statistical models.

The fifth disadvantage is a practical one that can have real consequences for developing academic careers. There is a real possibility that original data collection might be more highly regarded in some fields and some departments than others (see also McCall & Appelbaum, 1991). This can be a significant disadvantage for new professors looking to build a strong case for tenure or promotion. Local norms vary widely across departments, and the best advice is to be aware of the local culture. Our view is that academic departments should value scholarly contributions regardless of whether the underlying data were newly collected or whether they were extracted from a publicly available archive. We hope that this perspective will become more widespread as more and more psychologists engage in secondary data analysis. On a related point, most existing data sets are correlational in nature, and this places considerable limits on the causal inferences that can be drawn from any analyses. This fact may affect the extent to which secondary data analysis is valued within subdisciplines within psychology.

On balance, however, we believe that the advantages of secondary data analysis often outweigh the disadvantages. Accordingly, we are convinced that this is a valuable approach to research for psychologists to learn. This book is intended to make this argument by showcasing important research findings that have emerged from secondary data analyses and to provide an introduction to the key methodological issues. We endorse the perspective of strategic replication, or the idea that scientific advances occur when researchers submit hypotheses to a number of different tests using diverse forms of data. To the extent that findings replicate across different forms of data, researchers can have increased confidence in their verisimilitude. Likewise, failures to replicate findings using large and diverse samples often afford the opportunity to learn about the boundary conditions for particular propositions. In short, we believe that the analysis of secondary data sets has a definite place in psychological research. It is one important way of testing empirical hypotheses and thus can contribute to the development and refinement of theories.

OVERVIEW OF THE BOOK

The book is divided into two major sections. The first section is a practical guide to the analysis of secondary data. These chapters cover basic methodological issues related to getting started (Chapters 1 and 2), measurement issues (Chapter 3), sample weighting (Chapter 4), and handling missing data (Chapter 5). The final chapter in this section (Chapter 6) discusses innovative methodological techniques that are typically not associated with secondary data but that are becoming increasingly available. Although these chapters cover methodological issues that are particularly relevant for secondary data analysis, we believe that many of these chapters will be of general methodological interest. Indeed, the discussions of measurement and missing data analysis offer insights that transcend secondary data analysis and apply to many areas of psychological research. We should also caution readers that our coverage of some topics is sparse, especially in terms of survey response artifacts and sampling schemes. Accordingly, we refer readers to good introductions to survey methodology by Dillman, Smyth, and Christian (2009) and de Leeuw, Hox, and Dillman (2008).

The second section contains illustrations of secondary data analyses from leading researchers who have used these analyses to make substantive contributions to topical areas in psychology. This list includes behavioral genetics (Chapter 8), clinical psychology (Chapter 9), life-span developmental psychology (Chapters 7 and 10), cross-cultural psychology (Chapter 11), political psychology (Chapter 12), and intellectual development (Chapter 13). These chapters describe key substantive findings and therefore provide concrete examples of the kinds of contributions that secondary data analysis can make to psychological science. All of these chapters conclude by identifying key data sets in respective content areas and offer recommended readings. These example data sets will provide readers of similar interests with useful starting points for their own work.

Readers interested in nuts and bolts issues may want to read all of the chapters in the first section and then selectively read chapters in the second section that are most relevant to their substantive areas. However, those who want an introduction to the promise of secondary analysis techniques may want to begin by reading chapters in the second section to gain exposure to the broad range of questions that can be answered using secondary data. These chapters offer vivid testaments to our proposition that secondary data analysis can make crucial contributions to psychological science. Moreover, the substantive findings described in these chapters are quite interesting, regardless of the techniques that were used. After gaining insight into the possibilities that can be achieved with secondary analysis, readers can approach the chapters in the first section for basic instruction about how to approach secondary data analysis. In short, we hope that the chapters in this book provide strong motivation and the necessary practical guidance that will enable them to use this important class of techniques in their own work.

FOR FURTHER READING

Brooks-Gunn, J., Berlin, L. J., Leventhal, T., & Fuligini, A. S. (2000). Depending on the kindness of strangers: Current national data initiatives and developmental research. *Child Development, 71,* 257–268.

The authors provide an overview of several data sets that are useful for developmental research and reflect on the how these resources can be used to make substantive contributions in both scientific and public policy contexts.

De Leeuw, E. D., Hox, J. J., & Dillman, D. A. (Eds.). (2008). *International handbook of survey methodology*. New York, NY: Taylor & Francis.

This edited volume provides an introduction to the myriad issues associated with survey research.

Dillman, D. A., Smyth, J. D., & Christian, L. M. (2009). *Internet, mail, and mixed-mode surveys: A tailored design method* (3rd ed.). Hoboken, NJ: Wiley.

This classic textbook can help researchers design their own surveys and better understand research based on surveys. Chapters on sampling and the psychology of asking questions are particularly helpful.

Elder, G. H., J. R., Pavalko, E. K., & Clipp, E. C. (1993). Working with secondary data: Studying lives. *Quantitative applications in the social sciences* (Sage University Paper Series No. 07-088). Beverly Hill, CA: Sage.

This short monograph provides clear guidance regarding the steps necessary to take advantage of existing archives with particular attention to conceptual issues related to measurement. The lead author is well known for his work as an architect of life course theory.

Hofferth, S. L., (2005). Secondary data analysis in family research. *Journal of Marriage and the Family, 67*, 891–907.

This piece provides a clear introduction to the major issues in secondary data analysis that have wide applicability beyond family research.

Kiecolt, K. J., & Nathan, L. E. (1985). Secondary analysis of survey data. *Quantitative applications in the social sciences* (Sage University Paper Series No. 07-053). Beverly Hill, CA: Sage.

Although it is over 20 years old, this book provides important guidance about making use of existing resources.

McCall R, B., & Appelbaum, M. I. (1991). Some issues of conducting secondary analyses. *Developmental Psychology, 27*, 911–917.

The authors provide a straightforward discussion of many basic methodological issues related to secondary data analysis.

RECOMMENDED DATA SETS

The following web links are useful starting points for finding secondary data sets:

- *University of Michigan's Interuniversity Consortium for Political and Social Research (ICPSR):* http://www.icpsr.umich.edu/. The ICPSR's Data Use Tutorial is particularly helpful: http://www.icpsr.umich.edu/ICPSR/help/newuser.html.
- *Howard W. Odum Institute for Research in Social Science at the University of North Carolina at Chapel Hill:* http://www.irss.unc.edu/odum/jsp/home.jsp

- *Roper Center of Public Opinion Research at the University of Connecticut:* http://www.ropercenter.uconn.edu/
- *Henry A. Murray Research Center at the Institute for Quantitative Social Science:* http://www.murray.harvard.edu/frontpage

REFERENCES

Brooks-Gunn, J., & Chase-Lansdale, P. L. (1991). (Eds.). Secondary data analyses in developmental psychology [Special section]. *Developmental Psychology, 27,* 899–951.

Bulmer, M. I. A., Sturgis, P., & Allum, N. (Eds.). (2009). *The secondary analysis of survey data.* London, England: Sage.

Clark, L. A., & Watson, D. (1995). Constructing validity: Basic issues in objective scale development. *Psychological Assessment, 7,* 309–319. doi:10.1037/1040-3590.7.3.309

de Leeuw, E. D., Hox, J. J., & Dillman, D. A. (Eds.) (2008). *International handbook of survey methodology.* New York, NY: Erlbaum.

Dillman, D. A., Smyth, J. D., & Christian, L. M. (2009). *Internet, mail, and mixed-mode surveys: The tailored design method* (3rd ed.). New York, NY: Wiley.

Hofferth, S. L. (2005). Secondary data analysis in family research. *Journal of Marriage and the Family, 67,* 891–907. doi:10.1111/j.1741-3737.2005.00182.x

McCall R, B., & Appelbaum, M. I. (1991). Some issues of conducting secondary analyses. *Developmental Psychology, 27,* 911–917. doi:10.1037/0012-1649.27.6.911

Rosenberg, M. (1965). *Society and the adolescent self-image.* Princeton, NJ: Princeton University.

Rosenthal, R. (1994). Science and ethics in conducting, analyzing, and reporting psychological research. *Psychological Science, 5,* 127–134. doi:10.1111/j.1467-9280.1994.tb00646.x

Russell, S. T., Crockett, L. J., Shen, Y.-L., & Lee, S.-A. (2008). Cross-ethnic invariance of self-esteem and depression measures for Chinese, Filipino, and European American adolescents. *Journal of Youth and Adolescence, 37,* 50–61. doi:10.1007/s10964-007-9231-1

Trzesniewski, K. H., & Donnellen, M. B. (2010). Rethinking "Generation Me": A study of cohort effects from 1976–2006. *Perspectives in Psychological Science, 5,* 58–75. doi:10.1177/1745691609356789

Trzesniewski, K. H., Donnellan, M. B., & Robins, R. W. (2003). Stability of self-esteem across the life span. *Journal of Personality and Social Psychology, 84,* 205–220. doi:10.1037/0022-3514.84.1.205

I

METHODOLOGIES FOR SECONDARY DATA USE

1

GETTING STARTED: WORKING WITH SECONDARY DATA

AMY M. PIENTA, JOANNE McFARLAND O'ROURKE,
AND MELISSA M. FRANKS

Secondary data are those data that have been made available for use by people other than the original investigators. These data are typically preserved and disseminated by an organization that has a stated mission to preserve the data for the long term or in perpetuity. Most data that have been archived are quantitative (e.g., survey data), but increasingly, qualitative data (e.g., interview transcripts, open-ended question responses) and other nonquantitative data (e.g., audio, video) are being archived for secondary use. This chapter focuses mainly on the use of existing data that have a quantitative component, including data from studies that involved mixed data collection methods.

Secondary data analyses have been important for a number of years to scholarship in various disciplines, such as sociology, economics, and political science. Additionally, use of secondary data has been expanding in other disciplines that have not traditionally used such data, including psychology, family science, and various health science disciplines. Nonetheless, the value of secondary data remains an important topic of debate in the social sciences. Such debate initially was spurred by a series of National Research Council reports and more recently by the 2003 publication of the National Institutes of Health's (NIH; 2003) *Statement on Sharing Research Data*. This document from NIH and a similar one from the National Science Foundation Directorate for Social,

Behavioral, and Economic Sciences (n.d.) reinforce the long-held expectations placed on grantees to make data available for others to use.

NIH's policy is designed to encourage scientists to share research data with the goal of advancing science. The benefits of sharing data have been widely discussed and understood by researchers for many years. A central part of Kuhn's (1970) scientific paradigm is the replication and confirmation of results. Sharing data is at the core of direct replication (Anderson, Greene, McCullough, & Vinod, 2008; Freese, 2007; Kuhn, 1970). The foundation of the scientific process is that research should build on previous work, where applicable, and data sharing makes this possible (Bailar, 2003; Louis, Jones & Campbell, 2002). The argument has been made, and there is some evidence to support it (King et al., 1995), that sharing data and allowing for replication makes one's work cited more frequently. The nature of large data sets virtually guarantees that a single researcher (or team) will not be able to use the data set to its full potential. Thus, sharing data ensures that resources spent on data collection are put to the best use possible and the public benefit is enhanced.

Finally, secondary data are crucial in the education of undergraduate and graduate students (Fienberg, 1994; King, 2006). It is not feasible for students in a semester-long course to collect and analyze data on a large scale. Using secondary data sets allows students to experience science firsthand. Instructors can also use the metadata accompanying secondary data to teach students about research and exemplary study designs, and the results obtained from even simple analyses can be used to illustrate the use of scientific evidence in support of arguments (Sobal, 1981).

FINDING EXISTING DATA

Research data are currently shared in many different ways, ranging from informal dissemination to formal archiving. Data are often stored and disseminated through established data archives, such as the Interuniversity Consortium for Political and Social Research (ICPSR) and the other major U.S.-based archives described later. Research data in these archives generally reach a large part of the scientific community because of the wide reach of these organizations. Also, data in formal archives typically include information about the data collection process, as well as any missing data imputations, weighting, and other data enhancements. These are referred to as *metadata*, or data about data. These data archives have written policies and explicit practices to ensure long-term access to the data they hold that include replicated copies stored offsite and a commitment to the migration of data storage formats as technology changes. Five major archives in the United States are described next, and their web addresses are provided in the section Recommended Data Sets.

The Howard W. Odum Institute for Research in Social Science at the University of North Carolina at Chapel Hill was founded in 1924 for the "cooperative study of problems in the social sciences." The Odum Institute is the oldest university-based social science research institute in the United States and is probably the oldest archive of digital social science data. The institute specializes in data on the U.S. South and in state and regional public opinion polls. The institute archives the Louis Harris polls dating back to 1958. The Odum Institute data are available at no charge.

The Roper Center of Public Opinion Research at the University of Connecticut was founded in 1947. The Roper Center is the leading educational facility in the field of public opinion, with the largest archive of public opinion survey data. With its origins in the archives of pollster Elmo Roper, the center has strong relationships with commercial survey organizations, especially the Gallup Organization. The Roper Center offers individual and institutional subscriptions for access to its data.

ICPSR was founded in 1962 and is located within the Institute for Social Research at the University of Michigan. ICPSR is the largest nongovernmental social science data archive in the world and currently has more than 600 institutional members. ICPSR began as a repository for political science and university-based research data. It now has world-class data holdings in many fields, including health, education, aging, criminal justice, economics, substance abuse and mental health, and population. ICPSR is the archival home to many studies of interest to psychologists, such as the Midlife in the United States study and the Project on Human Development in Chicago Neighborhoods (PHDCN). Faculty, staff, and students at ICPSR member institutions can download archival data at no charge. Others are charged a fee for accessing a particular data collection of interest. Most data held by ICPSR's topical archives, which are funded by foundations and federal agencies, are publicly available at no cost. All documentation related to ICPSR's archival data is free for exploration.

The Electronic and Special Media Records Service Division, National Archives and Records Administration (NARA), was established in 1968. The division preserves and provides access to permanent electronic records created by or received by the U.S. federal government. Thus, the electronic data collection is wide ranging and includes a variety of data collections that would be of interest to psychologists. For example, NARA archives the American Soldier in World War II Surveys, 1942–1945. This collection provides soldiers' responses to psychometric screenings and a large scope of attitudinal measures.

The Henry A. Murray Research Center at the Institute for Quantitative Social Science, Harvard University, was founded in 1976. The Murray Center has important data collections related to human development, especially longitudinal and qualitative data, and data that illuminate women's lives. The

Murray's holdings are extensive and include the Block and Block Longitudinal Study. These data can also be used at no charge.

A second type of data archive has more narrowly focused collections around a particular substantive theme. Data in these thematic archives may be unique, or they may overlap with other archives, thus making the data more broadly available than they might otherwise be. For instance, the Association of Religion Data Archives is a specialty archive focusing on American and international religion data. The Cultural Policy and Arts National Archive at Princeton University is another example of a specialty data archive. It has data on the arts and cultural policy available for research and statistical analysis, including data about artists, arts and cultural organizations, audiences, and funding for the arts and culture. And finally, WebUse at the University of Maryland provides data to researchers interested in how technology generally, and the Internet specifically, affects human behavior. The web addresses for these data archives are provided in the section Recommended Data Sets.

Another type of archive is designed solely to support the scientific notion of replication. Journal-based systems of sharing data have become popular in economics and other fields as a way of encouraging replication of results (Anderson et al., 2008; Glenditsch et al., 2003). The *American Economic Review*, for example, requires authors to make data underlying their published work available on its website prior to publication in the journal. These collections can sometimes be shorter lived than the formal archives, particularly if the sustainability of their archival model relies on a single funding source. Some examples of still less formal approaches to data sharing include authors who acknowledge they will make their data available on request or who distribute information or data through a website. Researchers often keep these sites current with information about findings from the study, and publication lists, in addition to data files and metadata.

HOW TO ACCESS AND USE SECONDARY DATA SETS

Many researchers, especially those who collect their own data, may find using secondary data to be daunting. A researcher who collects his or her own data understands the nuances of the data collection methodology, the documentation and its completeness, and the data and data structure itself. Gaining familiarity with an existing data source can be challenging but can allow one to use a broader set of variables and for a larger, more representative sample than one would have access to in their own data collection. This section provides a summary of various components of secondary data collections and exploration tools that the secondary analyst should consider when evaluating an existing data collection.

Study-Level Metadata

Study-level metadata, or the study description, is typically the first aspect of existing data that is examined when a researcher evaluates how well secondary data matches his or her research needs. Most secondary data collections include a description of the scope of the data collection, including major content areas covered in the data, the time period covered by the data collection, the mode of data collection (e.g., in-person interview, telephone survey), and the sampling strategy. Thus, by examining the study description of a potential secondary data source, or comparing several descriptions, the researcher can determine whether the data are likely to meet research needs. The five formal archives listed previously have online catalogs with study descriptions that can be searched or browsed. The catalogs of these archives are a good starting point for exploring potential data collections that are available. Websites for a single data collection usually include similar information.

Documentation

The online catalogs of the major archives also point to other important elements of an existing data collection that can be useful when evaluating the use of secondary data. The documentation provides more detailed information than the study description and can be used to further determine whether a data collection suits one's research questions. Detailed information about the design of the data collection and the data are found in the documentation.

Codebooks are among the most important pieces of documentation for secondary data. Thus, the codebook is the next step for exploring an existing data collection. Codebooks typically provide a summary of the methodology underlying the data collection and important information about the provenance (ownership) of the data collection. In addition, the codebook provides a listing of all the variables in a data set(s) and should include the exact wording of the question, universe information (i.e., who was actually asked the question), unweighted frequency distributions, missing data codes, imputation and editing information, details about constructed variables, and labels that describe response codes. The codebook also typically includes information on administrative variables used to linking data files within a collection and how to properly apply survey weights.

Data collection instruments are often distributed with secondary data as well. Instruments can help one ascertain question flow and stems, skip patterns, and other crucial details for fully understanding the data collection. Review of the instruments and seeing the survey instrument as a whole helps provide the context in which a particular question was asked. This is difficult for automated data collection instruments, such as computer-assisted telephone interviews and computer-assisted personal interviews because the software programs used to produce these instruments often do not provide a version of the interview that is straightforward and easy to comprehend.

Data Format and Data Structure

Another consideration when selecting a secondary data source is data format and data structure. *Data format* typically refers to the statistical format in which data are saved or stored. For example, SPSS, SAS, and Stata are the three major statistical software packages in which quantitative data files are most commonly stored and distributed. Some sources are available in only one format, whereas some are available in a variety of formats and thus are readily accessible to a wider audience of data users. Even when data are available in only one format, there are several choices for migrating the data to one's preferred statistical package. SAS, SPSS, and Stata have the ability to import data files that are in a different format (see, e.g., Proc Import in SAS). Also, there are software packages, such as Stat/Transfer, that can be used to transfer data across formats among an even wider set of statistical packages and versions of major and minor packages.

Data structure refers to the number and organizational nature of distinct files that compose a data collection and the relationship among those data files. Many secondary data collections include only one data file, and in that data file each record (or line in the data file) represents one unit of analysis (i.e., one person, one school, one family). More complex data collections include multiple files that can be linked together using linking identifiers provided in all data files. For example, the PHDCN includes separate data files for each of the many instruments for which study participants provided data. Thus, an analyst would need to merge the data files that he or she is interested in analyzing.

Complexity of data structures is increasing among many of the major data collections. The amount of information being collected is growing larger, and storing the data in a single file becomes too cumbersome. Multiple data files are often provided when there is more than one unit of analysis or when there is a hierarchy among the files. For example, there may be a file describing schools (e.g. number of teachers and students, curricula offered) from which students were sampled and a file describing the children who were sampled from within the schools. In this instance, the analyst would need to merge files where there is not a one-to-one match across the files but rather there is a one-to-many relationship across the data files (i.e., several students may attend the same school). And finally, multiple data files are often encountered in longitudinal studies (and repeated cross-sectional studies), in which data files are created after each collection point. Like the other examples, these data files must be merged for comprehensive data analysis.

Other Data Exploration Tools

The complex nature of many data sets has spurred some data collectors to develop data extraction tools that seamlessly allow users to access all underlying data files and create analytic subsets of data without needing to have the skills required to merge the data files in SAS, SPSS, or Stata. For example, the website for the Panel Study of Income Dynamics (http://psidonline.isr.umich.edu) offers such a data extraction.

Online data analysis enables users to explore data sets using certain statistical procedures without downloading data files and without being familiar with any statistical packages. As an example, ICPSR currently offers online analysis for selected data collections using the data analysis tool, Survey Documentation Analysis (SDA), a software product developed and maintained by the University of California, Berkeley (see http://sda.berkeley.edu). Data at other archives use a variety of online analysis packages with similar capabilities. SDA allows users to select variables for analysis, perform statistical analyses, view the data graphically, recode and compute variables, and create customized subsets of variables and/or cases for download. Thus, online analysis allows a potential data user to (a) understand the types of variables available in a data collection, (b) explore the basic descriptive characteristics of the sample, and (c) easily examine bivariate and multivariate relationships within the data collection.

Analytic Constraints of Secondary Data

The most important element of understanding the match between secondary data and one's analytic needs is the extent to which the data collection includes information that is central to the theoretical (or analytic) model being tested. The analyst needs to be able to create a defensible model that includes all relevant constructs (and ensure they are represented with valid measures), as well as control variables. An existing data set may not be useful if a key construct was not assessed. For example, if there is an omitted variable, that is, a measure from the model that cannot be captured by the data, that biases the interpretation of the results, the data would not be suitable for the research question. Fortunately, most federally funded data collections are designed in consultation with panels of experts and close attention is given to including constructs and broad measures to provide the widest understanding of the issues being studied. Investigation based on scientific literature can provide the basis for these decisions.

Another consideration when selecting an existing data source is whether the data meet one's specific analytic needs. One aspect of this is whether the sample size is adequate to model the behaviors, statuses, or attitudes in which one is interested. Many of the large survey data collections have ample sample sizes to support a complex analytic model. However, certain demographic subgroups within a national or large regional sample may be difficult to study, depending on their representation in the sample and population (e.g., some groups may be oversampled to increase statistical power). This is sometimes true when analyzing certain racial and ethnic minority groups that are relatively less common in the U.S. population. As a consequence, most major data collections oversample at least the major racial and ethnic minority groups (e.g., African Americans, Latinos) so that meaningful within-group and between-groups analyses can be conducted. For statistical analyses, data must then be weighted to properly account for oversampling and other characteristics of the sample.

Finally, it is important to consider whether the study covers the appropriate time frame and/or covers aspects on change over time in a way that is consistent with one's research question. Or, a data collection may be cross-sectional in design and therefore not well suited to answering questions about change over time and/or developmental trajectories. This may limit the applicability of secondary data for certain research questions.

WORKSHOPS AND TRAINING OPPORTUNITIES

As noted earlier, working with secondary data can be challenging. Moreover, using secondary data has become increasingly difficult because of sophisticated approaches to collecting data that result in complex data structures and require a nuanced understanding of the study—but help is available. Assistance for navigating complex data collections reduces the required time and resource investment associated with learning to work with a secondary data collection. Many major data collection projects offer data user workshops that allow researchers to interact in a structured setting with both instructors and other data users. Through these interactions, researchers learn about the structure of the data and its possibilities and limitations. These meetings also allow one to spend time exploring and analyzing the data while help is on hand. One-day preconference workshops are also offered before major annual meetings. Two- to five-day day workshops are another type of training that brings prospective analysts together with data collection and analytic staff.

ICPSR has offered its Summer Program in Quantitative Methods of Social Research as a complement to its data services since the organization was formed. The Summer Program provides a program of courses in research design, statistics, data analysis, and social science methodology. Instruction is grounded in interactive, participatory data analysis using a hands-on computer laboratory component for most courses. The Summer Program at ICPSR is partitioned into two 4-week sessions. In addition, the curriculum includes special workshops that provide participants with opportunities to examine the impact of various methodologies on specific substantive issues, as well as learn more about a particular data collection. For example, the PHDCN data collection and the Changing Lives of Older Couples data have been covered in this kind of a short workshop. Participants in each year's Summer Program represent about 25 different departments and disciplines from over 200 colleges, universities, and organizations around the world. Sociology, psychology, and political science continue to represent the disciplines that attract the largest number of participants to the Summer Program.

The Summer Institute in Survey Research Techniques sponsored by the Survey Research Center, Institute for Social Research, University of Michigan, provides rigorous and high-quality graduate training in all phases of survey research. The program teaches state-of-the-art practice and theory in the design, implementation, and analysis of surveys. The Summer Institute has presented courses on the sample survey since the summer of 1948. Frequently, 1-week courses devoted to a particular archival data collection are offered in this program.

ARCHIVING PRIMARY RESEARCH DATA

In light of the benefits of working with secondary data, it is important to consider whether to archive one's own research data. Many of the data archives in the United States have comprehensive data collections and offer, without any charge to an individual researcher, the ability to archive and disseminate data to a large audience. Archiving data helps address the numerous questions raised regarding how to best preserve data: It provides standard formats and centralized locations for data. Moreover, archiving requires the investigator to document the data collection so that others can use the data. The rewards of these efforts are the greatest use of the data and ultimately, the greatest advancement of science.

Archiving data satisfies a funding obligation to share data (exemplified in the case of the NIH Data Sharing Policy). It also reduces the amount of time required by the data depositor to respond to user requests and questions. Data in most archives are also carefully reviewed and prepared so that the quality of the data and documentation files are enhanced. At most of the U.S. archives, data usage statistics can be tracked and reports about the usage of the data prepared for funders, data depositors, and others.

ICPSR distributes data and documentation to interested users at its member institutions, freeing investigators from using their own time and resources to do so and permitting other researchers to conduct secondary analysis using the data. All ICPSR products are retrievable or findable from the ICPSR website, including study descriptions. ICPSR maintains permanent backups of the data both on- and off-site (at multiple locations). ICPSR staff review deposited data to determine whether any inconsistencies or problems of respondent confidentiality exist. ICPSR prepares finding aids, including searchable study descriptions and bibliographic citations, to assist in locating the collection within ICPSR's archive. Availability of data is publicly announced on the ICPSR website through the "Recent Updates & Additions" feature. ICPSR's data are promoted at more than 10 professional association meetings each year (e.g., National Council on Family Relations, Society of Research in Child Development, American Psychological Association).

One particularly notable feature of ICPSR's service is the Bibliography of Data-Related Literature. The bibliography is a searchable database that currently contains over 43,000 citations of known published and unpublished works resulting from analyses of data held by ICPSR. The bibliography primarily includes scholarly works such as journal articles, books, book chapters, government and agency reports, working papers, dissertations, conference papers, meeting presentations, and unpublished manuscripts. The bibliographic records have been collected through standardized searches of full-text and abstracting/indexing databases, by browsing a core set of journals in the topical areas reflected in the ICPSR archive, and by soliciting submissions of publications from data depositors and authors. Thus, for any given data collection, it is easy to obtain a list of citations for publications relating to the archival data and, in many instances, ICPSR is able to provide a full-text link to the publication, depending on the arrangement the user's institution has made with ICPSR.

ICPSR preserves both public- and restricted-use data. Public-use data files are data for which direct and indirect identifiers can be removed or masked. Direct identifiers are always removed from public-use data files, typically prior to submission to ICPSR. Examples of direct identifiers include record numbers, Social Security numbers, and proper names. Single variables or combinations of indirect identifiers can also create unique records in a data set, thus creating the risk of disclosing respondent identity. By examining variables containing detailed personal characteristics such as education, income, race, ethnicity, and military service or organizational characteristics such as capacity, services offered, and programs for special populations, it quickly becomes possible to begin to narrow identity (O'Rourke, 2003). When indirect identifiers present disclosure risk, ICPSR takes steps to modify the data. ICPSR staff work closely with data depositors to resolve such disclosure issues because depositors are most familiar with the data, and in some cases, altering data reduces the amount of information available for analyses. Great care is taken to alter the data only as much as necessary to address the disclosure risk and balance analytic use with confidentiality protection (O'Rourke et. al, 2006).

Restricted data contain confidential information that could lead to the identification of respondents. For example, a data collection may have indirect identifiers removed (or masked) from a public-use version but have the full set of variables retained in a restricted data collection. This is the case when the indirect identifiers that create the disclosure risk are highly valuable for research purposes. ICPSR protects these data by maintaining them on a secure non-networked server. Individuals who apply for and complete a Restricted Use Data Agreement may obtain access to these data for legitimate research purposes. The application and agreement delineate the conditions of use pertaining to respondent confidentiality, as well as measures required for the physical safekeeping of the restricted data sets when in the researcher's possession. After both ICPSR and responsible officials at the researcher's institution sign the agreement, a copy of the data is sent on CD-ROM via registered mail to the researcher. The agreement requires that the applicant destroy the data after a set period of time and to provide ICPSR with proof of such (e.g., a sworn statement).

ICPSR also maintains a secure data enclave for data with the highest security considerations. These highly restricted data have confidentiality issues for which there is great concern regarding the sensitivity of the data and risk of disclosure, as indicated either by the depositor or ICPSR. The only form of access to such data is through on-site analysis in ICPSR's secure data enclave. To gain access to data in the enclave, a researcher applies in the same way as she or he does for access to other restricted-use data. If the application is approved, analysis is conducted under very controlled conditions. Thus, it is possible to permit access by qualified researchers to even the most highly sensitive data.

CONCLUSIONS

Whether data are archived and distributed by ICPSR, by another U.S. archive, or by the individual investigator, and whether they are in public- or restricted-use format, they represent an important record of the research accomplishments of an individual or a team. O'Rourke et al. (2006) discussed the particular importance of public-use data: The public-use [or archival] version of the data is very important because it is likely to be the only one to which most researchers, policy analysts, teaching faculty, and students will ever have access. Hence, it is the version from which much of the utility of the data is extracted and often it effectively becomes the historical record of the data collection. Large national studies containing thousands of variables are often not, nor are they necessarily intended to be, very thoroughly analyzed prior to their public release. The data are subsequently used for research, policy, and teaching purposes in the years after their release, and even decades later for comparative analysis.

Using secondary data has been common among sociologist, demographers, and political scientists. Psychologists have begun more recently to turn to secondary data in their work. The increasing availability of high-quality, longitudinal information on a wide range of topics of interests to psychologists has facilitated increasing amounts of scholarship built on these rich data sources. And, although there are significant barriers to consider when evaluating a secondary data source, the potential benefits, such as access to long-term representative samples at little to no economic cost, make secondary data an attractive option. Finding, evaluating, and accessing secondary data has become relatively easy, given the availability of data and metadata that is searchable on the websites of the various U.S.-based archives and through search engines such as Google. In exchange for loss of control about the types of questions asked of study participants, researchers using secondary data may gain the ability to understand human behavior over time (longitudinal information) and diversity across population subgroups (e.g., socioeconomic status, age, region, race/ethnicity). Moreover, in an increasingly multidisciplinary arena, psychologists have come to play a central role in the collection of large-scale social science data and have influenced the types of information that is being collected. Thus, secondary data represent an increasingly important resource for future scholarship among psychologists and in the social sciences more generally.

RECOMMENDED DATA SETS

- The Howard W. Odum Institute for Research in Social Science, University of North Carolina at Chapel Hill: http://www.irss.unc.edu/odum
- The Roper Center of Public Opinion Research, University of Connecticut: http://www.ropercenter.uconn.edu/
- Interuniversity Consortium for Political and Social Research: http://www.icpsr.umich.edu
- Electronic and Special Media Records Service Division, National Archives and Records Administration: http://aad.archives.gov/aad/
- The Henry A. Murray Research Center at the Institute for Quantitative Social Science, Harvard University: http://www.murray.harvard.edu/
- Association of Religion Data Archives: http://www.thearda.com/

- The Cultural Policy and Arts National Archive, Princeton University: http://www.cpanda.org/
- WebUse, University of Maryland: http://www.webuse.umd.edu/

REFERENCES

Anderson, R. G., Greene, W. H., McCullough, B. D., & Vinod, H. D. (2008). The role of data/code archives in the future of economic research. *Journal of Economic Methodology, 15*, 19–119.

Bailar, J. C., III. (2003, October). *The role of data access in scientific replication*. Paper presented at the Access to Research Data: Risks and Opportunities: Committee on National Statistics, National Academy of Sciences conference, Washington, DC.

Fienberg, S. E. (1994). Sharing statistical data in the biomedical and health sciences: Ethical, institutional, legal, and professional dimensions. *Annual Review of Public Health, 15*, 1–18. doi:10.1146/annurev.pu.15.050194.000245

Freese, J. (2007). Replication standards for quantitative social science: Why not sociology? *Sociological Methods & Research, 36*, 153–172. doi:10.1177/004912410 7306659

Glenditsch, N. P., Metelits, C., & Strand, H. (2003). Posting your data: Will you be scooped or will you be famous? *International Studies Perspectives, 4*, 89–95.

King, G. (2006). Publication, publication. *Political Science & Politics, 39*, 119–125.

King, G., Herrnson, P. S., Meier, K. J., Peterson, M. J., Stone, W. J., Sniderman, P. M. et al. 1995. Verification/replication. *Political Science & Politics, 28*, 443–499.

Kuhn, T. (1970). *The structure of scientific revolutions*. Chicago, IL: University of Chicago Press.

Louis, K. S., Jones, L. M., & Campbell, E. G. (2002). Sharing in science. *American Scientist, 90*, 304–307.

National Institutes of Health. (2003, February 26). *Final statement on sharing research data*. Retrieved from http://grants.nih.gov/grants/policy/data_sharing/

National Science Foundation Directorate for Social, Behavioral, and Economic Sciences. (n.d.) *Data archiving policy*. Retrieved from http://www.nsf.gov/sbe/ses/common

O'Rourke, J. M. (2003). Disclosure analysis at ICPSR. *ICPSR Bulletin, 24*, 3–9.

O'Rourke, J. M., Roehrig, S., Heeringa, S. G., Reed, B. G., Birdsall, W. C., Overcashier, M., & Zidar, K. (2006). Solving problems of disclosure risk while retaining key analytic uses of publicly released microdata. *Journal of Empirical Research on Human Research Ethics, 1*, 63–84.

Sobal, J. (1981). Teaching with secondary data. *Teaching Sociology, 8*, 149–170. doi:10.2307/1316942

2

MANAGING AND USING SECONDARY DATA SETS WITH MULTIDISCIPLINARY RESEARCH TEAMS

J. DOUGLAS WILLMS

The use of secondary data can be rather daunting for the beginning researcher. Quite often, new investigators have used only small "textbook" data sets during their graduate work and have not encountered very large data sets that have a multilevel structure, variables with differing amounts of missing data, and a complex weighting scheme. Usually, secondary data sets arrive as a text file with one or more sets of syntax files for reading the data and creating a system data file that can be used with particular software such as SAS, SPSS, or Stata. Even achieving this first step can be frustrating for the beginning researcher.

During the past 15 years, I have worked with researchers at the Canadian Research Institute for Social Policy at the University of New Brunswick (UNB-CRISP) to develop strategies for managing and using large-scale, complex data sets with multidisciplinary teams. This work has included the analysis of data from several national and international studies such as the National Longitudinal Survey for Children and Youth (NLSCY; Statistics Canada, 2005), the Programme for International Student Assessment (PISA; Organisation for Economic Cooperation and Development, 2001), the Progress in International Reading Literacy Study (Mullis, Martin, Gonzalez,

& Kennedy, 2003), and Tell Them From Me (Willms, & Flanagan, 2007). Each of these studies has its own peculiarities, but the studies share many of the same features, such as design weights, missing data, and a multilevel structure. Moreover, the analytic work involves the management and analysis of secondary data that could not reasonably be done by one person; they require work by teams of analysts, with a consistent approach to data management.

The aim of this chapter is to describe some of the management techniques that may be useful to the beginning researcher when preparing an unfamiliar data set for analysis. I also discuss some of the common pitfalls that we typically encounter in working with secondary data. Throughout the chapter, I use the NLSCY as an example. The NLSCY is a nationally representative longitudinal study of Canadian children and youth that was launched by the Canadian government in 1994 with a sample of more than 22,000 children in more than 13,000 families. The design included surveys administered to parents, teachers, and school principals; direct assessments of the children after age 4; and a separate self-report questionnaire for youth from age 10 onward. Children and their families have been followed longitudinally with data collected every 2 years. The U.S. National Longitudinal Survey of Youth (NLSY) and Australia's Longitudinal Survey of Australian Youth are comparable surveys. These studies provide extraordinary coverage of the characteristics, life experiences, and the healthy development of children as they grow from infancy to early adulthood.

Human Resources and Skills Development Canada has funded two multidisciplinary team projects to further the research on the NLSCY. The first of these, called "Vulnerable Children," led to the publication of an edited volume (Willms, 2002) and the development of a pan-Canadian network called the "New Investigators Network." The network published nearly 100 articles over a 4-year period. Recent examples of research based on the longitudinal data from the NLSCY include works published by Arim, Shapka, Dahinten, and Willms (2007); Dahinten, Shapka, and Willms (2007); and Dupéré et al. (2007). The second team project, "Successful Transitions," has aimed to exploit the longitudinal structure of the NLSCY data.

I believe there are three elements critical to the success of a multi-disciplinary team. One is that the members need to be chosen for both their knowledge and expertise in a substantive area and their predilection for quantitative research. Also, I prefer to have a balance of researchers who are at varying stages in their careers, as this affords the opportunity for senior researchers to mentor junior colleagues. The second element is training. In both projects, we held several 3-day training sessions on statistical approaches relevant to the project. These included, for example, training in the handling of missing data, the use of design weights, item response theory (IRT), and hierarchical linear modeling (HLM). Although team members varied in their initial skills in statistics, the training helped to bring them to a common level and appreciate later discussions about statistical methods. The third important element is to have a small central team of two or three analysts charged with creating a common database for subsequent analyses. This proved to be efficient and ultimately led to richer team discussions about methodological approaches.

Many students, when they are beginning their careers, are enthralled with fairly advanced complex techniques such as HLM, IRT, structural equation models, and multiple imputation of missing data. My advice is to do all analyses with simple techniques first and examine the basic results. In particular, I like to look at the univariate statistics (e.g., median, mean, standard deviation, skewness) for each variable first to discern whether there are any extreme outliers to consider or an unusual distribution of the data. At this point, I usually compare the results with those published in the codebook provided with the secondary data set. I then conduct some simple bivariate analyses (e.g., correlations, scatter plots), usually with the outcome variable and each covariate, to discern whether there are any nonlinear relationships to be aware of or outliers that can have a dramatic effect on estimated regression coefficients. Then I might move on to basic regression models and, finally, to more advanced techniques. Starting with a complex tool like HLM is like trying to build a house from top to bottom before looking at the materials and setting the foundation. The step-by-step approach recommended here, including the development of tall skinny files, is useful in that it forces one to do many of the preliminary analyses while the data set is being constructed.

BUILDING A USABLE DATA SET IN THREE STEPS

The most difficult task in working with secondary data is taking the raw data set provided and building a data set that can be used for analysis. During the early stages of my career, I developed very long syntax files that could read the secondary data, do the necessary coding and scaling of variables, and save a data set with 10 or 15 variables that I would then use for analysis. This worked reasonably well for small projects, but the syntax files were unwieldy for large-scale longitudinal studies like the NLSCY. Also, these syntax files were never adequately documented. Quite often, a paper would come back from review, 6 months to 1 year later, requesting additional analyses. Because the syntax files and the resulting variables were not adequately documented, it would usually take me several hours to reconstruct what I had done. Also, without adequate documentation, the knowledge transfer to new researchers was difficult at best, and often unsuccessful. Therefore, when the Successful Transitions team embarked on its work, the analysis group set in place an approach that included the development of a master usable data set in three incremental steps. The approach also involved the development of an accompanying "measures document," which included documentation that enables a multidisciplinary team to use the data across several projects.

Step 1: Creating the Base Data Set

The first step in the process of moving from raw text data to a usable data set is to create a data set that has all of the secondary data in the base program that the analyst intends to use, such as SPSS, SAS, or Stata. Although some data sets come in one or more of these formats, more often the analyst must perform this step. If so, the secondary data set usually comes with a syntax file for reading the raw, text-format data. When using this syntax file, I sometimes make small changes to the syntax. For example, I like to avoid the use of string variables as much as possible, especially for variables that will be used as identification (ID) variables because some programs will not read string variables for the ID. At the end of the syntax file, I like to sort the data on the basis of the structure of the data set. For example, with the NLSCY data, we sort cases by Cycle, Household-ID, and Child-ID. Although we may need to sort the data in other ways for particular projects, this structure is used for managing the tall skinny files. This database is referred to as the *base data set*. The data set is prepared without recoding of variables, such that it faithfully represents the raw data.

Step 2: Creating Tall Skinny Files

The next step is building tall skinny data files for each of the variables to be used in analysis. A *tall skinny file* is simply a data file that includes a small set of focal variables and one or more relevant ID variables. The syntax file to create a tall skinny file simply reads in the data from the base data set; does some manipulation on the data for a particular variable; sets the variable name, variable label, and missing values codes as desired; and saves a tall skinny file—a data set with the ID variables plus the new variable or set of variables.

Building the tall skinny files is the real work of the analyst: In our case, the first step—reading the secondary data into SPSS—required about 2 hr, whereas the step of building the tall skinny files took us 6 months. The use of tall skinny files is crucial to our work as it enables teams of researchers to work on separate variables; it allows us to identify errors when they occur; and it allows us to add new data to our system when they are collected in successive cycles. (We use the term *cycle* to refer to data collected on successive occasions; some studies such as the NLSY use the term *rounds*; others use the term *waves*.)

As a simple example, consider the syntax for creating the tall skinny file for the child's sex. Our syntax file reads in the base data; recodes the data for the variable "sex" to a new variable called "female," which is coded "0" for males and "1" for females, with missing data codes set to "9"; assigns value labels; and saves an SPSS file that includes the three ID variables and the new variable "FEMALE." Although this may seem trivial, the data for sex are coded "1" for males and "2" for females in some cycles of the NLSCY and "M" and "F" in other cycles. Also, we prefer the "0"–"1" coding rather than "1"–"2," as the variable can then be used directly as a dummy variable in regression analyses. We call the variable "FEMALE" rather than "sex" or "gender" so we can easily recall which children were coded "1" and which were coded "0."

It seems that there is no consistent naming convention for variables in secondary data sets. We like to include a variable name that is meaningful, such as "mumedyrs" for mothers' education coded in years. We include a suffix, which currently ranges from "A" to "F," to denote the cycle (i.e., "A" for 1994/1995, "B" for 1996/1997, etc.). Also, when data are imputed for a variable we add a suffix "_i" to denote that missing data were imputed for that variable. Thus, the variable "Cmumedyrs_i" is a variable with information on mother's education for children studied in the third data collection cycle (1999/2000).

For a slightly more complicated example of tall skinny file construction, there are many variables that are either nominal or ordinal but come as a single variable in the base data set. In this case, our syntax for the tall skinny file creates a small set of dichotomous variables with each variable name denoting the category. For example, for mother's or father's level of education, one might have separate variables denoting "did not finish secondary school," "secondary school," "some college or university," "completed college or trade program," and "completed university." We prefer to include the full set of dummy variables, rather than leaving out one dummy variable to be used as the base category in a regression analysis, as this allows the analyst to decide later which variable to use as the base category.

There is also a tall skinny file for childhood overweight and obesity. This variable is slightly more complicated. In this case, we read in the base data set and then merge the data from the tall skinny files for age and sex. We then examine the data for each child's weight and height, and do the necessary checking to ensure that there are not any extreme outliers. Usually, extreme outliers stem from coding errors, but in this case there are some children with data coded in the imperial system (inches and pounds) rather than the metric system (meters and kilograms). After making necessary repairs, we then construct a measure of body mass index (BMI). This is followed with a long syntax that codes levels of BMI into markers of overweight and obesity according to each child's age and sex. The cutpoints for BMI that determine whether a child is considered overweight or obese are based on international standards recommended by Cole, Bellizzi, Flegal, and Dietz (2000). The resulting tall syntax file includes the ID variables, the variables for height and weight, the estimates of BMI, and two dichotomous variables denoting whether the child was overweight or obese.

Other syntax files are much more complex. For example, we have coded our measure of adolescent depression using a particular variant of IRT appropriate for Likert scales with three or more possible responses to each item. In this case, the initial cleaning was done as in the example above, and then a provisional tall skinny file was created. The specialized IRT software was then used to examine the items and create a set of IRT scaled scores. These data were then merged back to the base file data, and cutpoints were set to classify youth as "not depressed," "moderately depressed," or "severely depressed." The final tall skinny file for depression that is saved includes the ID variables, the classical scores for the measure, the IRT scores for the measure, and three dummy variables denoting the three categories relevant to depression status.

Our syntax for socioeconomic status (SES) is the most complicated, as it is based on five separate variables describing family income, mother's and father's employment status, and mother's and father's education. We first created separate tall skinny files of each of these variables across the six cycles. The income variable was challenging work, as we had to use government tables to convert reported income to constant 1994 dollars. The measures for parental occupation were even more difficult, as the system used to code occupation had changed after the second cycle, and we had to devise a strategy to code all occupations onto a common scale. Finally, the scaling of SES used data from all five variables, with a strategy for accounting for missing data.

Many data sets come with their own derived variables, and at this point one might ask why one should go to the extra effort in creating a new measure of SES. I recommend reading the codebook to discern how the derived variable was actually constructed; in many cases, the methods used are inadequate for the purpose of the study. It is also a useful exercise to try and recreate the derived variable from the data available in the secondary data set. In doing so, try to learn what assumptions were made in the creation of the derived variable. For example, in the PISA data, the approach skirts the issue of missing data for fathers' education, which is usually missing for single parent families, by creating a new variable called "parents' education." This is the maximum value of the mother's and father's level of education. One has to ask whether this assumption is reasonable for the particular analysis that one is planning.

Missing data is another issue analysts must address in their work. For several variables there is often considerable missing data. In many cases, we create a dummy variable denoting whether the data were missing and a new variable that has the missing data replaced with an imputed value. Thus for family income, we have four variables: "INCOME," "INCOME94," "INCOME94_m," and "INCOME94_i," for the base variable, the constant dollar variable, the missing data indicator, and the variable with missing data imputed, respectively. Techniques for imputing missing data are described in Chapter 5.

A device we have found invaluable in our work is the cohort and cell diagram, which is shown in Figure 2.1. The NLSCY comprises 11 cohorts of children sampled in 2-year age groups.

We created a syntax file that assigns the cohort number (1–11) and the cell number (1–48) for the data for each child at each cycle. As each research paper in the Successful Transitions project uses a different subsample from the data set, the researcher can quickly select the subsample needed and communicate to others what data were used in the analysis.

Step 3: Creating the Usable Data Set

The final step is to merge the several tall skinny files into a data set ready for analysis. In most cases, this is easily done, as the tall skinny files include the relevant matching variables and are sorted by these variables.

However, this last step can be a little more complicated for longitudinal data sets. For the NLSCY, the construction of tall skinny files is done separately for each cycle, in our case yielding six tall skinny files. The tall skinny files are then stacked (e.g., using "add files" in SPSS) and sorted by the child ID to create a very tall skinny file. The new, stacked variable then does not require the prefix denoting cycle. We prefer stacking the skinny files rather than matching them laterally, as many of the programs we use to analyze longitudinal data require this format. Also, this approach reduces the number of variables, as there are no longer six separate variables for each measure.

THE MEASURES DOCUMENT

Keeping good notes is the sine qua non of the trade. One can keep informal notes in the syntax files, and the time required for this is seldom wasted. Those who do advanced programming in complex languages learn this early in their careers.

We also built a more formal document called the *measures document*, which describes each variable in the tall skinny files. The codebooks provided with secondary data sets never include all of the relevant information that analysts require. I use the word *never* rather than *seldom* because analysts need more information on variables and data structure than reasonably can be

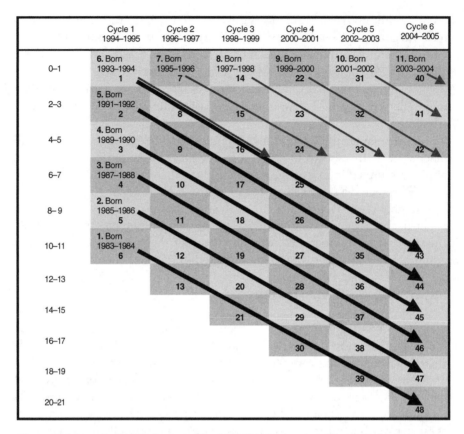

Figure 2.1. Longitudinal cohorts for the NLSCY, Cycles 1–6. The first six of these cohorts include children born between 1983 and 1994 who were followed longitudinally from 1994 to 1995; these are shown with thicker arrows. At each cycle, a new cohort of children aged birth to age 1 was sampled, and these children were followed longitudinally for two additional cycles; these are shown with thinner arrows. From *The NLSCY Measures Document,* p. 3, by J. D. Willms, L. Tramonte, and N. Chin, 2008, Fredericton, Canada: Canadian Research Institute for Social Policy. Copyright 2008 by Canadian Research Institute for Social Policy. Reprinted with permission.

provided with a codebook. Moreover, existing codebooks cannot include all of the lessons learned about variables that come through actually using them in various studies. The measures document includes information on several variables used in analysis. I liken the official codebook to a public telephone directory, whereas the measures document is akin to one's personal address book, with detailed information on a small number of people. Like the personal address book, the measures document is updated regularly with new entries and changes to old ones. Although building a measures document may seem time consuming and somewhat pedantic, it saves time in the long run.

The secondary data set for the NLSCY comprises a set of complex data sets that include data collected from children and youth, and their parents, teachers, and school principals. The survey began in 1994/1995, with a nationally representative sample of Canadian youth ages birth to 11. The majority of these children are part of a longitudinal sample that is being followed with biennial data collection. In addition, at each cycle, a new sample of children ages birth to 24 months are sampled, and in recent cycles these children are followed longitudinally to age 5. Consequently, the codebooks for the various NLSCY data sets are massive, with several thousands of pages requiring about 2 m of shelf space.

The NLSCY is not only large and complex—there are other challenges that make its use difficult. For example, the sample design changed as the study evolved such that not all children are followed longitudinally; many of the measures were altered from cycle to cycle, so that without some careful scaling work, they cannot be used longitudinally; and new survey content was added as children got older, whereas old content was either discarded or scheduled for collection at every other cycle, instead of every cycle.

Our measures document for the NLSCY (Willms, Tramonte, & Chin, 2008) was developed to help deal with these issues. In the short term, it was designed for describing a set of variables that could be used in a consistent fashion across the 15 papers for Successful Transitions. It has allowed researchers across the country to quickly begin their own studies as they can build on what has been done by the UNB-CRISP team. In the longer term, the measures document is an ongoing project that describes a set of measures used by analysts interested in the NLSCY. It has also proven useful also as a teaching tool.

The NLSCY measures document begins with a brief description of the data set and the variables to be used in Successful Transitions. This is followed with individual summaries for each variable that include (a) a description of the variable, (b) the age range covered by the variable, (c) the cycles in which the variable was measured, (d) the variable type (e.g., dichotomous, ordinal, continuous), (e) the unweighted number of children with data on the variable, (f) basic descriptive statistics (e.g., frequencies, mean, standard deviation) for the variables across cycles, and (g) notes regarding its development.

AVOIDING COMMON PITFALLS

My advice is to be wary of surprise findings. Although many researchers are sustained by new discoveries, too many times I have been excited by results only to find that I have made some mistake, usually a simple one. Thus, before getting too excited, assume it was a mistake. If you cannot find a mistake, try to do some auxiliary analyses that approach the analysis from different directions.

The most common errors I encounter are described in the following listing.

- *Miscoded data*. Quite often, questionnaire data are reverse coded. I have seen data sets in which males are coded "1" and females "2" in one cycle, and then females, "1," and males, "2," in the next cycle. The best safeguard is careful, simple preliminary analyses as suggested earlier.

- *Mismatched data*. Strange results occur when data are mismatched across cycles or across levels, such as the pupil and school levels. This can happen if one forgets to include the matching key when combining data.

- *Missing data codes*. If the values established for missing data have not been set correctly, one will typically get unusual results. The convention seems to be to use "9" for missing data for one-digit variables, "99" for two-digit variables, and so on. Many data sets include several missing data codes such as "7" for "not answered," "8" for "not applicable," and "9" for "missing." Of course, a careful check of the syntax files is the first step. However, one can also use bigger values, such as "999" instead of "9," for missing data, and then if there is a problem, it is easily detected. My advice is to never use "0" for the missing data value.

- *Filter questions*. In many studies, respondents are asked a question, and depending on their answer, they are asked to continue to the next question or skip ahead to a different set of question. This creates a special type of missing data—"not applicable"— and one needs to be careful in how these data are handled. Quite often, one can estimate a percentage or mean for the variable, but the statistic refers to the percentage or mean only for those who were filtered to that question.

- *Age of respondent*. The single most important variable in longitudinal surveys is the age of the respondent. However, one needs to distinguish between age of respondent when the survey was conducted; age of the respondent when the sample was selected; and age of the respondent when some event or intervention occurred, such as when a child started school. Most often, researchers will want the age of respondent when the survey was conducted, and this usually requires one to compute it using the age of the respondent when the sample was selected and the date when the respondent was actually tested or surveyed.

CONCLUDING REMARKS

We do not view the approach we used for creating tall skinny files as the best way or only way to establish a usable data set. For example, with the NLSCY, we coded our measure of adolescent depression using a particular variant of IRT. Another researcher may prefer to use a different approach to scaling. The important point is that another researcher can develop his or her own strategy and examine how the results compare with ours without having to start from the beginning.

Our approach to data analysis also provides a logical structure for managing files. We like to keep the raw secondary data sets in a separate directory. Our principle is to never alter these, as sometimes we have to go back and reconstruct what was done from first principles. We also have separate directories for each cycle. Each of these directories include the base SPSS file drawn from the secondary raw data with the first step; a subdirectory for the syntax files; and a subdirectory for the tall skinny files constructed for that cycle. Finally, we have a directory for the file that includes the syntax for stacking the tall skinny files across cycles and the resulting full database.

The use of secondary data for the novice researcher can be exceedingly frustrating, but it can also be rewarding. Many data sets require the use of complex design weights, a strategy for handling missing data, and an analytical approach that takes account of a multilevel structure. Longitudinal survey data can be even more trying, as quite often the data structure, the measures, and even the coding framework changes from cycle to cycle. This chapter recommends writing syntax files that create tall skinny files that can be used to form a usable data set. This has several advantages. First, it is very efficient in that all researchers in the team do not have start from the beginning and do all of the basic groundwork. Second, it enables fairly novice researchers to take advantage of sophisticated work, such as IRT scaling, done by seasoned researchers. Third, it facilitates work in multidisciplinary teams. The approach enables one to move from secondary data to usable data, and from frustrating to rewarding, in small steps with safeguards that help avoid the common pitfalls.

REFERENCES

Arim, R. G., Shapka, J. D., Dahinten, V. S., & Willms, J. D. (2007). Patterns and correlates of pubertal development in Canadian youth. *Canadian Journal of Public Health, 98,* 91–96.

Cole, T. J., Bellizzi, M. C., Flegal, K. M., & Dietz, W. H. (2000). Establishing a standard definition for child overweight and obesity worldwide: International survey. *British Medical Journal, 320,* 1240–1243. doi:10.1136/bmj.320.7244.1240

Dahinten, S., Shapka, J. D., & Willms, J. D. (2007). Adolescent children of adolescent mothers: The impact of family functioning on trajectories of development. *Journal of Youth and Adolescence, 36,* 195–212. doi:10.1007/s10964-006-9140-8

Dupéré, V., Lacourse, E., Willms, J. D., Vitaro, F., & Tremblay, R. E. (2007). Affiliation to youth gangs during adolescence: The interaction between childhood psychopathic tendencies and neighborhood disadvantage. *Journal of Abnormal Child Psychology, 35,* 1035–1045. doi:10.1007/s10802-007-9153-0

Mullis, I. V. S., Martin, M. O., Gonzalez, E. J., & Kennedy, A. M. (2003). *PIRLS 2001 international report: IEA's study of reading literacy achievement in primary schools.* Chesnut Hill, MA: Boston College.

Organisation for Economic Cooperation and Development. (2001). *Knowledge and skills for life: First results from the OECD programme for international student assessment (PISA) 2000.* Paris, France: Author.

Statistics Canada. (2005). *National Longitudinal Survey of Children and Youth microdata user guide—Cycle 5.* Ottawa, Canada: Author.

Willms, J. D. (Ed.). (2002). *Vulnerable children: Findings from Canada's National Longitudinal Survey of Children and Youth.* Edmonton, Canada: University of Alberta Press.

Willms, J. D., & Flanagan, P. (2007). Canadian students "Tell Them From Me." *Education Canada, 3,* 46–50.

Willms, J. D., Tramonte, L., & Chin, N. (2008). *The NLSCY measures document.* Fredericton, Canada: Canadian Research Institute for Social Policy.

3

ON CREATING AND USING
SHORT FORMS OF SCALES
IN SECONDARY RESEARCH

KEITH F. WIDAMAN, TODD D. LITTLE, KRISTOPHER J. PREACHER,
AND GITA M. SAWALANI

Short forms are so-named because they consist of shortened versions of original scales. Creating and using such measures is something of a cottage industry for many practicing scientists. A PsycINFO search conducted in late December 2008 using *short form* and *short forms* as alternate keywords returned 5,101 references, over 4,200 of which were articles in refereed journals. Many of these references had an applied measurement or methodological focus, describing the creation and psychometric evaluation of a short form of an extant instrument. For example, Rammstedt and John (2007) recently created a 10-item version of the 44-item Big Five Inventory (John, Donahue, & Kentle, 1991) as a way to measure the five broad dimensions of personality (i.e., Extraversion, Agreeableness, Conscientiousness, Neuroticism, and Openness) in 1 minute or less. Researchers often create short forms so they can assess a larger number of constructs in a reasonably short testing session. One particular advantage is that use of short forms can ensure that measures of many potentially critical variables are obtained so the researcher has greater latitude in testing alternative hypotheses.

Regardless of any compelling reasons for using short forms, the most likely outcome of using them is that the researcher will have a measure of the construct that has poorer psychometric properties than does the original long form. As a consequence, researchers must make careful and wise decisions about how to analyze the data and interpret the results. In this chapter, we provide an overview of issues related to reliability and validity, and provide explicit recommendations for creating and using short forms in behavioral science research, particularly as they apply to existing data sets. In this regard, we focus primarily on the typical secondary data set—an existing data set collected by other researchers to pursue their goals, yet a data set that can be mined to answer current theoretical questions. In most secondary data sets, many constructs are assessed using self-report questionnaire formats, although these data sets often include constructs assessed using other measurement methods, such as observer ratings, informant reports, and objective tests.

Researchers who use secondary data often must make decisions about which scales to use, whether to construct new scales from existing sets of items, and how to evaluate scales once they are assembled from existing data, among other concerns. This task can be daunting, particularly when considering whether one can "sell" reviewers of a manuscript on the nonstandard nature of certain measures. Therefore, our goal in this chapter is to provide applied researchers with a tutorial on developing and evaluating short forms derived from secondary data.

FUNDAMENTAL ISSUES IN PSYCHOLOGICAL MEASUREMENT: RELIABILITY

One very important psychometric property of a measure is its reliability. *Reliability* refers to precision of measurement—or how accurately determined an individual's score is on a measure or scale. In classical test theory (e.g., Lord & Novick, 1968), reliability is defined as the ratio of true score variance over total scale variance. As the ratio of true score variance over total variance increases, the relative proportion of error variance decreases, so precision of measurement is positively related to reliability and inversely related to error variance in a scale.

Precision of measurement is often presented in terms of the standard error of measurement for an instrument. The *standard error of measurement* is the standard deviation of a sampling distribution centered at a person's true score and estimates the standard deviation of scores the person would obtain on an infinite number of administrations of the instrument, other things being equal. If reliability of scale X is denoted r_{XX}, the standard error of measurement is calculated as $s_X \sqrt{1 - r_{XX}}$, where s_X is the standard deviation of scale X. Reliability is a key component in the formula for the standard error of measurement: As reliability increases, the standard error of measurement decreases, and precision of measurement improves.

Types of Reliability Coefficient

Reliability involves the extent to which individual differences in measured scores are consistent and reproducible. Scales and tests with adequate reliability should yield more or less the same scores across periods of time and groups. Empirically speaking, reliability can be indexed in a number of ways.

Internal Consistency

Many different kinds of reliability coefficient have been developed, such as split half, internal consistency, parallel forms, and test–retest reliability (see McDonald, 1999). The most commonly used reliability coefficients are internal consistency and test–retest coefficients. Internal consistency indexes estimate reliability on the basis of associations among scale items. Coefficient alpha (Cronbach, 1951) is the most often reported internal consistency index. However, many researchers are unaware that alpha is based on the assumptions that a single factor underlies the scale and that all items are equally good indicators of the latent variable being assessed (Schmitt, 1996). That is, if an item factor analysis were performed, all loadings of the p items on the single factor underlying the scale would be equal (i.e., tau equivalent). If the factor loadings are not equal for all items, coefficient omega is a more appropriate estimator of reliability (see below), and coefficient omega is always greater than or equal to coefficient alpha for a scale that is unidimensional (i.e., that is a one-factor scale; see McDonald, 1970, 1999).

Coefficient alpha can be calculated in many ways, but perhaps the easiest way is

$$\alpha = \left(\frac{p}{p-1}\right)\left(\frac{s_X^2 - \sum s_j^2}{s_X^2}\right) = \left(\frac{p}{p-1}\right)\left(1 - \frac{\sum s_j^2}{s_X^2}\right), \qquad (1)$$

where p is the number of items, s_X^2 is the variance of total scores on scale X, and $\sum s_j^2$ refers to the summation of item variances for the p items ($j = 1, \ldots, p$).

In the left section of Table 3.1, descriptive statistics are presented for a 6-item short form of the 10-item Rosenberg Self-Esteem Scale (Rosenberg, 1965; note that Items 5 and 6 are reversed scored), which are based on a sample of 6,753 participants in the 2005 Monitoring the Future survey. These data are freely available to researchers (more details are available at http://monitoringthefuture.org/).

The correlations among items, shown below the main diagonal, are moderate to large, ranging between .256 and .696, with a mean correlation of .468. Item variances are shown on the diagonal, and covariances among items are above the diagonal. To use Equation 1 to calculate coefficient alpha, we

TABLE 3.1

Six Rosenberg Self-Esteem Scale Items From the 2005 Monitoring The Future Study: Descriptive Statistics and One-Factor and Two-Factor Solutions

Item	Item descriptive statistics						One-factor model		Two-factor model		
	1	2	3	4	5r	6r	λ_1	θ_j^2	λ_1	λ_2	θ_j^2
1	**1.094**	.660	.495	.783	.470	.553	.853	.367	.810[b]	.058[a]	.377
2	.613	**1.061**	.569	.661	.440	.456	.776	.458	.825[b]	−.042[a]	.420
3	.516	.602	**.843**	.525	.297	.300	.604	.478	.708[b]	−.121[a]	.432
4	.696	.596	.532	**1.158**	.526	.597	.886	.372	.806[b]	.105[a]	.393
5r	.381	.362	.274	.415	**1.390**	.878	.605	1.024	.094[b]	.750[a]	.734
6r	.415	.347	.256	.435	.584	**1.626**	.670	1.177	−.094[b]	1.149[a]	.427
M	3.978	4.072	4.171	4.045	3.944	3.753					
SD	1.046	1.030	.918	1.076	1.179	1.275					

Note. $N = 6,753$. In the Item Descriptive Statistics section, values are correlations among items (below diagonal), item variances (on diagonal in bold print), and covariances among items (above diagonal, in bold print), with the mean and standard deviation for each item. Items 5 and 6 were reversed scored (resulting in Items 5r and 6r, respectively) prior to calculating item statistics. In the "One-factor" and "Two-factor" sections, tabled values are estimates from factor analyzing covariances among items. Symbols λ_1 and λ_2 refer to Factors 1 and 2, respectively, and θ_j^2 to unique factor variance. Factor variances were fixed at unity to identify and scale the estimates. Factors correlated .608 in two-factor solution.

[a]Parameters constrained to sum to zero. [b]Parameters constrained to sum to zero.

need two quantities: (a) the sum of all elements of the item variance–covariance matrix, which is equal to s_X^2, is 23.592, and (b) the sum of the item variances on the diagonal, which is 7.172. Given these values and the presence of $p = 6$ items, coefficient alpha is estimated as $\alpha = \left(\dfrac{6}{6-1} \right) \left(\dfrac{23.592 - 7.172}{23.592} \right) = .835$ for this six-item short form.

An interesting alternative to coefficient alpha is coefficient omega (McDonald, 1970, 1999). Coefficient omega is more appropriate for most research applications because it is unrealistic to assume that all items on a measure are equally good at tapping true score variance. In our experience, equal factor loadings for all scale items rarely, if ever, occur, so coefficient omega will, in general, be preferable to coefficient alpha. Assuming that a linear model underlies responses on each item on scale X, the linear model for item x_{ji} takes the form $x_{ji} = \tau_j + \lambda_j F_i + \varepsilon_{ji}$, where x_{ji} is the score of person i on item j, τ_j is the intercept (i.e., mean) of item j, λ_j is the raw score (or covariance metric) common factor loading for item j, F_i is the score on the common factor for person i, and ε_{ji} is the score of person i on the unique factor for item j. On the basis of factor analysis of the item variance–covariance matrix, coefficient omega can be estimated as

$$ \omega = \frac{\left(\sum \lambda_j \right)^2}{\left(\sum \lambda_j \right)^2 + \sum \theta_j^2} = 1 - \frac{\sum \theta_j^2}{s_X^2}, \tag{2} $$

where all summations are from 1 to p (the p items), θ_j^2 is the estimated unique variance of item j (i.e., the variance of ε_{ji}), and other symbols are as defined previously. In the first expression in Equation 2, one must first sum the p factor loadings and square this sum; the square of summed loadings estimates the variance of the scale. The denominator is the sum of the preceding value and the sum of the unique variances of the items. The ratio of these two values gives the proportion of variance in the scale that is reliable variance (i.e., coefficient omega). When a single factor underlies the scale and all factor loadings (λ_j s) are identical, coefficients omega and alpha are identical.

The second expression in Equation 2 is simply 1.0 minus the ratio of the sum of unique factor variances, $\sum \theta_j^2$, over total scale variance, s_X^2. If a scale is truly a single-factor instrument (i.e., is unidimensional), both expressions for coefficient omega in Equation 2 will provide identical results. But recent work by Zinbarg and Revelle and associates (e.g., Zinbarg, Revelle, & Yovel, 2007; Zinbarg, Yovel, Revelle, & McDonald, 2006) showed that the second expression is a more appropriate estimator of coefficient omega as developed by McDonald (1970) if a scale is "lumpy" (cf. Cronbach, 1951) and thus consists of two or more highly correlated group factors that reflect excess overlap in item content or stylistic variance that contributes to the multidimensionality.

To estimate coefficient omega, we used maximum likelihood estimation in Mplus (Muthén & Muthén, 1998–2007) to obtain a one-factor solution for the self-esteem items. To identify this model, we fixed the factor variance to 1.0 and estimated all remaining parameters. As seen in Table 3.1, the positively worded items had higher factor loadings and much lower unique variances than did the negatively worded items. Factor loadings varied considerably (range = .604–.886) and thus were not tau equivalent, implying that coefficient alpha is inappropriate for this data set. The one-factor solution had marginal levels of fit to the data, with a comparative fit index (CFI) of .881 and standardized root-mean-square residual (SRMR) of .069, so computation of coefficient omega may be suspect. For illustration, we used the first expression for coefficient omega shown in Equation 2 to compute a reliability estimate (the sum of factor loadings is 4.394, the square of this sum is 19.307, and the sum of unique variances is 3.876). This estimate of coefficient omega was .833, which is marginally lower than coefficient alpha reported above. Using the second expression in Equation 2, coefficient omega was .836, marginally higher than coefficient alpha. That the first of these two estimates of coefficient omega is lower than coefficient alpha is inconsistent with the claim that omega is greater than or equal to alpha (McDonald, 1999), an inequality that holds only if a scale is unidimensional. Thus, the first estimate of coefficient omega suggests that the one-factor solution for this data set is inappropriate.

To investigate this, we fit a freely rotatable, exploratory two-factor model to the data, again using maximum likelihood estimation and the Mplus program. To identify this model, we fixed factor variances to 1.0, allowed the factors to correlate, and constrained hyperplanar loadings on each factor to sum to zero. That is, we constrained the loadings of Items 5r and 6r on the first factor to sum to zero, and we constrained the loadings of Items 1 through 4 on the second factor to sum to zero. The results of this analysis are shown in the last three data columns of Table 3.1. The two-factor solution had quite acceptable levels of fit, with CFI of .980 and SRMR of .018. As seen in Table 3.1, the four positively worded items loaded highly on the first factor, the two negatively worded items loaded highly on the second factor, and the two factors were relatively highly correlated (.608). Notably, the unique factor variances for the two negatively worded items were greatly reduced relative to the one-factor model, and the sum of unique variances was now 2.783. Using the second expression in Equation 2, omega was 882, considerably higher than coefficient alpha.

Coefficient alpha is often touted as a lower bound estimator of scale reliability, and this sounds at first to be desirable, as one generally would not like to overstate the reliability of a measure. However, we think the most accurate estimate of scale reliability is a more useful value. As such, we advocate reporting coefficient omega given that the assumption of tau-equivalent items is unlikely to hold. We also recommend reporting mean interitem correlations (MIC) more frequently, so that estimates of reliability across scales with varying lengths can be compared more easily.

Test–Retest Reliability

The second most commonly reported index of reliability is test–retest reliability. Here, one administers the same scale at two points and calculates the Pearson product–moment correlation between the two administrations. In secondary data sets that contain longitudinal measurements, correlations between scores on a given scale across measurement occasions are test–retest correlations, and even single-item measures can be evaluated using test–retest reliability.

The strength of test–retest correlations depends on the time lag between assessments, with longer lags tending to yield lower correlations. Therefore, such estimates are not optimal as indices of measurement precision; instead, they reflect stability over time. Additionally, internal consistency and test–retest reliabilities may diverge as a function of the type of construct. A scale assessing a trait construct would ideally have high internal consistency reliability and should also exhibit high test–retest reliability. In contrast, if a scale assesses a state or mood construct that varies across time, the scale would ideally have high internal consistency reliability, whereas its test–retest reliability should be quite low, even near zero. If the test–retest reliability of a state or mood scale is quite high, the contention that the scale assessed a state construct is open to question.

Scale Characteristics Affecting Reliability

To better understand reliability, we delve into some of the characteristics of scales that can change the reliability by which a construct is measured. These features are not exhaustive, but they are central to understanding the reliability of any measurement tool.

Three Key Features

Three principal features influence the reliability of a scale: (a) the number of items in the scale, (b) the magnitude of the MIC among the items, and (c) the relative standard deviations of the items. With regard to the first of these, other things being equal, the larger the number of items on a scale, the higher the reliability of the scale. Because items composing a short form are a subset of items in the original scale, a short form will usually have lower reliability than the original, longer form. This reduced reliability is a crucial consideration: If a short form is too short, its reliability may be so compromised that it has unacceptable levels of measurement precision—and its use in research becomes a risky endeavor. Providing bounds of reliability that are acceptable is fraught with problems. In general, short-form scale reliabilities of .80 or above are generally quite acceptable, values between .70 and .80 are adequate for research purposes, and reliabilities between .60 and .70 are at the low end of general use (cf. Nunnally & Bernstein, 1994, pp. 264–265). However, occasionally a scale with a reliability of .45 to .50 has surprisingly high correlations with outside variables, so the proof of its use is in the empirical relations it has with other variables (i.e., its validity, as discussed later).

The second scale characteristic—the magnitude of the MIC—reflects the amount of variance that is shared among items. Here, the higher the MIC, the smaller the number of items needed to achieve an acceptable level of reliability. Conversely, scales with a low MIC will require more items to achieve a comparable level of reliability. Clark and Watson (1995) argued that the MIC for scales generally should fall somewhere between .15 and .50. When measuring broad constructs like extroversion, lower MICs (in the range from .15 to .35) are expected, as one should attempt to cast a broad net and assess many, somewhat disparate, aspects of a content domain. When measuring a narrow construct like test anxiety, higher MICs (ranging from .30 to .50) should occur because narrow domains of content have items of greater similarity.

The MIC is directly related to the standardized factor loadings one would obtain if item correlations were factor analyzed. If correlations among items were fairly homogeneous and the MIC were .16, then standardized factor loadings for items would be around .40, and MICs of .25, .36, and .50 would translate into factor loadings of about .50, .60, and .70, respectively. Thus, the guideline by Clark and Watson (1995) that the MIC should fall between .15 and .50 means that standardized item factor loadings should vary between about .40 and .70, a useful benchmark when evaluating factor analyses of items comprising a short form from a secondary data set.

With regard to the third scale characteristic, differences in item variance can affect both reliability and the nature of the construct assessed by the scale. Other things being equal, items with larger variance contribute proportionally more variance to the scale than do items with smaller variance. When this occurs, individual differences on items with larger variance contribute disproportionately to individual differences on the total scale, which is shifted in the direction of these items and away from items with relatively small variance. When items with small variance assess crucial aspects of a construct, failure to take account of differences in item variance lowers the contribution of these components to the scale's content domain.

If all items fall on the same (or a similar) scale, differences in variance across items are generally small. For example, if each item is rated on a 1-to-5 scale, then marked differences in variance across items are unlikely and would not have large differential effects on scale scores.

However, items in a short form may have rather different scales (e.g., some items might fall on 1-to-3 rating scales, others on 1-to-5 rating scales, and still others on 1-to-10 or even 0-to-100 rating scales). When scale formats vary considerably across indicators, items must be rescaled so that items rated using larger scales do not bias the summary measure too far in their direction. One alternative is to convert all indicators to z scores, with M of 0.0 and SD of 1.0; if items have identical means and standard deviations, then differential contributions to the scale score are minimized. However, standardization should be done with care, because it is a sample-specific operation that will not generalize to a new sample. Furthermore, if existing data have a longitudinal aspect, care must be taken to transform a given item in a comparable fashion (e.g., using the same mean and standard deviation) at each time point so that scores are on a comparable metric across time. A second option is to use percent of maximum possible (POMP) scoring (see, e.g., Cohen, Cohen, Aiken, & West, 1999). Here, each item is rescaled to fall between 0 and 1, and then averaged into a scale score. For example, if an item were originally scored on a 1-to-5 scale, the researcher could subtract 1 from each person's score (so scores would now fall on a 0-to-4 scale) and then divide by 4. POMP scoring has the advantage that all item scores fall on a scale with the same potential range (i.e., 0 to 1), although items may still differ markedly in variance. Thus, POMP scoring may not be an optimal approach in all applications and should be used with care.

Reliability as a Function of Number of Items and MIC

To illustrate effects of the number of items and the MIC on scale reliability, we calculated the reliability for various combinations of these factors for hypothetical scales using the Spearman–Brown prophecy formula (McDonald, 1999). As shown in Table 3.2, the reliabilities of scales of different length are shown for original scales with 10, 20, 30, or 40 items, crossed by levels of MIC that span the approximate range discussed by Clark and Watson (1995)—specifically, MIC levels of .2, .3, .4, and .5. When researchers use a short form, they typically look first at the number of items and the homogeneity coefficient or reliability of the long form; these are shown in the first and third columns of Table 3.2, respectively, along with the MIC among items consistent with the associated level of reliability. Each row in Table 3.2 has three additional

TABLE 3.2
Predicted Reliabilities for Short Forms as a Function of Properties
of Long Form

Long form			75% as long		50% as long		25% as long	
No. of items	MIC	r_{xx}	No. of items	r_{xx}	No. of items	r_{xx}	No. of items	r_{xx}
40	.50	.98	30	.97	20	.95	10	.91
	.40	.96		.95		.93		.87
	.30	.94		.93		.90		.81
	.20	.91		.88		.83		.71
30	.50	.97	23	.96	15	.94	8	.89
	.40	.95		.94		.91		.84
	.30	.93		.91		.87		.77
	.20	.88		.85		.79		.67
20	.50	.95	15	.94	10	.91	5	.83
	.40	.93		.91		.87		.77
	.30	.90		.87		.81		.68
	.20	.83		.79		.71		.56
10	.50	.91	8	.89	5	.83	3	.75
	.40	.87		.84		.77		.67
	.30	.81		.77		.68		.56
	.20	.71		.67		.56		.43

Note. MIC = mean interitem correlation. Tabled values are theoretical estimates derived from MIC and number of items using the Spearman–Brown prophesy formula. A Microsoft Excel spreadsheet with other combinations of conditions is available at http://www.Quant.KU.edu/resources/published.html.

pairs of columns, one pair of columns for a scale 75% as long as the original form (i.e., discarding one fourth of the items), a second pair for a scale 50% as long (i.e., discarding half of the items), and a final pair for a scale 25% as long (i.e., discarding three fourths of the items). Thus, a 40-item scale with an MIC of .3 would have a reliability of .94, and a 20-item scale with MIC of .2 would have a reliability of .83.

Values in Table 3.2 appear to present a rather positive picture, with relatively high levels of reliability in many parts of the table. But one should remember that most original (or long-form) scales used in psychology have between 10 and 20 items per dimension. Suppose a researcher wanted to keep reliability above .80 and knew that the reliability of a 20-item scale was .90. This level of reliability would arise from an MIC of around .3, and the researcher would expect a short form containing half of the items from this scale (10 items) to have a reliability of .81. If this level of reliability were deemed too low, then keeping more items would be advisable. Or, if the original form of a 10-item scale had a reliability of .87 (i.e., MIC of .4), deleting more than about three items from the scale would lead to reliability below .80, which may be unacceptable.

FUNDAMENTAL ISSUES IN
PSYCHOLOGICAL MEASUREMENT: VALIDITY

Reliability concerns precision of measurement (i.e., how well the set of items measures whatever it is they assess). *Validity*, in contrast, concerns whether the scale assesses the construct it was designed to measure. Traditionally, methodologists have discussed a tripartite conception of validity—content validity, criterion validity, and construct validity—although more recent work (e.g., Messick, 1995) has extended these notions in interesting ways.

Content validity refers to how well a scale embodies content from all definable aspects of the domain to be assessed. Thus, a math achievement test for second graders may contain simple and complex addition items, simple and complex subtraction items, and word problems that can be translated into simple numerical operations, but it should not contain multiplication or division items or addition and subtraction items with decimals and fractions because these operations are not usually covered in the second grade curriculum. Content validity is typically assessed by asking subject-matter experts whether the measure is sufficiently comprehensive of all aspects of a domain. When using secondary data, short forms will often have been constructed from longer, original measures, and the researcher should ensure that the same breadth of content is shown in the short form as in the original form. If breadth of coverage is limited, then the short form may measure a somewhat narrower construct than assessed by the full instrument, and this should be noted.

Criterion validity is established by examining the predictive or concurrent correlations of a focal scale with key variables that are identified as criteria. Grades in school and scores on established intelligence tests are often used as criteria for new intelligence tests; job performance ratings might be used as criteria when evaluating the criterion validity of a battery of measures used in personnel selection. The magnitude and direction of these criterion-related correlations should be consistent with theory and past research with similar constructs. The stronger the correlation of a scale with a criterion measure, the stronger the criterion validity of the scale. For example, an intelligence test is likely to have good criterion validity for predicting educational attainment, because educational attainment is a near measure for an intelligence test, where *near* refers to a close connection theoretically and, perhaps, temporally. In contrast, an intelligence test may have rather lower levels of validity for predicting a criterion such as annual salary, which would be a far measure for the intelligence test (i.e., where *far* indicates much less close connection theoretically and, probably, temporally).

Finally, *construct validity* concerns whether a scale is a good measure of the theoretical construct it was designed to measure. No single study can establish the construct validity of a scale; instead, construct validity is gauged by the pattern of results obtained across all studies using the scale. This pattern should satisfy several criteria: (a) the scale should correlate highly with other, well established measures of the same construct; (b) the scale should correlate much lower with measures of quite different constructs; and (c) scale scores should vary as a function of relevant contexts or conditions. To reiterate, the correlation of a scale with measures of other constructs need not always involve strong positive correlations, but rather can involve a well reasoned set of hurdles that include zero, small, medium, and large correlations in both positive and negative directions—all of which should be consistent with theory underlying the measure and its expected levels of correlation with other measures. In their description of a hypothetical measure of social intelligence, Westen and Rosenthal (2003) argued that it should correlate moderately positively with verbal IQ ($r = .50$), at a low positive level with Extraversion ($r = .10$), and moderately negatively with hostile attribution bias ($r = -.40$). Even using the elegant Westen and Rosenthal (2003) approach, construct validity of a scale cannot be captured with a single set of correlations but is summarized by examining all evidence that has accrued using the scale. A scale may have good construct validity for certain inferences but much poorer validity for others. Thus, construct validity is not an all-or-nothing affair but requires an understanding and summary of available research on the scale and considerations of the uses to which the scale will be put.

Much psychological research suffers an unfortunate confirmation bias (Widaman, 2008), whereby researchers hypothesize that relatively high, significant correlations will hold between certain measures and pay less attention to variables with which the focal measure should correlate at low levels. When correlations are evaluated, correlations hypothesized to differ significantly from zero are treated as theoretically important even if they are relatively small in magnitude, and correlations hypothesized to be negligible are treated as essentially equal to zero, even if they barely miss being deemed statistically significant. To combat this unfortunate bias, researchers should develop hypotheses regarding both the convergent and discriminant validity of their measures, as Westen and Rosenthal (2003) argued. *Convergent validity* refers to the degree to which a set of measures converges on the construct of interest. Convergent validity is supported if measures of the same purported construct exhibit high intercorrelations. *Discriminant validity* describes the degree of meaningful separation, or lack of substantial correlation, between indicators of putatively distinct constructs. Discriminant validity is supported if relations between different constructs are approximately zero in magnitude or at least much smaller than convergent correlations for the measures. The classic article by Campbell and Fiske (1959) should be consulted regarding convergent and discriminant validation, as should more recent work on structural equation modeling (SEM) of such data (e.g., Eid & Diener, 2006; Widaman, 1985).

Relations Between Reliability and Validity

A common axiom of psychometric theory is that a scale cannot be valid if it is not reliable. If reliability is the proportion of variance in a measure that is true score variance, and validity is an index of how highly a measure correlates with the construct it purports to measure, then the square root of reliability places an upper limit on the validity of the measure. A scale with no reliable variance should be unable to correlate with any other measure. Because reliability places an upper bound on validity, rules of thumb have been offered for acceptable levels of reliability for measures. By convention, researchers often state that reliabilities between .70 and .80 are acceptable for research purposes, between .80 and .90 are preferred for research purposes, and above .90 (and preferably above .95) are required for individual assessment and diagnostic purposes. A scale with a reliability of .70 would still have a maximal validity of .84 if the criterion were perfectly reliable (McDonald, 1999, p. 133).

Classical tools for investigating statistical relations between variables, including regression analysis and analysis of variance, require the assumption that all variables are measured without error. All associated estimation theory—including estimating the strength of relations between variables, parameter estimates, standard errors, and confidence intervals of estimates—is based on the crucial assumption of perfect reliability. If measures have less than perfect reliability, parameter estimates are generally reduced in magnitude, standard errors and associated confidence intervals will be increased, and these effects will influence Type I and Type II error rates. Specifically, *Type I error rates*— or the likelihood that one would conclude that a relation between variables is significant when in fact it is due entirely to chance—would be lower as a function of lowered reliability of measures, so tests of significance would be negatively biased. However, *Type II error rates*—or the likelihood that one would fail to find significance for a relation when in fact it differed from zero — would increase as a function of lowered reliability of measures. Clearly, higher reliabilities are better, and the closer the reliabilities of measures are to unity, the more closely actual Type I and Type II error rates approximate their nominal values.

RECOMMENDATIONS: HOW TO CREATE AND EVALUATE A SHORT FORM OPTIMALLY

When creating a short form of a scale, the ultimate issue should be the validity of the short form, rather than its reliability (John & Soto, 2007). That said, reliability should not be disregarded; indeed, because reliability is a prerequisite for validity, reliability should be the first psychometric index to be evaluated. However, any short form will have fewer, often many fewer, items than the original scale, so reliability of a short form is likely to be appreciably lower than that for the full scale.

If a researcher were interested in creating a short form that has as high a level of reliability as possible, he or she might select the subset of items that have the highest MIC, because higher reliability arises from higher MIC values. But if selection of only items with high MIC leads to a biased selection of items (i.e., failure to preserve the breadth of the domain across the items in the short form), then the validity of the short form may be severely compromised, even as the reliability of the short form is maximized. Stated differently, the optimal set of indicators for a short form measure of a given construct may not be the indicators that have the highest internal consistency from among the possible items of the full scale; in fact, maximizing internal consistency can lead to suboptimal outcomes. Indeed, Loevinger (1954) described the attenuation paradox in which increasing reliability leads to increasing validity up to a point, beyond which point further increases in homogeneity reliability decreases validity. Or, selecting items that correlate most highly can lead to selection of items with extreme levels of item content overlap, leading to bloated specific factors that represent pairs of redundant items (Cattell & Tsujioka, 1964). Researchers must take care when developing short forms from longer original measures because common approaches for developing short forms are potentially problematic.

The most common methods for constructing short form measures are (a) selecting a subset of items with the highest MIC (described earlier), to maximize reliability of the short form; (b) selecting items with the highest loadings on the common factor underlying the items, to obtain items most closely aligned with the factor; (c) selecting items with the highest correlation with the total scale score (preferably the highest correlation with a composite of the remaining items on the scale); (d) selecting items with the highest face validity, or items that are the most obvious indicators of the construct; or (e) selecting items randomly from the original scale. Each of the preceding methods has flaws, and most methods have several. Methods (a), (b), and (c) use empirical methods, basing decisions on patterns of results from a particular set of data. Because the subset of items that appears to be optimal might vary across different sets of empirical data, basing item selection on a single data set is problematic and capitalizes on chance results in a single sample. Further, Methods (a) through (d) may result in a narrowing of item content, restricting improperly the breadth of the item content in the full scale. Method (d) is based on subjective judgments by researchers, and care must be taken lest the predilections of one researcher bias the item selection in idiosyncratic ways. Finally, Method (e) appears to be an unbiased approach to item selection, but researchers usually want to select the best items for a short form, not a random sample of items. Only if all items of the larger scale were equally good would a random selection of a subset of items be a reasonable approach. In practice, items are rarely equally good, so this approach probably would not lead to an optimal short form.

An underused approach that has potential merit is to identify a subset of items that maintains the factorial integrity of the construct. By *factorial integrity*, we mean that the construct maintains its levels of association with a select set of criteria or other constructs and that the estimated mean and variance of the construct are minimally changed. This focus on factorial integrity of the construct is a focus on validity—ensuring that the construct embodied in the short form maintains the same position in the nomological network of relations among constructs (cf. Cronbach & Meehl, 1955) as did the full, longer scale. SEM can be used iteratively to identify the subset of items that maintains factorial integrity of the short form. Here, one fits a model using the items from the full scale to represent the construct and includes a carefully chosen set of additional criteria. In a second analysis, all aspects of the model in the first analysis are identical except that one selects a subset of items to represent the focal construct. The mean, variance, and associations of the construct based on the full scale are compared with the mean, variance, and associations of the construct based on the selected subset of items. This model would be iteratively fit until an optimal subset of items is identified that maintains the factorial integrity of the construct.

When using secondary data, using the preceding methods to construct short form measures of constructs may not be possible. Secondary data are what they are—existing data that can be used for new purposes. As a result, if short forms were used when the data were collected, then existing short forms have already been constructed, and the user must live with those existing short forms. However, many secondary data sets have large selections of items that were never assigned to a priori scales. Instead, the questions probe various domains of content, and individual questions may have been used in prior research to answer particular questions. Nothing should stop the enterprising researcher from using these items to create scales to represent constructs of interest, but care must be taken when doing so. Of course, creating new scales from collections of items in an existing data set will involve new scales, not short forms of established scales. Still, the resulting new scales will likely consist of a fairly small number of items, so all principles and concerns related to analysis and evaluation of short forms still apply.

Additional steps can be pursued to explore the use of short forms constructed through the preceding steps. One step would be to perform a factor analysis to determine whether factors aligned with newly constructed short forms can be confirmed in the secondary data. Researchers should ensure that common factor techniques are used, because the use of principal-components analysis—the chief alternative to common factor analysis and the default in most computer programs—can lead to substantial bias in loadings and other parameter estimates, especially when the number of items analyzed is not large (Widaman, 1993, 2007). Factor analyses can be conducted at the item level, but item-based analyses are often problematic because of the issue of bloated specifics noted above. One useful alternative is the use of item parcels, which are sums of subsets of items composing a scale (Kishton & Widaman, 1994; Little, Cunningham, Shahar, & Widaman, 2002). Suppose one sifted through a set of items in an existing data set with the intent of developing short scales for Big Five dimensions of personality. Suppose as well that one identified a total of 30 items, six items for each of the five dimensions, that seemed to capture the respective dimensions reasonably well. Item-based analyses could be pursued, but a researcher would also be justified in forming 3 two-item parcels for each scale and then performing the factor analysis on the set of 15 two-item parcels. For additional suggestions on use of factor analysis in revising and evaluating measures, see Floyd and Widaman (1995) and Reise, Waller, and Comrey (2000).

RECOMMENDATIONS: WHAT TO DO WHEN WORKING WITH ALREADY-CREATED SHORT FORMS

When using existing data, researchers hope to find measures of key constructs needed to answer theoretical questions, even if some measures are short forms. If short forms of existing instruments are present, the user must evaluate the psychometric properties of the short forms and then analyze data with these properties in mind. We have several recommendations for data analyses that are informed by the properties of the scales analyzed.

The first recommendation is to estimate the reliability of each scale from the existing data set that will be used in the current research. Do not assume that original levels of reliability will be obtained, particularly if the scale is a short form composed of many fewer items than in the original form. Reliability is usually estimated using a homogeneity coefficient, and we recommend coefficient omega over the more commonly used coefficient alpha because it relies on more reasonable assumptions regarding the items on a short form— that items have a congeneric structure, rather than tau equivalent structure. Also, if coefficients omega and alpha diverge in magnitude, coefficient alpha is likely a biased underestimate of scale reliability, leading to biased overcorrection for unreliability when using the correction for attenuation. If data have a longitudinal component, then the correlation of a given scale from one measurement occasion with the same scale at the next measurement occasion can be used to estimate test–retest reliability.

As a second recommendation, when investigating correlations among measures, investigators should use the correction for attenuation to correct all correlations for unreliability and then evaluate both the raw and disattenuated correlations. The disattenuated correlation between variables X and Y provides an estimate of the correlation between the true scores of X and Y, and is calculated as

$$r_{XYc} = \frac{r_{XY}}{\sqrt{r_{XX}\, r_{YY}}}, \tag{3}$$

where r_{XYc} is the correlation between X and Y corrected for attenuation due to unreliability, r_{XY} is the Pearson product–moment correlation between the observed scores on variables X and Y, and r_{XX} and r_{YY} are the reliability coefficients for variables X and Y, respectively. Because any short form is likely to have somewhat lower reliability than the full form from which it was derived, the lowered reliability of the short form will lead to lower correlations of the short form with other variables. Correcting correlations for attenuation due to unreliability will allow one to evaluate the influence of lowered reliability on estimated relations among variables.

Our third recommendation is to consider analyzing data using latent-variable SEM, which automatically corrects for attenuation due to unreliability and also corrects for attenuation due to specific variance. The correction for attenuation obtained using SEM approaches arises because latent variables in such models represent error-free constructs, and relations among latent variables are relations from which measurement error and specific variance have been partialed out (Little, Lindenberger, & Nesselroade, 1999). When latent-variable SEM is used, whether one used a short form or the long form of a scale should not matter, at least in theory. Estimated relations among latent variables should be comparable across long and short forms because the analysis accommodates the different levels of reliability of the short and long forms. Of course, this contention is based on several assumptions, a chief one of which is that the short form provides an unbiased, if less reliable, measure of the construct assessed by the long form. If item selection in deriving the short form from the long form of the scale resulted in any narrowing or bias in item content of the short form, then the equality of relations for short and long forms need not hold (for researchers with little acquaintance with SEM, see Kline, 2004).

Our fourth recommendation is that to the degree possible, a researcher should investigate the validity of a construct by inspecting criterion-related associations of the construct with other measures in the data set. Here, one would examine other published data that used the full scale and note the associations of the full scale with as many other constructs as possible. If the existing data set has similar constructs or criteria, the short form should show patterns of association with these variables that are sufficiently similar to encourage further consideration. Admittedly, differences between studies can result in changes in correlations among variables, but similar patterns of correlations among constructs should tend to hold across studies.

Our fifth recommendation, which pertains specifically to longitudinal studies, is that researchers take care to ensure that variables are on the same metric across times of measurement. In longitudinal data sets, items in a short form may change from one occasion to the next. In such situations, researchers must ensure that measurements are on the same underlying scale if growth or change is the object of study. Simple approaches—such as the computation of average item scores or of proportion scores—rest on problematic assumptions that the items from the different forms function in precisely the same fashion in assessing the construct. Thus, these simple approaches are too simpleminded and problematic for current scientific work.

Linking the metric of latent variables across time in the presence of changes in the sets of items on a short form can be accomplished using either SEM or item response theory (IRT) approaches. Many different scenarios for the migration of items off of or onto short forms can be envisioned. For example, under one scenario, Items 1 through 12 (a short form of a 30-item instrument) might be used to assess a construct for three times of measurement during early adolescence; as participants move into later adolescence and are assessed three additional times, the first six items are dropped and Items 13 through 18 are substituted for them. Thus, 12 items are used at each measurement occasion, and one subset of six items (Items 7–12) is used at all measurement occasions. Under a second scenario, Items 1 through 12 are included at the first three times of measurement, Items 1 through 12 are supplemented with Items 13 through 24 at the fourth time of measurement, and all remaining times of measurement involve only Items 13 through 24. Under this scenario, no core set of items is administered across all measurement occasions, but all items that appear at any time of measurement are used at the fourth time of measurement. Clearly, many additional scenarios could be posed as likely to occur in existing data.

Under the first scenario, an SEM approach might use Items 7 through 12 to define two parcels, the same items would be assigned to these two parcels at each time of measurement, and these two parcels would appear at all times of measurement. Items 1 through 6 could be summed to form a third parcel for measurement occasions 1 through 3, and Items 13 through 18 could be summed for a third parcel at the last three measurement occasions. If the factor loadings, intercepts, and unique variances for the two common parcels were constrained to invariance across all times of measurement, the resulting latent variables would be on a comparable scale across all times of measurement. An appropriate IRT approach would have a similar rationale, requiring the presence of all 18 items in one analysis, and resulting theta scores (which are estimates of participant level on the construct) would be on a comparable scale across time.

The second scenario is, in some ways, simpler than the first, with all items that are used at any time of measurement appearing at a single occasion of measurement (the fourth time of measurement). The key analyses would be the linking of scores across the two forms—Items 1 through 12 and Items 13 through 24—in analyses using data from the fourth measurement occasion. Then, whether using SEM or IRT approaches, invoking invariance of parameter estimates from the fourth occasion of measurement on corresponding estimates at other occasions of measurement would lead to latent-variable scores on the same metric. Details of these methods are beyond the scope of the present chapter. The Embretson and Reise (2000) text offers a very good introduction to IRT procedures in general, and recent work (e.g., Cho, Boeninger, Masyn, Conger, & Widaman, 2010; Curran et al., 2008) provides relevant details and comparisons between SEM and IRT approaches.

CONCLUSIONS

Creating and using short forms of longer measurement instruments is a fact of life in many areas of psychology. Sometimes short forms are used to yield optimal screening instruments; other times they are used to incorporate measures of many constructs in a single protocol that is not too long. The key question to address with short forms is this: Has the reduced form of the scale undermined its validity for your intended purpose (John & Soto, 2007)? Our discussion has covered multiple ways in which a short form can compromise validity. The most obvious reason is the decrease in reliability that should occur with the decrease in the number of items, an effect embodied in the Spearman–Brown prophecy formula that was proposed 100 years ago (Spearman, 1910; Brown, 1910). But the validity of a short form can also be diminished by biased selection of items from the longer form, thereby narrowing the range or breadth of content covered by the scale and changing fundamentally the nature of the underlying dimension tapped by the scale (see Little et al., 1999). Thus, short forms are not a panacea for research in psychology, and researchers should be careful when selecting short forms of longer scales for their own research.

However, secondary data are what they are and cannot be changed. They often also have notable advantages, such as large sample sizes and probability-based sampling plans. If the data contain short forms, then these short-form scales should be handled with the most optimal mathematical and statistical techniques available. Many existing data sets are invaluable; they can be used to answer questions of current theoretical interest, and new data with long forms of scales would take years or decades to gather anew. Thus, rather than ruing the absence of long form instruments, we recommend that researchers concentrate instead on the most appropriate and state-of-the-art ways to analyze the existing data, warts and all.

Our strongest recommendations range from tried-and-true to innovative approaches to data analysis that can and should be used with short-form instruments. The tried-and-true methods include estimation of reliability in the sample of data at hand and use of the correction for attenuation when estimating relations among variables. Similarly, SEM methods, particularly multiple-indicator SEMs, accomplish a great deal in terms of correcting for poorer measurement properties of short forms (Little et al., 1999), and these methods are not generally novel any more. However, the ways in which SEM or IRT can be used to ensure that the scale of a latent variable remain the same across measurement occasions in the face of changes in the composition of a short form are innovative. Current research is being done to illustrate how this can and should be done and to establish optimal procedures for meeting these analytic goals.

We have considered likely outcomes when short forms are used, offered basic ideas about how to gauge the psychometric properties of short form data, provided some guidelines about constructing new scales from older collections of items in existing data, and recommended analytic strategies for evaluating short form data and including them in models. Valuable secondary data are out there, often containing short form instruments but waiting to be used as the unique basis for answering interesting, crucial, state-of-the-science questions. We encourage researchers to exploit such resources, using analytic approaches that are appropriate for the data and provide optimal tests of their conjectures.

FOR FURTHER READING

Informative articles on reliability, validity, and scale development and revision that we recommend include

Clark, L. A., & Watson, D. (1995). Constructing validity: Basic issues in objective scale development. *Psychological Assessment, 7*, 309–319. doi:10.1037/1040-3590.7.3.309

Floyd, F. J., & Widaman, K. F. (1995). Factor analysis in the development and refinement of clinical assessment instruments. *Psychological Assessment, 7*, 286–299. doi:10.1037/1040-3590.7.3.286

Messick, S. (1995). Validity of psychological assessment: Validation of inferences from persons' responses and performances as scientific inquiry into score meaning. *American Psychologist, 50*, 741–749. doi:10.1037/0003-066X.50.9.741

Reise, S. P., Waller, N. G., & Comrey, A. L. (2000). Factor analysis and scale revision. *Psychological Assessment, 12*, 287–297. doi:10.1037/1040-3590.12.3.287

Schmitt, N. (1996). Uses and abuses of coefficient alpha. *Psychological Assessment, 8*, 350–353. doi:10.1037/1040-3590.8.4.350

Informative introductions to psychometrics, structural modeling, and IRT that we recommend include

Embretson, S. E., & Reise, S. P. (2000). *Item response theory for psychologists.* Mahwah, NJ: Erlbaum.

Kline, R. B. (2004). *Principles and practice of structural equation modeling* (2nd ed.). New York, NY: Guilford Press.

McDonald, R. P. (1999). *Test theory.* Mahwah, NJ: Erlbaum.

Nunnally, J. C., & Bernstein, I. H. (1994). *Psychometric theory* (3rd ed.). New York, NY: McGraw-Hill.

REFERENCES

Brown, W. (1910). Some experimental results in the correlation of mental abilities. *The British Journal of Psychology, 3*, 296–322.

Campbell, D. T., & Fiske, D. W. (1959). Convergent and discriminant validation by the multitrait–multimethod matrix. *Psychological Bulletin, 56*, 81–105. doi:10.1037/h0046016

Cattell, R. B., & Tsujioka, B. (1964). The importance of factor-trueness and validity, versus homogeneity and orthogonality, in test scales. *Educational and Psychological Measurement, 24*, 3–30. doi:10.1177/001316446402400101

Cho, Y. I., Boeninger, D. K., Masyn, K. E., Conger, R. D., & Widaman, K. F. (2010). *Linking of scales in longitudinal research: Comparing item response theory and second-order latent growth model approaches.* Manuscript submitted for publication.

Clark, L. A., & Watson, D. (1995). Constructing validity: Basic issues in objective scale development. *Psychological Assessment, 7*, 309–319. doi:10.1037/1040-3590.7.3.309

Cohen, P., Cohen, J., Aiken, L. S., & West, S. G. (1999). The problem of units and the circumstances for POMP. *Multivariate Behavioral Research, 34*, 315–346. doi:10.1207/S15327906MBR3403_2

Cronbach, L. J. (1951). Coefficient alpha and the internal structure of tests. *Psychometrika, 16*, 297–334. doi:10.1007/BF02310555

Cronbach, L. J., & Meehl, P. E. (1955). Construct validity in psychological tests. *Psychological Bulletin, 52*, 281–302. doi:10.1037/h0040957

Curran, P. J., Hussong, A. M., Cai, L., Huang, W., Chassin, L., Sher, K. J., & Zucker, R. A. (2008). Pooling data from multiple longitudinal studies: The role of item response theory in integrative data analysis. *Developmental Psychology, 44*, 365–380. doi:10.1037/0012-1649.44.2.365

Eid, M., & Diener, E. (Eds.). (2006). *Handbook of multimethod measurement in psychology*. Washington, DC: American Psychological Association. doi:10.1037/11383-000

Embretson, S. E., & Reise, S. P. (2000). *Item response theory for psychologists*. Mahwah, NJ: Erlbaum.

Floyd, F. J., & Widaman, K. F. (1995). Factor analysis in the development and refinement of clinical assessment instruments. *Psychological Assessment, 7*, 286–299. doi:10.1037/1040-3590.7.3.286

John, O. P., Donahue, E. M., & Kentle, R. L. (1991). The Big Five Inventory—Versions 4a and 5. Berkeley, CA: Institute of Personality and Social Research.

John, O. P., & Soto, C. J. (2007). The importance of being valid: Reliability and the process of construct validation. In R. W. Robins, R. C. Fraley, & R. F. Krueger (Eds.), *Handbook of research methods in personality psychology* (pp. 461–494). New York, NY: Guilford Press.

Kishton, J. M., & Widaman, K. F. (1994). Unidimensional versus domain representative parceling of questionnaire items: An empirical example. *Educational and Psychological Measurement, 54*, 757–765. doi:10.1177/0013164494054003022

Kline, R. B. (2004). *Principles and practice of structural equation modeling* (2nd ed.). New York, NY: Guilford Press.

Little, T. D., Cunningham, W. A., Shahar, G., & Widaman, K. F. (2002). To parcel or not to parcel: Exploring the question, weighing the merits. *Structural Equation Modeling, 9*, 151–173. doi:10.1207/S15328007SEM0902_1

Little, T. D., Lindenberger, U., & Nesselroade, J. R. (1999). On selecting indicators for multivariate measurement and modeling with latent variables: When "good" indicators are bad and "bad" indicators are good. *Psychological Methods, 4*, 192–211. doi:10.1037/1082-989X.4.2.192

Loevinger, J. (1954). The attenuation paradox in test theory. *Psychological Bulletin, 51*, 493–504. doi:10.1037/h0058543

Lord, F. M., & Novick, M. R. (1968). *Statistical theories of mental test scores*. Reading, MA: Addison-Wesley.

McDonald, R. P. (1970). The theoretical foundations of principal factor analysis, canonical factor analysis, and alpha factor analysis. *British Journal of Mathematical and Statistical Psychology, 23*, 1–21.

McDonald, R. P. (1999). *Test theory*. Mahwah, NJ: Erlbaum.

Messick, S. (1995). Validity of psychological assessment: Validation of inferences from persons' responses and performances as scientific inquiry into score meaning. *American Psychologist, 50*, 741–749. doi:10.1037/0003-066X.50.9.741

Muthén, L. K., & Muthén, B. O. (1998–2007). *Mplus user's guide* (4th ed.). Los Angeles, CA: Authors.

Nunnally, J. C., & Bernstein, I. H. (1994). *Psychometric theory* (3rd ed.). New York, NY: McGraw-Hill.

Rammstedt, B., & John, O. P. (2007). Measuring personality in one minute or less: A 10-item short version of the Big Five Inventory in English and German. *Journal of Research in Personality, 41*, 203–212. doi:10.1016/j.jrp.2006.02.001

Reise, S. P., Waller, N. G., & Comrey, A. L. (2000). Factor analysis and scale revision. *Psychological Assessment, 12*, 287–297. doi:10.1037/1040-3590.12.3.287

Rosenberg, M. (1965). *Society and the adolescent self-image*. Princeton, NJ: Princeton University Press.

Schmitt, N. (1996). Uses and abuses of coefficient alpha. *Psychological Assessment, 8*, 350–353. doi:10.1037/1040-3590.8.4.350

Spearman, C. (1910). Correlation calculated with faulty data. *The British Journal of Psychology, 3*, 271–295.

Westen, D., & Rosenthal, R. (2003). Quantifying construct validity: Two simple measures. *Journal of Personality and Social Psychology, 84*, 608–618. doi:10.1037/0022-3514.84.3.608

Widaman, K. F. (1985). Hierarchically nested covariance structure models for multitrait–multimethod data. *Applied Psychological Measurement, 9*, 1–26. doi:10.1177/014662168500900101

Widaman, K. F. (1993). Common factor analysis versus principal component analysis: Differential bias in representing model parameters? *Multivariate Behavioral Research, 28*, 263–311. doi:10.1207/s15327906mbr2803_1

Widaman, K. F. (2007). Common factors versus components: Principals and principles, errors and misconceptions. In R. Cudeck & R. C. MacCallum (Eds.), *Factor analysis at 100: Historical developments and future directions* (pp. 177–203). Mahwah, NJ: Erlbaum.

Widaman, K. F. (2008). Integrative perspectives on cognitive aging: Measurement and modeling with mixtures of psychological and biological variables. In S. M. Hofer & D. F. Alwin (Eds.), *The handbook of cognitive aging: Interdisciplinary perspectives* (pp. 50–68). Thousand Oaks, CA: Sage.

Zinbarg, R. E., Revelle, W., & Yovel, I. (2007). Estimating ω_h for structures containing two group factors: Perils and prospects. *Applied Psychological Measurement, 31*, 135–157. doi:10.1177/0146621606291558

Zinbarg, R. E., Yovel, I., Revelle, W., & McDonald, R. P. (2006). Estimating the generalizability to a latent variable common to all of a scale's indicators: A comparison of estimators of ω_h. *Applied Psychological Measurement, 30*, 121–144. doi:10.1177/0146621605278814

4

ANALYZING SURVEY DATA WITH COMPLEX SAMPLING DESIGNS

PATRICK E. SHROUT AND JAIME L. NAPIER

American psychologists are known for taking a casual view of sampling. Most studies published in our journals report findings that are based on U.S. college students, but the results are written as if they describe universal processes in perception, memory, decision making, attitudes, moods, distress, romantic attraction, group processes, and so on. The studies do not even represent a formal snapshot of the college students on a campus but rather those who are interested enough in psychology to register for a class. The justification for this tradition lies in the fact that most studies are experimental in nature—that is, subjects are randomly assigned to groups that receive different treatments. Inferences about processes arise from contrasts of the treatment groups, and there is little interest in the absolute level of the responses in any group. If the manipulations produce predicted results in these samples of convenience, then psychologists infer that similar results would be found with samples from some specific population. This inference assumes that the effect of the manipulation would not interact with characteristics of the population, and under these inferential rules, critics are assigned the burden of proof to show that the assumption does not hold.

In contrast to the typical approach of psychologists, the approach taken by sociologists, epidemiologists, and demographers who produce secondary data sets is one of formal sampling. A population is defined, a representation of the individuals in the population is constructed (i.e., the sampling frame), and random samples from the frame are drawn using either simple or complex sampling plans (Cochran, 1977; Levy & Lemeshow, 1999). Although some researchers engage in survey experiments (e.g., Duan et al, 2007; Schuman & Bobo, 1988; Sniderman & Piazza, 1993) and therefore focus on contrasts of conditions, most survey researchers are interested in describing levels of responses and patterns of association of variables in the population. For example, political scientists might be interested in what proportion of the population endorses some controversial position and whether that proportion varies with gender, age, and residential region. Epidemiologists might want to know how many episodes of posttraumatic stress disorder were reported among a group of returning war veterans. Unlike the psychologists' default assumption that associations do not interact in any important way with demographic characteristics, survey researchers assume that levels and associations vary across many strata in the population. From this perspective, the burden of proof for a universalist point of view is to show that associations do not vary over levels of key demographic variables. Formal survey analysis methods provide for meaningful average results, even when the effect that is being averaged varies in strength from one subgroup to the next. These methods, however, require a sample that has been constructed to provide information about the average result in the population. Such samples are informally called "representative samples."[1] A corollary of the demographer's position is that samples of convenience are likely to give biased representations of both levels of variables and strength of associations, and that no statistical adjustment is available to eliminate the bias.

When psychologists find it useful to use secondary survey data to make statements with more external validity than those that can be made with college students, or to investigate levels of variables outside of college campuses, they must decide how seriously to take the documented sample survey plan. For example, secondary data often include sets of sampling weights, and information about primary and secondary sampling units. When results of secondary analysis of existing data are published in psychology journals, reviewers and editors may or may not require that these sampling variables be considered in the analysis. What difference does it make? How would one take the information into account if one wanted to? In this chapter, we attempt to provide an overview of answers to these questions. For more details about these topics, we refer interested readers to a number of useful texts (Lee, 2006; Levy & Lemeshow,

---

[1]Statisticians do not like this informal term, as the sample does not ever represent the population precisely. However, methodologists often use this term to state that some effort was taken to design a sample that can be used to produce unbiased estimates of population values.

1999; Skinner, Holt, & Smith, 1989; StataCorp, 2007; for a more technical reference, see Sarndal, Swensson, & Wretman, 1992).

A NUMERICAL EXAMPLE

Let's start with a simple example. Suppose we were interested in the responses to the following survey question regarding immigrant amnesty: "I believe that immigrants who are working in the United States illegally but who are otherwise law abiding should be offered a chance to register for legal status without returning to their country of origin." Suppose response options ranged from 1 (*strongly disagree*) to 7 (*strongly agree*), with 4 serving as the neutral middle point. Table 4.1 shows fictional responses of 36 subjects. The average response in this sample is 3.78, which suggests that on average this group is inclined to modestly oppose amnesty.

If the numbers in Table 4.1 were a simple random sample[2] from a large population, the sample mean and standard error would provide an unbiased estimate of the group attitude. However, simple random samples are expensive to obtain, and it is more common to enumerate households and then carry out a two-step selection process. First, a household is selected, and then one person living in the household is selected. The data in Table 4.1 were created with this sampling design, and the number of persons per household (N_h) is shown in the table. Note that persons who live in a household with more members are less likely to be included in the sample than persons who live alone. Not only must their household be selected but also the probability that one individual will be selected within a household is inversely related to the household size, ($1/N_h$). Thus, this sample design oversamples persons in smaller households, but it does so in a way that can be addressed in the analysis.

If attitude toward amnesty is associated with the household size, then the simple mean of the 35 observations in Table 4.1 will be biased.[3] The data in Table 4.1 were created to have persons living alone more opposed to amnesty than persons living in groups of three, four, or five persons. In this case, the sample mean will suggest more opposition to amnesty than in the full population, as the persons living alone are overrepresented in the sample. Because we generated the data in Table 4.1 from a simulation study, we know the population mean. It was 4.07, which is, it is important to note, larger than

---

[2]A simple random sample would require that all persons were enumerated and that selection was obtained by using some random rule to select 35 persons directly from the sampling frame.
[3]Bias from a statistical perspective is the difference in the expected value of a statistic from the true population value.

TABLE 4.1
Data for Amnesty Survey Item for 36 Fictional Respondents

Subject ID	Household ID	Household size	Survey response	Survey response
1	14	1	3	3
2	33	1	2	2
3	131	1	3	3
4	221	1	3	3
5	249	1	2	2
6	405	1	3	3
7	453	1	3	3
8	474	1	2	2
9	487	1	3	3
10	489	1	4	4
11	97	2	4	4
12	108	2	5	5
13	134	2	5	5
14	161	2	5	5
15	247	2	5	5
16	287	2	3	3
17	291	2	2	2
18	343	2	3	3
19	369	2	4	4
20	396	2	3	3
21	286	3	3	3
22	325	3	3	3
23	337	3	6	6
24	348	3	5	5
25	356	3	3	3
26	375	3	4	4
27	383	3	4	4
28	407	3	2	2
29	418	3	3	3
30	67	4	5	5
31	157	4	5	5
32	169	4	5	5
33	268	4	6	6
34	340	4	7	7
35	417	4	3	3
36	27	5	5	5

Note. ID = Identification number.

the biased sample mean of 3.78 in Table 4.1.[4] In the next section, we discuss how sampling weights can be used to eliminate the bias, but these weights make inference more complicated. This is one reason that special software is needed for analysis of complex samples.

---

[4]The sample mean in this small example is not statistically different from the known population mean, but our simulation study allows us to calculate the expected value of the biased estimator. It is 3.80, which is quite close to the sample mean in this case, and it is important to note, smaller than the population mean.

The cost of obtaining survey data such as represented in Table 4.1 is usually associated with the initial contact of the household. Once a survey worker is in the household, the cost of adding an additional survey response from the household is often small. Suppose that such data were obtained from households with two or more residents. These additional observations are shown in Table 4.2. Although these additional observations help counteract the overinclusion of persons living alone, they introduce a new statistical challenge. In many cases, the response of one person in a household will be more like the response of other family members than persons sampled at random from other households. This is a cluster effect, and it violates the usual assumption that observations are independent. When we calculate the average of the observations in the two tables, the mean is 3.92, and this is closer to the known population mean. However, the estimate of the standard error of this mean that we obtain from a simple statistical program will be too

TABLE 4.2

Data for Amnesty Survey Item for 26 Additional Fictional Respondents From Households With Two or More People

Subject ID	Household ID	Household size	Survey response
37	97	2	3
38	108	2	3
39	134	2	4
40	161	2	5
41	247	2	4
42	287	2	6
43	291	2	4
44	343	2	4
45	369	2	4
46	396	2	4
47	286	3	4
48	325	3	4
49	337	3	5
50	348	3	4
51	356	3	5
52	375	3	5
53	383	3	3
54	407	3	5
55	418	3	2
56	67	5	5
57	157	4	3
58	169	4	5
59	268	4	4
60	340	4	4
61	417	4	3
62	27	5	5

Note. ID = Identification number.

TABLE 4.3

Means of Simulated Data in Tables 4.1 and 4.2, Ignoring Sample Design
and Considering Sample Design

Estimator	M	SE
Unweighted mean of 36 persons	3.78	0.2150
Unweighted mean of 62 persons in 36 clusters	3.92	0.1460
Weighted mean of 36 persons	4.12	0.2155
Weighted mean of 62 persons in 36 clusters	4.05	0.1471

small. The clustered data usually provides less information than independent data, and therefore the standard error estimate needs to be adjusted with special software.

Table 4.3 shows a comparison of the population mean, and four estimates of the mean. The first is a simple mean and standard error estimate of data in Table 4.1, with no adjustment for sample selection probability. The second is a simple mean and standard error estimate of data in Tables 4.1 and 4.2, with no adjustment for either selection or clustering. The third estimate is an estimate of the Table 4.1 mean, taking into account sampling weights, and the last is an estimate of data in Tables 4.1 and 4.2, with adjustments for both weights and clustering. If these were real data, the different methods used would lead political commentators to give different spins on the outcomes of the survey. The biased mean, which is less than the neutral point of 4.0, suggests that on average the population is modestly against amnesty, whereas the unbiased mean suggests that this population is on average undecided on the issue of amnesty.

DETAILS OF SURVEY ANALYSIS ISSUES

To set the stage for understanding alternate approaches for the analysis of data from complex survey designs, we briefly consider five technical sample survey issues. These issues are (a) a possible correction for finite populations, (b) random versus systematic samples, (c) stratified samples, (d) sample weights, and (e) cluster samples. For a full discussion of these topics, see Levy and Lemeshow (1999).

Finite Population Corrections

When the numerical example was introduced, we asked the reader to suppose that the population being sampled was large. Now consider the opposite. Suppose that the sample was taken from a small town with around

200 persons age 18 or older. Such a sample might be drawn by investigators who have a specific interest in this small town and who have no intention of making inferences to other similar towns or populations. If the scope of inference were specified in this way, then Tables 4.1 and 4.2 would represent the opinion of a sizable number of the population. Sampling statisticians would take the small size of the town population very seriously. They would note that the sampling was done without replacement (see Levy & Lemeshow, 1999, pp. 48) and that therefore the standard error of the average town attitude would be smaller (by a factor of about .866)[5] than that of an average attitude of a large population. This adjustment is called a *finite population correction* (fpc), and it reflects the trade-off of limited inferential scope for improved precision of an estimate.

The survey software packages that we discuss later (SPSS Complex Samples, SAS, Stata) all have provisions for making finite population corrections. Although these corrections make the standard errors smaller and hence can lead to more findings that are statistically significant, they should be used with care when reporting to the psychology community. If a secondary data set, for example, is designed to represent the South Side of Chicago, the investigators would have to limit any inferences to that specific community if they used finite population corrections in the analysis. To avoid making the finite population correction, the analyst either specifies in the software that the sampling was done with replacement or refrains from specifying the population total size.

Random Versus Systematic Samples

Once a sampling frame has been identified, survey researchers may draw either random samples without replacement or systematic samples. The former uses some list of random numbers to select persons and ignores persons who have already been selected. The latter typically orders the population according to some variable and then selects participants according to some fixed rate. If the first selection is random and the ordering is done without regard to any judgments or preferences of the investigators, then the systematic sample is a special kind of random sample. For example, an exit poll survey might recruit every 15th person who exits from a polling location. Although the overall sampling rate may be the same in each strategy, the conditional probability of being selected varies across strategies, most notably with regard to whether the ordering variable used for systematic sampling is related to the

---

[5]If N is the number of persons in the population and n is the number of persons in the sample, then the finite population correction for the standard error of the mean is $\text{SQRT}[(N - n)/N]$ for a simple random sample. Similar adjustments are made for estimates from more complex sampling designs.

outcome of interest. See Levy and Lemeshow (1999, pp. 81–120) for some issues that can arise with systematic sampling. These are generally small issues, and we do not distinguish systematic samples from other random samples.

Stratified Samples

Stratified sampling designs are ones in which the population is divided into groups or strata and possibly different proportions of respondents are selected within each stratum. For example, samples might be stratified to obtain larger numbers of minority group members, equal numbers of men and women, or equal numbers of urban and rural residents. This design can provide more precision for contrasts of these groups and also provides more precision for stratum-specific estimates. Sampling statisticians distinguish between design-based stratification and poststratification. The former describes the breakdown of the sample according to variables used to collect the sample, whereas the latter describes breakdowns of the sample using variables that were obtained during the survey itself. Formal analysis of poststratification often takes into account the fact that the actual numbers of persons in each stratum may themselves be affected by sampling variation.

Sample Weights

In stratified samples, and certain multiple stage sample designs, the probability of selection into the sample varies systematically. In these cases, sample weights can be developed to adjust for the differences between the distribution of the sample and the population. Typically, the weight is the reciprocal of the probability of sample selection. For example, if households in a large urban area are chosen at the rate of 1 per 1,000 from some sampling frame, and 1 person is chosen from the N_h persons in the hth household, then the probability of selection for the selected persons is the product of two sampling rates: $(1/1,000) \times (1/N_h)$. The first sampling rate is the same for all households, but the second rate varies according to household size.

If the outcome varies across strata levels and if an overall estimate of the population mean is desired, then the researcher should consider using sampling weights in the analysis. Let p_i be the probability of the ith person being selected. An appropriate sampling weight is $w_i = (1/p_i)$. If Y_i is the response of the ith person ($i = 1, n$) then the weighted estimate of the population mean is

$$\overline{Y}_W = \frac{\sum_{i=1}^{n} w_i Y_i}{\sum_{i=1}^{J} w_i}. \tag{1}$$

The denominator of this estimate is equal to the total number of persons in the population. One interpretation of this estimate is that the obtained survey responses are weighted to represent the persons in the population stratum who were not selected. When the precision of this estimate is assessed, it is important to keep track of how many observations were actually interviewed. Special survey software keeps track of the relative size of the sample to the population when computing standard errors of measures, but routine application of weight functions in nonsurvey sections of SPSS or SAS do not necessarily keep track of these numbers.

A common way to keep track of the actual numbers of survey participants is to use a relative weight, which sums to the sample size rather than the population size. If N is the population size and n is the sample size, then $(rw)_i = w_i \times (n/N)$. Many times, this alternative weight is provided in the secondary data set. The weighed mean is unaffected by which weight is used, because they are proportional to each other. The relative weight cannot be used if finite population correction methods are to be used.

Are sampling weights always required? There are differences of opinion in the statistics community. Traditional survey statisticians recommend using weights that are consistent with the sampling design, and this approach is called *design-based* analysis. Other statisticians have argued that if the researcher is interested in modeling the variables that were used to create the sampling strata, and if one can be reasonably sure that the statistical model is correct,[6] then a regression-based analysis gives interpretable results without using weights (DuMouchel & Duncan, 1983). Still other statisticians suggest using weights, but only after the most extreme weight values have been shrunken toward the mean weight (e.g., Meng, Alegria, Chen, & Liu, 2004). This last position is taken by those who worry about excessive influence of only a few survey points, but it might lead to biased estimators.

In some cases, a stratified sample is designed so that weights are not needed. These so-called self-weighting samples are constructed so that the sampling units are selected with probability associated with their size. However, even with such initial sampling designs, weights are presented in the secondary data set. Typically, these are poststratification weights that attempt to adjust for missing data due to differential nonresponse. Other approaches to missing data are addressed in Chapter 5, this volume.

Cluster Samples

As we noted in our numerical example, it is often relatively inexpensive to obtain survey information from an additional respondent once one has

---

[6]*Correct* in this case means that important variables related to the outcome are included and that the functional forms of the relationships (e.g., a linear or nonlinear relation) are properly specified.

made contact with the household. This principle can be generalized to produce a cluster sample design. The survey organization can enumerate primary sampling units (PSUs), such as census tracts, zip codes, or counties, and obtain random samples of these geographic units. Next, the households within the sampled units are enumerated and a sample obtained of these nested units. Within the households, the sampling plan might call for obtaining multiple participants from among those eligible. The primary benefit of a cluster sample design is cost saving in the fieldwork. The disadvantage is that the additional surveys that are obtained do not add as much information to the parameter estimates as independent observations.

The loss of information of additional observations within clusters is sometimes called the *design effect* (Levy & Lemeshow, 1999, p. 302). The design effect is a function of both the proportion of observations that are clustered together and the empirical similarity of observations within the cluster relative to observations across clusters. Depending on how similar respondents are within clusters, the effective sample size might vary from the total sample n (a design effect of 1.0) to the (much smaller) number of PSUs (a design effect of $n/[\# \text{PSU's}]$). What we mean by similarity of observations depends on the outcome variable being analyzed. A cluster sample might be very efficient for one outcome but not very efficient for another. Design effects are largest for outcomes that are influenced by neighborhood and family factors. Because cluster sample designs produce sequences of observations that cannot be assumed to be independent, it is especially important to use survey sample software that takes the dependency of the data into account when computing standard errors of estimates.

SOFTWARE APPROACHES

Standard software for carrying out analyses of descriptive statistics, cross-tabulations, correlations, linear regression, logistic regression, and other multivariate models typically assumes that the observations are independent and the target population is orders of magnitude larger than the sample. In contrast, special survey software can take into account finite population corrections, sample design weights, poststratification weights, and multiple levels of clustering. These programs typically use explicit formulas for estimates and their standard errors that are based on Taylor series linear approximations (e.g., SUDAAN from Research Triangle Institute, 1989), or they use resampling methods (e.g., WesVar from Weststat, 2007). Although these specialized programs are still preferred by many survey statisticians, in recent years, general purpose statistical analysis systems such as SPSS, SAS, and Stata have added survey analysis modules that implement Taylor series methods for estimates and standard errors. Readers are encouraged to consult Levy and Lemeshow (1999), who provide both Stata and SUDAAN syntax examples for a wide variety of analyses of complex sample data. On our website (http://www.psych.nyu.edu/couples/SurveySyntax.rtf) we provide illustrations of SPSS, SAS, and Stata syntax for the estimation of descriptive statistics and a simple regression analysis of a secondary data set.

EMPIRICAL EXAMPLE: AMERICAN NATIONAL ELECTION STUDY OF 2000

The American National Election Studies (ANES, n.d.) has conducted surveys of the American electorate every presidential and midterm election year since 1952. The foci of these surveys are to identify who participates in political campaigns and elections, the political and social values of potential voters, and perceptions and evaluations of political candidates and public policy issues. Respondents are interviewed prior to the election and are then re-interviewed immediate after the election. Data from these surveys are publicly available on the ANES home page (http://electionstudies.org).

Sample Design of National Election Study 2000

Although the complex sample designs in textbooks seem complicated, the designs used in some secondary data sets can make the textbooks look simple. The sample design of the ANES 2000 provides a case in point. The sample includes responses from 1,807 persons, but they entered the sample through two different sampling designs. One group ($n = 1,006$) was sampled through a four-stage cluster sample design, and the selected individuals were interviewed face-to-face (FTF group). Another group ($n = 801$) was sampled by using random digit dialing methods, and these respondents were interviewed on the telephone (TEL group). Both samples are formally representative of the 48 contiguous states and can be compared to determine whether sampling design and interview mode affected responses. Details of the sampling designs of both samples are available online,[7] but are summarized here.

Design for the Face-to-Face Group

The 48 contiguous states were divided into 108 mutually exclusive units for the first stage of sampling. The largest eight of these units were selected

---

[7]http://www.electionstudies.org/studypages/2000prepost/2000prepost.htm

with certainty (e.g., New York City, Los Angeles, Chicago, Dallas/Fort Worth). Of the 20 next largest PSUs, 10 were selected (e.g., Houston, Seattle/Tacoma, Cleveland, Denver) using a stratified design that randomly selected one unit from pairs of cities that were formed to be similar geographically. In addition to these 18 locations, 26 PSUs were sampled from the 80 remaining units with the probability of selection proportionate to size (on the basis of 1990 census information). For the second stage of selection, PSUs were divided into "area segments" on the basis of 1990 census information, and six to 12 segments were selected within PSUs with a selection probability proportionate to size. A total of 279 such segments were selected. For the third stage of selection, 2,269 housing units were enumerated within the segments and housing units were selected with equal probability. Of the 1,639 occupied selected housing units, 1,564 contained eligible persons. To be eligible, persons needed to have been both a U.S. citizen and 18 years of age on or before November 7, 2000. For the final stage of selection, one resident per housing unit was selected at random using a procedure described by Kish (1949). The response rate for the FTF survey was calculated to be .64.

Design for the Telephone Group

In contrast to the FTF sample, the TEL sample was not clustered but was a stratified equal probability sample. A commercial vendor provided "banks" of telephone numbers that were composed of the first eight digits of 10-digit phone numbers. These banks contain 100 possible numbers, and they were used if at least two of the 100 were known to be residential numbers and if the numbers were associated with the 48 contiguous states. An initial sample of 8,500 numbers was selected from the eligible banks, and these were linked to geographic locations on the basis of their area codes and exchanges. The numbers were then stratified according to the competitiveness of the upcoming congressional election, whether the race was open, and the Census division. An initial set of 2,349 numbers was sampled, and 1,475 of these numbers were determined to belong to occupied households. Of these, 1,418 contained eligible respondents, and 801 provided responses, for a .56 response rate.

Analysis Considerations

ANES 2000 provides a composite sampling weight for each respondent. It incorporates sampling probability, nonresponse adjustments based on Census region, and poststratification adjustments based on age group and education level. The weight is scaled so that its sum equals the sample size, 1,807. This scaling makes it difficult to make finite population corrections, but that is not a concern in the tradition of the way psychologists provide evidence. Moreover, the size of the U.S. population is so large relative to the sample size that these adjustments would have little impact. The scaling of the weights to the obtained sample size allows the weight to be used in standard statistical programs to get estimates of the standard errors of estimates that are in the ballpark of the correct estimates. In the codebook of the ANES 2000, the survey researchers report that the standard errors from standard programs are likely to be too small by a factor of 1.098 on average.[8]

To obtain the best measures of estimation precision, one needs to explicitly take the sampling design into account in the analysis. Although the ANES 2000 sample is defined as a composite of two different designs, one for the FTF mode and one for the TEL mode, the public access data set provides combined survey design variables that incorporate the needed information for an appropriate analysis. A variable called *sampling error stratum code* (SESC) is provided that links each person to a sample design PSU and a sample area segment. To ensure confidentiality of the responses, the specific identities of sample area segments within PSUs are not provided in the public access version of the data. In combination with interview mode (FTF vs. TEL), combined sampling weight and the SESC variable is all that is needed to use Taylor series methods to take into account the complex sampling design in the analysis.[9] Insofar as the responses within SESC groupings are more homogeneous than responses across the groupings, the standard errors of parameter estimates need to be larger than those based on observations that are completely independent.

In the analyses that are presented in the next section, we specified the interview mode as a major stratification variable, the SESC groups as the key clustering variable, and the composite weight as the adjustment for differing selection probabilities and non-response. We treated the sample as if it were sampled with replacement, which implies that the population is substantially larger than the sample. This latter treatment removes any adjustments for finite populations.

Political Orientation and Need for Cognition

In 2000, the ANES added items to the survey that assessed the respondents' cognitive style, namely the "need for cognition" (Cacioppo & Petty, 1982).

---

[8]The survey researchers examined a variety of outcomes and calculated an average square root of the design effect to be 1.098 for the combined sample, 1.076 for the FTF sample, and 1.049 for the TEL sample. Multiplying the standard errors from the usual statistical packages by these values will give a better approximation to the correct standard error.

[9]The information that is needed for this analysis is provided in the public access codebook, but it is embedded in several pages of technical description. Analysts need to patiently review all the technical material provided on the public access files to find the necessary information.

Need for cognition is a measure of the extent to which an individual tends to enjoy engaging in effortful cognitive activities. Prior research suggests that the need for cognition may be related to political orientation. Specifically, research on the differences in cognitive style between political liberals and conservatives suggest that those who lean toward the liberal side of the political spectrum tend to enjoy thinking more and to prolong cognitive closure as compared with those who lean more toward the conservative side (Jost et al., 2007; Kruglanski, Pierro, Mannetti, & De Grada, 2006). For our example, we examine the relationship between political orientation and the need for cognition among respondents in the pre-election ANES 2000 survey.

Need for cognition was assessed in the ANES 2000 with two items: a dichotomous question that asked whether the respondent preferred difficult (vs. simple) problems and an item that measured the extent to which the respondent liked responsibility for thinking, measured on a 5-point scale ranging from 1 (*dislike a lot*) to 5 (*like a lot*). These variables were strongly correlated ($r = .49$), and the responses were combined to create an overall need for cognition measure. They were scaled to range from 1 to 5 and then averaged (Bizer, Krosnick, Petty, Rucker, & Wheeler, S. C., 2002). Out of 1,807 respondents, 1,802 responded to these items. Political orientation was assessed on a 7-point scale ranging from 1 (*strong liberal*) to 7 (*strong conservative*). Out of 1,807 survey respondents, 1,623 responded to this item.

Descriptive Statistics

In Table 4.4, we show six different estimates of means and standard errors for the need for cognition and political orientation variables. The first two use standard (nonsurvey) software procedures, whereas the last four use complex survey software (see http://www.psych.nyu.edu/couples/SurveySyntax.rtf for SPSS, Stata, and SAS syntax).[10] As shown in the first two rows of the table, the application of sample weights in the standard software has a small effect on the mean for need for cognition but scarcely any effect for political orientation. The estimates of the standard errors, which ignore the sample clusters, are not much affected the application of the weights. This is not surprising because the weights have been scaled to sum to the sample size. When complex sample software is used with weights, we obtain the same estimates of means as provided by the standard software (when weights were used), but the estimates of standard errors are slightly larger, even without taking strata and cluster information into account. When clustering is considered, the standard error estimates for both variables increase further. This implies that individuals

---

[10]For these results, as well as the regression results presented next, the three software systems produced exactly the same estimates and standard errors for the different conditions.

TABLE 4.4
Descriptive Statistics for Need for Cognition and Political Orientation

Sample design feature	Need for cognition		Political orientation	
	M	*SE*	*M*	*SE*
Without complex samples software				
No weight	3.40	.033	4.34	.041
Sample weight	3.30	.033	4.35	.040
With complex samples software				
Weight only	3.30	.036	4.35	.043
Weight and strata	3.30	.036	4.35	.043
Weight and cluster	3.30	.043	4.35	.046
Weight, strata, and cluster	3.30	.042	4.35	.046

within each cluster were more likely to respond in a similar way than individuals across clusters. Thus, not considering the nonindependence of observations would lead to a biased estimate of the standard errors. The ratio of the standard error in the last row of Table 4.4 to that of row 3 provides an estimate of the square root of the design effect. For need for cognition, the estimate is $0.047/0.033 = 1.17$, and for political orientation it is $0.046/0.043 = 1.07$. One is larger and one is smaller than the average values provided in the ANES codebook and illustrate the fact that design effects vary with the outcomes.

Regression Analysis

Next, we examined the relation of political orientation to need for cognition while adjusting for age, sex, marital status, and region. Ages ranged from 18 to 97, with a mean of 47.21. Sex was dummy coded so that "0" = males and "1" = females. Marital status was entered as dummy codes with those who are widowed, divorced or separated, single, and partnered compared with those who are married. Region was entered as dummy codes with individuals living in the Northeast, North Central, and Western United States compared with those living in the South.

We estimated three regression models: a model without weights, one with sample weights only, and a model that accounted for clusters and strata using survey software (see http://www.psych.nyu.edu/couples/SurveySyntax.rtf for the syntax to run this latter model in SPSS, SAS, and Stata). As shown in Table 4.5, these three models could lead to different conclusions. For instance, in the unweighted model, one might conclude that people who are widowed do not differ significantly from married people on political orientation. When the sample weight was taken into account (either with or without using complex samples survey software) as shown in the second and third columns

TABLE 4.5
Predicting Political Orientation With Age, Marital Status, Region, and Need for Cognition

Independent variable	Without complex samples software						With complex samples software					
	No weights			Weight only			Weight only			Weight, strata, and clusters		
	b	SE	p	b	SE	p	b	SE	p	b	SE	p
Need for cognition	-.057	.030	.060	-.073	.030	.014	-.073	.031	.018	-.073	.032	.023
Age (decades)	.055	.029	.058	.051	.028	.069	.051	.030	.092	.051	.030	.098
Female	-.244	.083	.003	-.238	.081	.004	-.238	.087	.006	-.238	.083	.005
Widowed	-.255	.161	.113	-.309	.175	.078	-.309	.167	.065	-.309	.150	.041
Divorced	-.471	.115	.000	-.452	.125	.000	-.452	.122	.000	-.452	.116	.000
Single	-.584	.114	.000	-.653	.113	.000	-.653	.121	.000	-.653	.111	.000
Partnered	-.963	.262	.000	-.932	.247	.000	-.932	.272	.001	-.932	.281	.001
Northeast	-.320	.118	.007	-.331	.112	.003	-.331	.124	.007	-.331	.122	.007
North Central	-.107	.106	.312	-.220	.104	.035	-.220	.107	.040	-.220	.114	.056
West	-.294	.109	.007	-.352	.109	.001	-.352	.117	.003	-.352	.116	.003

of Table 4.5, we found that the estimate for being widowed on political orientation increased and that the relationship between being widowed and political orientation is marginally significant. When the strata and clusters are considered, the standard errors are further refined, as shown in the third set of columns of Table 4.5. In this model, there is evidence that widows are significantly more liberal than married persons. In this case, the standard error decreased, which means that the design effect was less than one. This is unusual in cluster samples, and it suggests that the widow effect on political orientation may be somewhat more pronounced across clusters than within clusters.

In addition, the unweighted model shows that need for cognition is only marginally related to political orientation. When the sample weights are applied, the estimate increases and the association between political orientation and need for cognition are significant at the .05 level. In this case, when the strata and clusters are considered, the standard error increases slightly, but the effect remains statistically significant.

CONCLUSION

Secondary data sets are an excellent resource for psychological research. The use of nationally representative samples allows social psychologists to examine how levels of their variables of interest may differ among different demographics and to test their theories in samples that are more diverse then the typical college campus. The data from many carefully done surveys are publicly available and easy to obtain (see, e.g., Interuniversity Consortium for Political and Social Research: http://www.icpsr.umich.edu). However, the use of these data presents its own set of challenges for the researcher.

Probably the most exigent part of using secondary data in an analysis is to gauge a thorough understanding of the sampling design. Documentation of the strata, clusters, and weights are generally available for all surveys, but understanding these technical reports can be difficult and time-consuming. Nevertheless, if a researcher wants to make statements that extend to the general population or that are free of bias introduced by arbitrary sampling design decisions, it is important to consider the sampling methods in the analyses (see also Brogan, 1998). Once the strata, clusters, and weights are identified, analyzing data using general-purpose statistical software is often straightforward. However, special modules of the computer software systems are needed. One never knows how biased results might be when the sampling design is ignored, both in terms of the estimates and the standard errors, and so we recommend that these analytic methods become part of the standard psychological methodological repertoire.

REFERENCES

Bizer, G. Y., Kronsnick, J. A., Petty, R. E., Rucker, D. D., & Wheeler, S. C. (2000). Need for cognition and need to evaluate in the 1998 National Election Survey pilot study. *ANES Pilot Study Report, No. nes008997.* Retrieved from ftp://ftp.electionstudies.org/ftp/nes/bibliography/documents/nes008997.pdf

Brogan, D. J. (1998). Pitfalls of using standard statistical software packages for sample survey data. In P. Armitage & T. Colton (Eds.), *Encyclopedia of biostatistics* (Vol. 5; pp. 4167–4174). New York, NY: Wiley.

Cacioppo, J. T., & Petty, R. E. (1982). The need for cognition. *Journal of Personality and Social Psychology, 42,* 116–131. doi:10.1037/0022-3514.42.1.116

Cochran, W. G. (1977). *Sampling techniques.* New York, NY: Wiley.

Duan, N., Alegria, M., Canino, G., McGuire, T. G., & Takeuchi, D. (2007). Survey conditioning in self-reported mental health service use: Randomized comparison of alternative instrument formats. *Health Services Research, 42,* 890–907. doi:10.1111/j.1475-6773.2006.00618.x

DuMouchel, W. H., & Duncan, G. J. (1983). Using sample survey weights in multiple regression analyses of stratified samples. *Journal of the American Statistical Association, 78,* 535–543. doi:10.2307/2288115

Jost, J. T., Napier, J. L., Thorisdottir, H., Gosling, S. D., Palfai, T. P., & Ostafin, B. (2007). Are needs to manage uncertainty and threat associated with political conservatism or ideological extremity? *Personality and Social Psychology Bulletin, 33,* 989–1007. doi:10.1177/0146167207301028

Kish, L. (1949). Procedure for objective respondent selection within the household. *Journal of the American Statistical Association, 44,* 380–387. doi:10.2307/2280236

Kruglanski, A. W., Pierro, A., Mannetti, L., & De Grada, E. (2006). Groups as epistemic providers: Need for closure and the unfolding of group-centrism. *Psychological Review, 113,* 84–100. doi:10.1037/0033-295X.113.1.84

Lee, E. S., & Forthofer, R. N. (2006). *Analyzing complex survey data.* Thousand Oaks, CA: Sage.

Levy, P. S., & Lemeshow, S. (1999). *Sampling of populations: Methods and applications.* New York, NY: Wiley.

Meng, X.-L., Alegria, M., Chen, C., & Liu, J. (2004). A nonlinear hierarchical model for estimating prevalence rates with small samples. In T. Zheng (Chair), *ASA Proceedings of the Joint Statistical Meetings* (pp. 110–120). Alexandria, VA: American Statistical Association.

National Election Studies. (n.d.). *The 2000 National Election Study* [data set]. Ann Arbor, MI: University of Michigan, Center for Political Studies [producer and distributor]. Retrieved from http://electionstudies.org/studypages/download/datacenter_all.htm

Research Triangle Institute. (1989). *SUDAAN: Professional software for survey data analysis.* Research Triangle Park, NC: RTI.

Sarndal, C., Swensson, B., & Wretman, J. (1992). *Model-assisted survey sampling*. New York, NY: Springer-Verlag.

Schuman, H., & Bobo, L. (1988). Survey-based experiments on White racial attitudes toward residential integration. *American Journal of Sociology, 94*, 273–299. doi:10.1086/228992

Skinner, C. J., Holt, D., & Smith (1989). *Analysis of complex samples*. New York, NY: Wiley.

Sniderman, P. M., & Piazza, T. L. (1993). *The scar of race*. Cambridge, MA: Belknap Press.

StataCorp. (2007). *Stata statistical software: Release 10*. College Station, TX: StataCorp, LP.

Weststat. (2007). *WesVar 4.3 user's guide*. Rockville, MD: Author.

5

MISSING DATA IN SECONDARY DATA ANALYSIS

PATRICK E. McKNIGHT AND KATHERINE M. McKNIGHT

The greatest benefit of secondary data analysis is eliminating data collection troubles. Data in such contexts, by definition, come to us as is, and thus researchers are spared the data collection costs and hassles. One may argue, therefore, that the best data are those collected by others. However, secondary data also have their disadvantages. One disadvantage is that those who collected the data may not share your interests and may not have collected all of the data you need to address your research questions. Even if their interests are the same as yours, those who collected the data still may have overlooked key variables, designed or used poor measures, or failed to ensure the integrity of all records. In short, the data you need may be incomplete or completely missing. The purpose of this chapter is to introduce readers to various methods of handling missing data. Throughout, we address methodological and statistical problems researchers are likely to encounter due to missing data.

In previous work (McKnight, McKnight, Sidani, & Figuredo, 2007), we presented a simple, comprehensive five-step plan for conceptualizing and handling missing data. The comprehensive plan includes (a) understanding, (b) preventing, (c) diagnosing, (d) treating, and (e) reporting treatment methods and potential implications of missing data. Other missing data discussions tend to provide a brief overview (Step 1) and then a detailed description of treatment methods (Step 4) without addressing the other steps that may be most relevant to researchers. All five steps are relevant to research regardless of who collects the data—including data collected by others. Here, we discuss the five-step plan but tailored to secondary research.

STEP 1: UNDERSTAND MISSING DATA

An essential part of attending to missing data is understanding missing data. In particular, there are two essential areas of knowledge—the effects and language of missing data—that readers ought to be familiar before moving forward. We address each in the following sections.

Effects of Missing Data

Knowing how to prevent or treat missing data has almost no impact if researchers are not convinced that missing data pose a problem. As scientists, we are trained to avoid the kinds of problems that missing data present; most of us fail to recognize this fact. We learn that great care must be taken to ensure that causal inference is strong; we must minimize or prevent alternative hypotheses. Great care comes from rigorous research design, proper statistical analyses, and sound logic. Yet, missing data can still negatively affect scientific inference, despite great care in these areas. Missing data alter our designs and taint our data so that both no longer represent our true intentions. Our design no longer protects against known threats and our samples no longer represent the population of interest.

Research design allows researchers to infer causal relationships when they are able to control or account for the counterfactual (i.e., what would have happened if the hypothesized causal variable, such as a treatment, were not present). Controlling for the counterfactual requires rigorous research design such as random assignment to conditions, use of a control group, controlling for confounds, and so on. Without experimental control, researchers introduce the possibility of alternative explanations for study outcomes. Missing data present such a problem. The basic between-subjects experimental design, for example, relies on the assumption that subjects are randomly assigned to each study condition (e.g., treatment vs. control). When data are missing for subjects, such as when participants drop out, the random assignment assumption may no longer be tenable; there may be a systematic phenomenon responsible for missingness. Therefore, participants remaining in the study are not a random subset of the original sample. As a result, an initially strong experimental design becomes weaker because of the missing data. What was initially a "true" experiment is now a quasi-experiment, and quasi-experimental designs tend to produce weaker causal inference compared with experimental designs (Campbell & Stanley, 1963; Cook & Campbell, 1979). The primary weakness of quasi-experimental designs comes from threats to *internal validity*, or the extent to which one can infer that X is the cause of Y. As Campbell and Stanley (1963) noted, weaker designs introduce more threats to validity—also referred to as *alternative explanations* or *plausible rival hypotheses*. Missing data often produce weaker designs and introduce more threats to internal validity.

Missing data also affect *external validity* or *causal generalization*—that is, the extent to which researchers can generalize study results across different settings, procedures, and participants (Shadish, Cook, & Campbell, 2002). Recall that inferential statistics rely on random samples from a population of interest. Those samples are used to draw inferences about the population.[1] Of course, true random samples from a population are rarely if ever realized, but for the purposes of statistical inference, researchers have to assume that their data are derived from random samples. The missing data literature emphasizes that missing data affect statistical inference by potentially changing samples from random to some form of nonrandom. Although missing data do not guarantee that a sample is no longer representative, they increase the chances that the sample is less representative. A less representative sample of the target population threatens causal generalization.

Missing data may also affect *statistical conclusion validity* (Cook & Campbell, 1979), or the extent to which statistical analyses allow one to make correct decisions about relationships in the data. Findings based on statistical analyses are weakened if those findings are due to statistical artifact. One potential statistical artifact due to missing data is decreased statistical power. *Statistical power* is the probability of correctly rejecting the null hypothesis. *Power* is the probability of concluding, for example, that a relationship exists between a given treatment and an outcome based on statistical tests, when in fact, the relationship is nonzero.[2] The power of a statistical test depends on the statistical significance criterion used (e.g., $\alpha = .05$), the magnitude of the effect researchers are studying (i.e., effect size) in the population, and the sensitivity of the data. Missing data can have a detrimental effect on the ability of the data to show an effect (i.e., the sensitivity of the data). Reliability of measures, statistical control (e.g., including relevant variables in the statistical model), and sample size are all related to the sensitivity of the data. Missing data can affect all three of these factors.

---

[1]The inferential process we refer to here pertains primarily to frequentist statistical procedures. Bayesians typically do not hold to this dictum because Bayesian procedures allow for updating from previous studies or from within studies.

[2]A discussion of statistical power goes beyond the scope of this chapter. For a clear definition and description of statistical power, see Cohen (1988).

Regarding reliability of measures, classical test theory tells us that the observed score variance for a given measure is an additive combination of true score variance plus error variance. *Reliability* is defined as the proportion of the observed score variance that is "true" score variance, with higher proportions reflecting greater reliability. We want more "signal" (true score variance) than "noise" (error variance) in our measures; missing data can increase the noise and thus attenuate reliability in numerous ways. If data collectors fail to ensure that all items of a given scale are completed, then the observed score for a given measure would be based on only the observed data; potentially, the data may contain less true score variance. Items could be missing for systematic reasons, or they could be missing randomly. Ignoring or trying to make up for those missing items (e.g., by substituting item mean scores) can lead to various problems related to decreased sensitivity and decreased statistical power. Furthermore, using the item mean score as the estimate of a missing item value decreases the variance in total scale scores and introduces a source of noise in our measures. Increasing measurement noise means it will be more difficult to find relationships among variables. Statistical power is hampered, thus threatening statistical conclusion validity.

The problems at the item level can also occur at the variable level. When researchers use existing data, entire scale scores or variables may be missing, either because they were not included in the original design (an error of omission) or because participants failed to complete the measures. In the case of errors of omission, when using inferential statistics, researchers often assume that all relevant variables are included in their analysis. This problem is an issue of statistical control. Failure to include relevant variables in the statistical model renders statistical results questionable at best. When variables are omitted from statistical models, either because of omission from the study or because of failure to collect complete data from participants, the missing data threaten statistical conclusion validity. Relationships among variables may be more difficult to detect or, conversely, might be detected as an artifact of an incomplete statistical model.

Notably, the missing data literature tends to look much more closely at the effects of missing data at the participant or case level than at the variable or construct level. At the case level, sample size is a well-known issue as it relates to statistical power. Smaller samples are generally associated with decreased sensitivity of the data. As the law of large numbers and the central limit theorem dictates, all else being equal, larger samples lead to increased precision in estimates of population properties (e.g., the magnitude of the relationship between a given treatment and an outcome). All else being equal, larger samples produce smaller standard errors and confidence intervals, thereby enhancing statistical power.

A less commonly discussed problem associated with missing data and related to statistical conclusion validity is the sampling of measures used in a given study. Sampling applies not only to cases but to measurement as well. Measures and constructs are selected from a universe of measures and constructs, respectively. Inferential statistics hold two important assumptions about this selection procedure. The first is that any measure one chooses will be representative of what one wishes to measure; that is, the measure captures the essence of a fundamental property relevant to the research question. Many researchers refer to this as *construct validity*. The second assumption is that all relevant measures or constructs are included in the analysis. Missing data threaten these two basic assumptions. Regarding the first, missing data potentially decrease the degree that a measure captures the essence of the relevant property. How missing data affect the second has already been discussed (i.e., omission of relevant variables).

Language of Missing Data

To make sense of the literature, one must understand the language of missing data. Most of the missing data language is technical, often expressed in mathematical notation. The usual technical discussions in the missing data literature are potentially inaccessible to many researchers who may lack the mathematical or statistical background required. Here, we present the information at the conceptual level and avoid the mathematical notation altogether.

One of the more technical discussions in the missing data literature concerns missing data mechanisms. These mechanisms are central to the literature on the statistical handling of missing data. Researchers must all understand these terms to wisely handle the situation. In the statistical literature, missing data are typically characterized by three terms: *missing completely at random* (MCAR), *missing at random* (MAR), and *missing not at random* (MNAR). These terms denote the structure of missing data—often referred to as the missing data mechanism (Rubin, 1976) rather than the function of missing data. That is, the terms focus on the features versus the effects of the missing data. Much like the structure of a building tends to be of less focus to the occupants than its function, the structure of missing data tends to be less salient than its function to researcher. To the researcher, how missing data affect study results is more readily understood than how they are structured (McKnight et al., 2007). The structure, however, allows researchers to characterize data for clearer communication with others, and the language of missing data mechanisms is standard in statistical discussions and, therefore, is regarded as essential terminology. The easiest way to conceptualize the three terms is to see how they might be manifested in data. Table 5.1 shows a

TABLE 5.1
A Generic Data Set to Illustrate Missing Data Mechanisms

ID	IV	DV	MCAR.DV	MAR.DV	MNAR.DV
1	−0.30	1.96	1.96	1.96	1.96
2	−0.94	−1.47	−1.47		
3	−0.07	0.29	0.29	0.29	0.29
4	−0.09	−0.65	−0.65	−0.65	−0.65
5	0.83	−1.14	−1.14	−1.14	
6	−0.18	1.17	1.17	1.17	1.17
7	−0.04	−0.08	−0.08	−0.08	−0.08
8	−0.19	1.67	1.67	1.67	1.67
9	−0.21	−0.28		−0.28	−0.28
10	−0.33	0.86			0.86

Note. ID = identification; DV = dependent variable; MCAR.DV = dependent variable missing completely at random; MAR.DV = dependent variable missing at random; MNAR.DV = dependent variable missing not at random.

hypothetical, complete data set of 10 observations of three primary variables. In addition, there are three variables (right side of the table) corresponding to three different missing data scenarios for the dependent variable (DV).

MCAR is a condition in which cases (individuals) and variables are missing at random. If the DV in Table 5.1 were missing several observations at random (represented by the variable MCAR.DV), then, by definition, the missing data mechanism is completely random and falls under the label of MCAR. That is, there is no systematic means that accounts for what is observed or missing. MCAR comes about if the missing data cannot be accounted for by any mechanism other than chance alone. Statistically, MCAR is the best-case scenario for missing data because no systematic causes or bias exist for the missing data. However, causal forces almost always account for missing data, thus rendering MCAR unlikely in social science research.

MAR is a condition in which cases and variables are missing, but the missing values can be predicted by available data. Consider the variable MAR.DV in Table 5.1. Values for that variable are missing if the values for the independent variable (IV) were the lowest values. MAR mechanisms are often likely when individuals are followed over time in treatment studies and those who are either struggling to improve or have already improved no longer remain in the study. Statistically, MAR tends to be a manageable situation because the missingness can be modeled in the analysis.

MNAR—the most difficult situation statistically—is a condition in which cases and variables are missing. Unlike the situation with MAR, the MNAR missing values cannot be predicted by available data. The variable MNAR.DV in Table 5.1 shows missing values based on the values of the DV itself, where the lowest values are missing. No information in the data set from the other variables would allow one to predict that the lowest values for the DV are missing. Therefore as researchers, we cannot know that the available data for the DV are actually biased, with the lowest end of the distribution missing. If we have only three variables in our data set—ID, DV, and MNAR.DV—then we would be unable to predict scores from the missing variables. What makes this missing data situation difficult is that the mechanism is not available to the data analyst, and the mechanism cannot be ignored statistically because of the aforementioned bias in the available data.

These three terms—MCAR, MAR, and MNAR—form the basis of the missing data statistical language. The three mechanisms play an important role in determining how to diagnose and treat missing data. Additional factors play important roles, and we address those when discussing diagnostics.

STEP 2: PREVENT MISSING DATA

In Step 1, we emphasized understanding missing data, both its impact and the language used to communicate missing data. In Step 2, the emphasis is on preventing missing data. The adage about health—an ounce of prevention is worth a pound of cure—applies to missing data as well. Many missing data problems can be prevented—even in secondary research. For obvious reasons, the raw values that are not observed in existing data generally cannot be recovered by the researcher; however, in some situations, raw data are manipulated, and those manipulations are the cause of missing data. Therefore, missing data prevention becomes relevant during data manipulation. Variable transformation and data reduction are two general methods of data manipulation we address here.

Several scenarios require the researcher to transform variables in secondary data sets, for reasons often related to normality or scaling. Transformations can produce missing data by putting unrealistic constraints on the values. Logarithmic transformations, for example, require manifest variable values to exceed zero (0). Any zero or negative value usually gets recoded as a system missing value under logarithmic transformation because the log of such a value is not a real number.[3] Another common transformation that can produce missing data is the z score transformation. If z scores are computed within groups, a quotient of infinity will arise because of division by zero if individuals within a group exhibit no variance on a measure. Both transformations result

---

[3]Software packages differ in their default handling of impossible transformations. Some packages report an error, whereas others complete the computation without any hint that the transformation was illogical for some cases. It is always best practice to scan the raw values and transformed values graphically before proceeding to subsequent data analyses.

in missing values. Careful inspection of the raw data prior to transformation can prevent further missing data. Preventing missing data in transformation, therefore, requires knowledge of the raw values prior to transformation and knowledge of the transformation constraints (e.g., the log of 0).

Data reduction—a slightly more complicated manipulation—often results in missing data. In secondary research, some form of data reduction often is necessary. A researcher may be faced with too many variables for a given analysis. Quantitative methods training teaches that in such cases, researchers ought to combine variables, where appropriate, through factor analysis, index score computation, or variable means. These three methods represent the most prominent tools for reducing data in social and behavioral science. All methods of data reduction require the analyst to make decisions about missing data, often unknowingly. It is unfortunate that many of those decisions are subtle and impact the integrity of the data. For example, factor analysis requires data to be transformed from raw values to measures of covariance (covariance or correlation). The transformation usually takes place without the data analyst explicitly conducting the transformation. Factor analysis takes raw data as the input and produces the transformed covariance matrix as an initial step before estimating the factor solution. Treating missing raw values in these procedures requires knowledge of the procedure itself and the default methods of handling raw missing values. In the case of factor analysis, some packages use whatever data are available (i.e., pairwise deletion) or complete cases only (i.e., listwise deletion). Either approach results in compromised solutions. Prevention in secondary research may be as simple as understanding the raw data and all possible transformations.

STEP 3: DIAGNOSE THE PROBLEM

When missing data cannot be prevented, the investigator ought to diagnose the extent of the problem. Many researchers immediately try to treat missing data without diagnosis. Treatment without diagnosis, however, is inefficient and potentially detrimental. Diagnosis falls under four categories: amount, level, pattern, and mechanism. Diagnosing the amount of missing data is not as straightforward as it might seem. When 20% of the data are missing, which 20% are missing is unclear. Perhaps 20% of the cases had missing values (i.e., only 80% of the cases provided complete data), or 20% of the variables had missing values, or perhaps 20% of the raw data matrix (cases by variables) contained missing cells. These three amounts—all reported as 20%—have far different implications. Our first recommendation to the researcher, therefore, is to define "amount" before diagnosing each facet of missing data. Amount often dictates what can or ought to be done about missing data. When only a relatively small number of cells (say 1 cell for every 1,000) are missing, then the analyst may need to do nothing. If, however, many cases have missing values, something ought to be done with those missing values or the researchers risks the loss of a substantial portion of the sample (and therefore decrease statistical power and bias results).

The amount of missing data fails to communicate the full extent of the missing data problem because it does not address the scientific relevance of the missing values. A supplemental diagnosis focuses on the level of missing data. *Level* refers to measurement and generally falls under the five categories of item (individual questions), scale (combinations of items), construct (all relevant measures of a construct), person (an individual respondent), or group (naturally or artificial collections of persons). These levels provide the scientific relevance of missing data from a sample and often indicate the extent and influence missing data might have on results. Missing data at the item level tend to be far less damaging than missing data at the group level. In a way, level communicates the severity of the problem.

Another method of diagnosing severity is the pattern of missing data. Missing data may be patterned in any manner, but some patterns present fewer problems than others. For illustrative purposes (see Figure 5.1), imagine the data were recoded as "1" or "0," indicating present or missing, respectively, and the raw data matrix were plotted as a rectangle with the rows representing the cases ($N = 300$) and the columns representing the variables ($N = 30$). Evident from the figures is that information is contained in the patterns. The most disorganized pattern shows that no general cause is likely for the missing values, whereas the most organized pattern suggests that a systematic or causal process to account for the missing data is likely. Patterns of missing data potentially are indicative of the mechanism but are not direct tests of mechanisms.

The final diagnostic pertains directly to the three missing data mechanisms (MCAR, MAR, and MNAR) discussed previously. Because patterns do not directly identify which mechanism produced missing values, one ought to investigate the underlying structure of the missing data. As mentioned previously, the mechanism determines what information from the data available and what needs to be done to remedy the situation. However, no direct test for all three mechanisms exists. The only test proposed to date is for ruling out MCAR. Little (1988) developed a chi-square test for assessing the extent to which available data could account for missing values. If the test is nonsignificant, then the researcher failed to rule out MCAR. It is important to note that the test does not indicate whether the missing data mechanism is MCAR; rather, the test rules out, or fails to rule out, the possibility that the mechanism is MCAR. Therefore, if MCAR can be ruled out, that leaves two other mechanisms: MAR and MNAR. Differentiating between these two

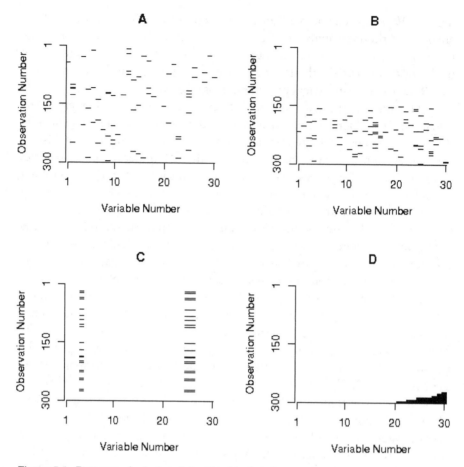

Figure 5.1. Patterns of missing data. The black cells represent the missing values, and the white cells represent the observed values. This figure shows four possible patterns plotted for a relatively large data set arranged from the most disorganized pattern (A) to the most organized pattern (D). The four patterns illustrated are a completely random pattern (i.e., randomly missing by case and variable) (A), a random pattern by variable but fixed by case (B), a random pattern by case but fixed by variable (C), and a monotonic pattern (fixed by case and variable) (D).

mechanisms relies on logic and inference—not a statistical test. The researcher must carefully consider whether data are available to account for the missing data. If so, then the mechanism may be MAR. If, however, no way to account for the missing data can be found, then the data are likely missing through the MNAR mechanism. We realize that diagnosing a problem on the basis of conjecture may be unsettling for most researchers; precisely for this reason we propose a more comprehensive diagnostic system that includes amount, level, and pattern, in addition to mechanism. The combination of the four diagnostic tools helps the researcher to understand better the extent, severity, and difficulty of the missing data problem.

STEP 4: TREATING MISSING DATA

Logically, treatment follows diagnosis. Diagnosis ought to lead the researcher through a process of choosing a suitable method for handling missing data. We emphasize the word *suitable* because many researchers look for the "best" or "appropriate" method. Both adjectives imply that some methods are superior to others. Although some methods are generally preferable to others, no single method serves as the treatment of choice across all missing data situations. We encourage researchers to use the simplest, most efficient method available, given the results of the diagnostic procedures.

Most of the missing data literature emphasizes the statistical treatment of missing data. Our inclination is to de-emphasize statistical treatment because it is only one step in the process and is not necessarily more important than the other steps. Here, we offer a cursory review of various treatment methods, because of space limitations and our desire to provide equal coverage to other, equally important steps for dealing with missing data. We encourage interested readers to consult the many references that provide far more detail (e.g., Allison, 2001; Little & Rubin, 1987; McKnight et al., 2007) than can be provided here.

Four general categories of treatment methods are available: *deletion, weighting, adjusting,* and *imputing.* Each of these methods can be used across a variety of missing data conditions. We present each general category with a brief description, a list of procedures that apply to that category, and conditions under which these procedures may be suitable.

Deletion Methods

The easiest and most obvious method for treating missing data is by deleting cases, variables, or cells with missing values. That is, the data contained in the case, variable, or cell are deleted from the analysis. Deletion methods are the easiest to implement because they require little from the analyst. Moreover, these methods are the easiest to understand. Data that are missing are essentially ignored.

Listwise deletion (complete case), pairwise deletion (available case), and available item are three procedures that fall under the deletion category. Listwise deletion involves deleting all cases with any missing data—in some cases, even if the case is missing data for a variable that is not used in the statistical modeling. Listwise deletion will always result in the same sample size, regardless of the analysis, because it leads to a reduced data set with complete data for all observations. In contrast to listwise deletion, pairwise deletion omits cases on the basis of the bivariate, or paired (e.g., correlational), analysis. Computations in which one or both of the variables are missing for a given case use only those cases for which data for both variables are present. Pairwise deletion, thus, results in different sample sizes for each bivariate analysis.

Both listwise and pairwise deletion pertain to cases. The third and final procedure—available item—is the only deletion procedure that pertains directly to variables. Data reduction procedures such as summing or averaging variables require complete data on all the variables (items) for the calculation. Depending on the statistical software, when variables used to calculate a total score have missing values, the summary score will either be missing or computed, but it may not be valid because it is composed of fewer variables (only those with observed data, or the "available items"). In the latter case, the score is based on differing numbers of variables for cases with missing data, which is also problematic.

Deletion procedures are the easiest to use, and they tend to be the default procedure in many statistical packages. These methods require little (if any) planning or effort on the part of the researcher. Additionally, these methods often result in the least disturbance to the data integrity (i.e., they do not manipulate the raw data). Despite these advantages, in many situations the use of deletion procedures ought to be considered with great caution. Listwise deletion results in the complete elimination of cases because of the presence of missing data, even if that missing data is irrelevant to the analysis of choice. If a sufficiently large number of cases contain missing values, they will be omitted from analyses, thus reducing statistical power. Furthermore, some deletion procedures may create new problems that are unrelated to missing data. Pairwise deletion, in particular, creates unbalanced correlation or covariance matrices that often cannot be used for more complicated models (e.g., factor analysis or structural equation models) because the matrices fail to provide mathematically sound structures.[4] Although deletion procedures are efficient, they require careful application in all situations (i.e., amount, pattern, level, and mechanism of missing data). Listwise deletion is an efficient and useful method only when data are MCAR and when a negligible amount is missing. Pairwise deletion is an efficient method for bivariate analyses when the data are MCAR and the results of the analyses will undergo no further procedures (e.g., correlations are the end result). Finally, available item

---

[4]The sound structures we refer to are balanced, invertible matrices that contain no singularities or linear dependencies. These topics fall outside the scope of the chapter, and interested readers are encouraged to consult more technical books on the mathematics underlying covariance modeling procedures.

analyses appear to be efficient under conditions of MCAR and MAR, as well as able to handle more complex patterns and larger amounts of missing data. Regardless, we encourage analysts to exercise caution with any deletion procedure.

Weighting Methods

Survey researchers often face missing data problems from nonresponse (i.e., those who were offered the survey failed to respond) and from sampling (i.e., those who were vs. were not offered the survey to begin with) problems. Perhaps the most popular method for handling missing data in survey research is weighting. Other methods apply to survey analysis as well, but weighting is the dominant method. Secondary data analysts often use survey data, and therefore we focus more heavily on this method. Weighting requires the application of probabilities that relate to the sampling method, design, or both. For example, a survey researcher may aim to survey a representative sample of a particular population and realizes that many important subgroups are under- or overrepresented. Bias associated with representation presents a condition of missing data in which the values are almost certainly missing by the MAR or MNAR mechanism. To counter bias, survey researchers resort to sampling weights whereby individual cases are weighted according to their inverse probabilities—the inverse probability of being selected or the inverse probability of that person's subgroup in the population. By weighting cases according to such a scheme, parameters from statistical models are said to be "adjusted" by population sampling probabilities. Adjustments may also be made for subsampling, skip-pattern, or multipart surveys. In each of these cases, only a subset of the total survey respondents complete particular parts of a survey. Thus, adjustments must be made to account for survey design. In both sampling and design, weights are applied to adjust parameters in the presence of missing data.

The National Comorbidity Study—Replication (NCS–R; Kessler et al., 2004) provides an excellent example of weighting due to missing data. The study aimed to capture medical and mental health problems in the U.S. adult population. Obtaining a representative sample of all U.S. adults is difficult, to say the least. The investigators decided to use a multistage survey. All survey respondents were asked a core set of questions (Part A), but only a subset of the respondents were asked another set of questions (Part B). The design necessarily results in missing data for Part B. Kessler et al. (2004) sought to adjust the sampling and design problems by creating weights. The derivation and computation of these weights is beyond the scope of our chapter; in summary, the weights reflect a sum total of the inverse probabilities of both the sampling and design biases that may account for the results. These weights would be applied to any model that estimates population parameters (i.e., inferences about the nature of the U.S. adult population), including those used in secondary research. The researcher using existing survey data should consult the original study, data set, or both, to obtain these weighting schemes to investigate whether the weights apply to the analyses for the current study and, if so, make use of those weighting schemes.

Multiple methods are available for applying weights to adjust parameter estimates in the presence of missing data. The original investigators for the NCS–R (Kessler et al., 2004) used method of probability weights based on multiple imputation (MI; a method we cover shortly). Other methods, such as propensity scores (Rosenbaum & Rubin, 1983), also can be used to adjust for sampling or design problems that lead to missing data. In all design or data situations in which weighting is relevant, the exact method of weighting is a matter of choice on the part of the analyst. Most reviewers expect to see some attention to missing data in survey research, and the data analyst ought to make a logical and defensible choice. Weighting by any method often demonstrates that the analyst has been attentive to the problems associated with the missing data. For further information, we encourage readers to investigate methods described and used by survey experts (e.g., Rubin, 1987; Kish, 1967).

Adjustment Methods

One problem with missing data is that missing values tend to produce estimates that do not reflect accurate population parameters, particularly when missing data are MAR or MNAR. A way to counter the inaccuracy is to adjust the estimates so they are more accurate or, perhaps, not as misleading. Adjustments tend to be based on a model or distribution, such as the normal distribution, and thus allow for flexibility in application. The normal distribution model used most frequently is maximum likelihood. Several variants on maximum likelihood, such as restricted maximum likelihood, full-information maximum likelihood, marginal maximum likelihood, and expectation and maximization, have been proposed. Each variant makes slight modifications to the basic underlying normal distribution method that adjusts parameter estimates to fit the expected distribution better and thus provides potentially better population estimates. The actual mechanics of these procedures are complex and fall outside the scope of the current chapter. The important point is that these methods do not replace missing values, but instead they are part of the parameter estimation procedure, and their purpose is to adjust parameter estimates to reflect better the expected population values, given the hypothesized distribution of scores (e.g., multivariate normal). Adjustment methods are regarded as both useful and efficient when missing data are MCAR or MAR (e.g., Allison, 2001; Schafer & Graham, 2002). These methods can be used to treat missing data across many different data analytic models; unlike deletion methods, however, they require some statistical sophistication to implement, troubleshoot, and interpret.

Most adjustment methods rely on the assumption that an underlying distribution is inherently normal (i.e., multivariate normal for more complex multivariate analyses). In many instances, these normal distribution procedures suit the data and, therefore, perform as expected. Data that are nonnormal or cannot be transformed to be normal are not well-suited for these procedures. Additionally, missing data must be ignorable; the mechanism must be either MAR or MCAR and in sufficiently small quantities to avoid over- or under-adjustment. Another limitation to adjustment procedures is whether adequate adjustment has been made to counter the missing data. Without this information, researchers cannot be aware of the impact of missing data on statistical results. We discuss this general limitation further when we address MI.

Imputation Methods

The three aforementioned methods (deletion, weighting, and adjustment) all have one thing in common—missing values are not replaced. Imputation methods depart from the preceding methods because individual cells with missing data are replaced with actual values, as if the data were never missing. Two general imputation methods are available: single imputation and MI. Because of their differences, we discuss each separately.

Single Imputation

As the name suggests, *single imputation* replaces each missing value once with a particular value. The imputed value may be a constant (e.g., zero), a between-subjects value (e.g., group-level mean), a within-subject value (e.g., mean of other items completed by the respondent or the last observed value carried forward), or a random value from either the current data (i.e., hot deck) or other similar data (i.e., cold deck). Single imputation methods impute a single value into each missing data cell and, therefore, result in a complete data set. The aim of all imputation strategies is to create a complete data set prior to statistical analysis. Selecting which value to impute presents a dilemma to the analyst. Some values may come from the data (hot deck or last observation carried forward), but those values may have inherent biases. Other values come from the data indirectly (e.g., mean imputation), by random process (e.g., hot deck), from other data (e.g., cold deck), or by principle (e.g., zero imputation). Choosing the source from the myriad of choices can be as perplexing as fully appreciating the implications and limitations of each.

Each single imputation procedure has limitations. Replacing missing values with a constant (e.g., 0) or a group mean decreases variance in the data when the amount of missing data is nontrivial. Limitations are documented elsewhere (e.g., McKnight et al., 2007), and space constraints do not allow for their summary in this chapter. We encourage researchers to consider carefully their missing data diagnostic results before dismissing any single imputation method from their treatment strategy. These methods can be useful and appropriate in limited missing data situations. Data that are mostly observed with only a few missing cells can hardly be detrimentally affected by any of these methods. The methods are easily implemented, intuitively appealing, and readily understood by researchers and research consumers.

Multiple Imputation

The primary disadvantage of most missing data treatment methods is that there is no process to determine the extent to which missing values impact study results. MI is the exception. The MI approach to missing data provides an estimate of the impact missing data had statistical results. This facility alone makes MI the preferred treatment method among expert data analysts. The following briefly summarizes the steps to conduct MI.

The MI process begins by selecting an appropriate imputation method, given the type of data for which values are missing—continuous normal, discrete, or mixed. Next, the analyst imputes values to replace missing ones using the selected method. In contrast to the single imputation methods, the imputation process runs several times (usually three to five), and each run results in a complete data set. Next, the analyst conducts the desired statistical procedure on each of the complete data sets. Thus, if five fully observed data sets are generated, the statistical model (e.g., multiple regression) is carried out five times, once for each data set, resulting in five sets of statistical results. These results then serve as data to be aggregated and analyzed, for instance, to assess measures of central tendency and variance. The results that serve as data for analysis may be parameter estimates (e.g., regression coefficients), p values, statistical indices (e.g., t test values), or any other outcome the analyst deems appropriate. Results of these analyses provide evidence regarding the extent to which missing data influenced the results from the multiple runs of the desired statistical procedure. If parameter estimates varied widely from each of five multiple regressions carried out on the five imputed data sets, then the missing data had a considerable impact on the statistical results and may call into question their accuracy.

The above description of MI is brief, because of space constraints, and cannot provide sufficient detail for carrying out MI. We describe these procedures for the applied researchers in greater detail elsewhere (McKnight et al., 2007), and a large statistical literature describes the use and advantages of MI for handling missing data. Rubin, Schafer, and colleagues (e.g., Rubin, 1987; Schafer, 1997; Schafer & Graham, 2002) have spent considerable effort in describing MI and making the general procedure more accessible to most data analysts. The implementation of MI requires some skill, and it is not yet the standard procedure in even the most popular statistical software. Currently, many data analysts conduct MI procedures and generate multiple, fully observed data sets using separate software from that they use for analyzing data using the desired statistical models. However, because of rapid technology improvements, this situation is likely to change, and MI soon will become a standard procedure available in most statistical packages.

Currently, experts regard MI as the premier method for handling missing data in the more difficult situations in which the simplest methods (e.g., deletion, single imputation) are not appropriate (Schafer & Graham, 2002). MI is a preferred method because it borrows the advantages of the random single imputation procedures but supplements those procedures with an iterative process. The combination results in a method that allows the researcher to understand better the nature and influence of missing data on results. Difficulties lie in implementing MI because of the technical exper-tise required to troubleshoot when problems arise, as they often do when using these methods.

STEP 5: REPORTING RESULTS

Reporting is the final step in the treatment and handling of missing data. Science relies on the ability to communicate results effectively so that other researchers may review, evaluate, replicate, and extend the findings. Missing data present special circumstances that require additional reporting. Many times, resistance to the problem of missing data occurs at the level of reporting. Reviewers, editors, and readers often do not understand or appreciate the relevance or the importance of reporting missing data; in many cases, neither do the investigators themselves. A researcher's job is to document all com-ponents of a study that might have an impact on the results and conclusions. We provide some guidelines about reporting missing data to assist researchers in determining the most relevant details. As a brief checklist, we suggest researchers gauge the extent to which another researcher could replicate each of the points listed in Exhibit 5.1 using the existing secondary data. Researchers who can check off each of these points can be assured that the reporting of methods used to prevent, diagnose, and treat missing data were detailed sufficiently. The majority of these points ought to be addressed in the Method and Results section of a research article; however, they are relevant when discussing the limitations of the study as well. It is important to bear in mind

EXHIBIT 5.1
A Brief Checklist for Reporting Results With Missing Data

Description
- Clearly specify the source of your data, including Internet location and manuscript references if applicable.
- Identify variables selected for your analyses and the reasons they were selected.
- Describe variable transformation and computation steps.
- Provide details about how you prevented missing values in the transformation and computation of new variables.
- Briefly describe the nature and extent of missing data; that is, missing data diagnostics.
- Provide the necessary detail for handling the missing data; that is, how diagnostics informed choice of treatment.
- Describe any results of the treatment methods.
- Explain the impact of missing data on the results.
- Describe the limitations of the results based upon the missing data.

---

that the list we provide is not exhaustive. A researcher may deem other points to be relevant to include, given the nature and the purpose of the study. The best reporting covers all relevant details as succinctly as possible.

CONCLUSION

Missing data present problems in all types of research. The effective treatment of missing data ought to follow a systematic process to ensure that the extent of the problem and the methods used to treat the problem are well articulated. We presented a simple five-step process that can be applied to secondary research. Readers interested in a deeper understanding of missing data in general ought to consult the references provided.

REFERENCES

Allison, P. (2001). *Missing data*. Thousand Oaks, CA: Sage.

Campbell, D., & Stanley, J. (1963). *Experimental and quasi-experimental designs for research*. Boston, MA: Houghton Mifflin.

Cohen, J. (1988). *Statistical power analysis for the behavioral sciences* (2nd ed.). Hillsdale, NJ: Erlbaum.

Cook, T., & Campbell, D. (1979). *Quasi-experimentation: Design and analysis issues for field settings*. Boston, MA: Houghton Mifflin.

Kessler, R. C., Berglund, P., Chiu, W. T., Demler, O., Heeringa, S., Hiripi, E., et al. (2004). The U.S. National Comorbidity Survey—Replication (NCS–R): Design and field procedures. *International Journal of Methods in Psychiatric Research, 13*(2), 69–92.

Kish, L. (1967). *Survey sampling.* New York, NY: Wiley.

Little, R. (1988). A test of missing completely at random for multivariate data with missing values. *Journal of the American Statistical Association, 83,* 1198–1202. doi:10.2307/2290157

Little, R., & Rubin, D. (1987). *Statistical analysis with missing data.* New York, NY: Wiley.

McKnight, P., McKnight, K., Sidani, S., & Figuredo, A. (2007). *Missing data: A gentle introduction.* New York, NY: Guilford Press.

Rosenbaum, P. R., & Rubin, D. B. (1983). The central role of the propensity score in observational studies for causal effects. *Biometrika, 70,* 41–55. doi:10.1093/biomet/70.1.41

Rubin, D. (1976). Inference and missing data (with discussion). *Biometrika, 63,* 581–592. doi:10.1093/biomet/63.3.581

Rubin, D. (1987). *Multiple imputation for nonresponse in surveys.* New York, NY: Wiley.

Schafer, J. (1997). *Analysis of incomplete multivariate data.* London, England: Chapman & Hall.

Schafer, J. L., & Graham, J. W. (2002). Missing data: Our view of the state of the art. *Psychological Methods, 7,* 147–177. doi:10.1037/1082-989X.7.2.147

Shadish, W., Cook, T., & Campbell, D. (2002). *Experimental and quasi-experimental designs for generalized causal inference.* Boston, MA: Houghton Mifflin.

6

INNOVATIVE METHODS WITHIN THE CONTEXT OF SECONDARY DATA: EXAMPLES FROM HOUSEHOLD PANEL SURVEYS

THOMAS SIEDLER, JÜRGEN SCHUPP, AND GERT G. WAGNER

Previous chapters have discussed some of the important features of secondary data, including some of the unique problems of measurement and analysis. In this chapter, we extend the discussion of secondary data to include one important but distinctive class of data, the household panel survey. *Household panel* studies follow people's life over time, and the same individuals are interviewed every year; they are further distinctive because, unlike most studies, in which only one individual from a household is interviewed, household panels interview all adult household members every year. These surveys have their own distinct sets of challenges and opportunities, which we illustrate by drawing on five household surveys that are nationally and internationally respected and currently available for use by scholars, free of charge. In the section that follows, we briefly describe the five surveys and then discuss some of their distinctive features. The section Innovative Topics illustrates some of the innovative survey methods currently being incorporated, and the next section provides examples of innovative data collection methods. Then, Household Panel Studies as Reference Data describes the potential use of these surveys as a source of reference material. The chapter concludes by providing the reader with information on how to access the various data sets.

HOUSEHOLD PANEL SURVEYS

This section briefly discusses key features of household panel surveys and outlines differences from other forms of secondary data sets. We refer in particular to some of the best-known and most widely used long-running household panel surveys: the U.S. Panel Study of Income Dynamics (PSID; which began in 1968), the German Socioeconomic Panel (GSOEP; which began in 1984), the British Household Panel Survey (BHPS; which started in 1991), the new United Kingdom Household Longitudinal Study (UKHLS; first wave to be launched in 2010), and the Dutch Multidisciplinary Facility for Measurement and Experimentation in the Social Sciences (MESS; which began in 2007). The many other household panel surveys are in, for example, Canada (Canadian Survey of Labour and Income Dynamics), Switzerland (Swiss Household Panel), Australia (The Household, Income and Labour Dynamics in Australia Survey), and New Zealand (Survey of Family, Income, and Employment). We now provide a short overview over some of the most widely used or most innovative household panel studies in the world. How interested researchers can gain access to these household panel studies is briefly explained in the section Recommended Data Sets.

The Panel Study of Income Dynamics

The PSID is the oldest household panel study in the world. The first wave started in 1968 as a representative sample of private households in the United States, with about 5,000 households. Since then, the PSID has attempted to follow all individuals from these original households regardless of whether they have continued residing in the same household or with the same persons. Similarly, children born to original household members become part of the survey and are interviewed on their own when they have reached adulthood. The PSID collects data on economic and social behavior; demography; health; and the neighborhoods, housing, and labor markets in which respondents live. Most of the data might not be of interest to psychologists. However, the PSID also contains a child development supplement with a focus on children and caregivers that might be of special interest to psychologists collecting information on health, education, cognitive and behavioral development, and time use. (For further information on the PSID, see http://psidonline.isr.umich.edu/.)

German Socioeconomic Panel Survey

The GSOEP is a is a multipurpose household panel survey representative of the German population residing in private households. The survey started in

1984 with two subsamples: Sample A, the main sample, covers the population of private households in the former West Germany; Sample B, the guest worker sample, is an oversample of immigrants from South European countries (foreign-born residents and their children, mainly recruited abroad during the economic booms of the 1960s and 1970s, with a Turkish, Spanish, Italian, Greek, or [ex-]Yugoslavian head of household). The initial sample size in 1984 comprised around 6,000 households. Since 1990, the GSOEP has included a sample of households in the former East Germany, and in the following years more samples were included into the survey (e.g., in 1998, a refreshment sample; in 2000, an innovation sample; and in 2002, a high-income sample). As a result, the sample size has increased considerably, and in 2008—with the study's 25th wave—the GSOEP consists of about 11,000 households with more than 20,000 adult respondents. In each of these samples, original sample respondents are followed, and they (and coresident adults) were interviewed at approximately 1-year intervals. Children in original sample households are also interviewed in their own right when they reach adulthood (the year they turn 17), and former partners of original sample members are also followed over time.

Whereas the PSID is very much centered on income dynamics, the GSOEP supports research not only in economics but also in sociology and psychology. For psychologists, one of the most important variables in the GSOEP is the one on life satisfaction, which has been part of the GSOEP since the very beginning (for a recent application, see Easterlin, 2008). All the other panels discussed later in this chapter contain similar subjective data that are of interest to psychological research. (For further information on the GSOEP, see http://www.diw.de/english/sop/index.html.)

British Household Panel Survey and the UK Household Longitudinal Study

The Institute for Social and Economic Research at the University of Essex has been commissioned to launch a major new panel study, the UKHLS. This study aims to be the largest household panel in the world, with a target sample size of 40,000 households and around 100,000 individuals across the United Kingdom. The UKHLS will incorporate the existing BHPS, a household panel study that started in 1991 as a representative sample of the private household population in Great Britain. The original sample size of the BHPS comprised around 5,500 households with approximately 10,000 adult respondents. Likely key features of the UKHLS are (a) inclusion of an ethnic minority boost sample of over 3,000 households (with an Indian, Pakistani, Bangladeshi, Caribbean, African, or Chinese head of household) with a special focus on ethnicity-related issues, (b) interviews conducted annually with all household members ages 10 and above, (c) a multitopic survey meeting the needs of social scientists and biomedical science, (d) linkage with administrative records and geocodes, (e) a collection of biomarkers, and (f) an innovation panel for methodological research. (For further information about the UKHLS and the BHPS, see http://www.iser.essex.ac.uk.)

An Advanced Multidisciplinary Facility for Measurement and Experimentation in the Social Sciences

The MESS is a new, representative panel of 5,000 Dutch households that have agreed to be interviewed on the Internet, with the aim of creating a laboratory for developing and testing innovative research techniques.[1] The first wave of the MESS started in fall 2007. The project has four main aims, according to the MESS proposal (which can be downloaded at http://www.uvt. nl/centerdata/en/mess/submission/). First, it aims to integrate various data collection methods that are of relevance to different disciplines, such as the social sciences, economics, (bio)medical science, and behavioral science. Second, it intends to conduct experiments to test social science theories and improve survey methodologies, as well as to link survey data with administrative records. Third, the MESS aims to pioneer new forms of data collection using personal digital assistants, webcams, measurement devices for the collection of biomarkers, and experience sampling. (More information on the MESS project can be found at http://www.uvt.nl/centerdata/en/mess/.)

Household panel surveys have characteristics that distinguish them from other types of longitudinal survey, such as cross-sectional surveys with retrospective information, rotating panels, administrative longitudinal data, and prospective cohort studies.

Household Panel Surveys Are Prospective

Household panels are designed to collect many variables prospectively as the survey proceeds from wave to wave on an annual basis. This has the advantage of permitting detailed information to be collected on income, marital status, health, wealth, education, respondents' beliefs and expectations, and—of crucial importance for psychologists—family dynamics over time. Contemporaneous collection of information is crucial for reliability because respondents do not have to recall detailed pieces of information (the longer the recall period, the more likely memories will contain systematic error; see Scott & Alwin, 1998). Most household panel surveys also collect retrospective life history information to provide data on family background. Furthermore, the

---

[1]Note that Internet access was not a prerequisite for participation in the study and all households without Internet access were provided with a high-speed Internet connection.

panel itself can be used to provide data on later-life outcomes. Children and even grandchildren of original household members become panel respondents in their own right at around the age of 16 or 17 and are then followed over time. By design, these are children and grandchildren who have lived with a parent who was (and may well remain) a panel member too. Thus, with household panel surveys, researchers can not only match partners to each other (Ermisch et al., 2006) but also match parents to children, as well as grandparents to grandchildren, and analyze various aspects of intergenerational mobility (Solon, 1992).

Household Panels Obtain Information From Multiple Family Members

Another unique advantage of household panel survey is that, by design, they collect information about all individuals within a given household at the time of the interview, including all siblings. The observation of multiple siblings allows researchers to apply statistical estimation methods that control for unobserved family fixed effects (Francesconi et al., in press).

Tracking Rules

Household panel studies share certain rules for tracking respondents over time. First, to maintain the ongoing cross-sectional representativeness of the (nonimmigrant) population, household surveys define the adults and children in the households of the first-wave representative sample as the *original sample members* (OSMs). Note that the children living at home in wave one are not necessarily all the children the parents have, because some may have left home previously or died. Similarly, the adults present in wave one may not include both birth parents of a given child because of, for example, divorce or the death of a parent before the survey. In subsequent waves, interviews are attempted with all adult members of all households containing either an OSM or an individual born to an OSM, regardless of whether that individual was a member of the original sample or whether the individual lives in the same household or residence as at the previous interview. This rule allows researchers to analyze the influence of shared environment over a certain period (e.g., during cohabitation, marriage, or both) and later-life outcomes of individuals who separated or divorced (Schimmak & Lucas, 2007), and underlies the design of virtually all household panels. However, differences exist with respect to treatment of new panel members who later move out of the OSM household. In most household panel surveys, including the BHPS and the PSID, these people are not interviewed again (unless they retain an important relationship with a sample member, such as parent). By contrast, the GSOEP has, since Wave 7, followed and interviewed all panel members, regardless of their relationship to the OSM (Spiess et al., 2008).

Attrition

The other dimension of nonresponse that is of particular importance for household panel surveys is selective sample dropout (i.e., attrition). Attrition is a problem that potentially increases in severity the longer the panel lasts and, hence, is a feature that conflicts with the distinct advantages of longer panels. Attrition reduces sample size and also introduces potential non-representativeness if respondents drop out in a nonrandom way. The latter case occurs when individuals with particular characteristics are systematically more likely to drop out of the panel than others. For example, if respondents with lower levels of education are more likely to drop out of the panel, estimates of the degree of returns to education may be biased. Nonrandom panel attrition and nonrepresentativeness are issues that are often discussed but not always addressed in empirical research.

INNOVATIVE TOPICS

This section discusses a number of innovations that are currently being developed in the household panel studies previously discussed and have already demonstrated their research potential, especially in the discipline of psychology. We place our main emphasis here on the GSOEP, which has pioneered many household panel innovations, making cross-references to the other panels as well.

Trust and Fairness

Trust and trustworthiness are key components of social capital, and there is a growing literature on how best to measure trust (Ermisch et al., 2009; Glaeser et al., 2000; Sapienza et al., 2007). Both the BHPS and the GSOEP collect information about respondents' levels of trust and fairness. In 2003, several trust and fairness questions were incorporated into the GSOEP questionnaire. Overall, six different questions on trust, generosity, and fairness were included. The BHPS also repeatedly collected attitudinal trust measures in the years 1998, 2000, and 2003, asking respondents the general trust question "In general, would you say that most people can be trusted, or that you can't be too careful these days?"

One criticism of attitudinal survey questions like the ones above concerns the lack of behavioral underpinnings and the absence of meaningful survey questions that get at respondents' trustworthiness (Ermisch et al., 2009; Glaeser et al., 2000). Combining attitudinal survey questions that inquire into respondents' trust with behavioral experiments that include monetary rewards can potentially provide a fuller understanding of trust and trust-worthiness. We discuss this issue in more detail in the section Innovative Data Collection Methods.

Big Five Inventory

In 2005, both the BHPS and the GSOEP incorporated new questions to elicit respondents' personality traits through the Big Five Inventory (BFI). The BFI is a psychological inventory used to measure personality on the basis of the assumption that differences in personality can be summarized through five personality traits: Neuroticism, Extraversion, Openness to Experience, Agreeableness, and Conscientiousness (John & Srivastava, 1999). The study by Gosling et al. (2003) indicated that the Big Five personality traits can be reliably measured with a small number of items. Both the BHPS and GSOEP use a 15-item version, with three items per personality trait. For further information about data collection and internal validity of the short BFI version in GSOEP (BFI-S), see Gerlitz and Schupp (2005) and Dehne and Schupp (2007). The incorporation of the BFI into the GSOEP and the BHPS will likely be of great value to psychologists and will allow researchers to study relationships between personality traits and various behavioral outcomes (for a first application, see Rammstedt, 2007). Using the Big Five personality factors from the GSOEP, Winkelmann and Winkelmann (2008) reported that certain personality clusters are more dominant in some occupations than others and that a positive relationship exists between personal and occupational profiles and life satisfaction. The study by Rammstedt and Schupp (2008) aimed to investigate personality congruence between spouses and to examine which dimensions show a high degree of congruence. It also investigated the extent to which the congruence between spouses is moderated by the marriage duration. Results reveal that among the Big Five dimensions, there are strong differences in spouses' congruence. Although for Extraversion, congruence is close to zero, correlations averaging at .30 are found for Agreeableness, Conscientiousness, and Openness.

INNOVATIVE DATA COLLECTION METHODS: TRUST AND TRUSTWORTHINESS

A vast literature exists on trust and trustworthiness in several disciplines, including psychology, sociology, political science, and economics. Until recently, the trust literature was split into two research strands. One approach to measuring people's trust is through attitudinal measures from responses to survey questions. One of the most frequently used measure of trust comes from answers based on the World Values Survey or the General Social Survey (GSS) to the standard trust question "Generally speaking, would you say that most people can be trusted, or that you can't be too careful in dealing with people?" Versions of this attitudinal trust question are widely used in the literature to measure social capital or generalized trust, that is, respondents' expectation about the trustworthiness of other people in the population (Alesina & La Ferrara, 2002). A second approach is to measure trust and trustworthiness through behavioral experiments with monetary rewards (for a review of this literature, see Camerer, 2003).

Both approaches have their advantages and disadvantages. Glaeser et al. (2000) questioned the validity of the GSS trust measure to capture social capital and argued that attitudinal survey questions are "vague, abstract, and hard to interpret" (p. 812). The authors found no empirical evidence that the GSS attitudinal trust question predicts trusting behavior in the experiment, which used the standard trust game first introduced by Berg et al. (1995) based on a sample of Harvard undergraduate economics students. However, Glaeser et al. found a positive significant correlation between survey measures of trust and revealed trustworthiness (i.e., sender's behavior in the experiment). In the original two-person one-shot trust game, Player 1 (truster) is allocated $10, which she or he can keep or invest. If the truster decides to invest (e.g., transfers a positive amount to Player 2), the amount invested is doubled by the experimenter and transferred to Player 2 (trustee). The trustee can then decide how much of the amount received to return to the truster and how much to keep. The amount transferred by the first player measures trust, and the amount transferred back measures trustworthiness. Ermisch et al. (2009) pointed out that answers to attitudinal questions might be too generic and relatively uninformative about the reference group or the stakes respondents have in mind. Another potential limitation when using survey questions is measurement error and the issue of whether respondents' answers to survey questions are behaviorally relevant (Fehr et al., 2002).

Laboratory experiments have the advantage that researchers can control the environment under which individuals make their financial decisions and allow causal inferences by exogenously varying one parameter while keeping all others unchanged. However, a major limitation of most experiments is that they are administered to students, who usually self-select themselves into the study and are therefore not representative of the entire adult population. In fact, because of self-selection, experimental studies with student subjects might not even be representative of the entire student population. In addition, most laboratory experiments are conducted on very homogenous samples (typically students studying the same subject at the same university), and often information on potentially important socioeconomic background characteristics is missing or lacks sufficient variation. Another shortcoming of laboratory experiments is the lack of anonymity. In most laboratory studies, students play against each other and know that the other player is a student. Hence, the degree of anonymity is rather low. Both the degree of homogeneity and anonymity in the subject pool might influence revealed social preferences (Sapienza et al., 2007). For a detailed discussion of potential limitations of laboratory experiments measuring social preferences, see Levitt and List (2008).

New research bridges these two research strands and combines behavioral experiments and survey methods. Fehr et al. (2002) incorporated the standard trust-game experiment (Berg et al., 1995) into a representative survey (of the German population) for the first time. This was a pretest for incorporating behavioral experiments into the GSOEP. In addition, the authors asked respondents several GSS-like survey measures of trust. Fehr et al. found a positive association between attitudinal survey measures of trust and sender's behavior but no significant correlation between survey-based measures of trust and trustworthiness in the experiment. In addition, they reported that individuals ages 65 and above, highly skilled workers, and those living in larger households exhibit less trusting behavior in the experiment. Individuals with foreign citizenship, those who express affinity toward one of the two major political parties in Germany (Social Democratic Party and Christian Democratic Party) and those who are Catholic exhibit higher levels of trust in the experiment.

Bellemare and Kröger (2007) also carried out a trust experiment with a representative sample of the Dutch population. They found that women have higher levels of trust than men but display lower levels of trustworthiness. In line with Fehr et al. (2002), Bellemare and Kröger found a positive, inverted U-shaped association between age and trust.

Ermisch et al. (2009) integrated a new experimental trust design into a sample of the British population. Their rationale for using an alternative trust design was based on observations that the sender's behavior in the standard trust-game experiment (Berg et al., 1995) is not only influenced by trust but also depends on other motivations such as sender's reciprocity, risk aversion, altruism, or inequality aversion. In their one-shot trust experiment, the sender faces the decision whether to pass on a fixed amount of money (e.g., whether to send £10. If £10 are sent, the experimenter increases it by £30 (so that the second person receives £40) and the receiver must decide whether to pay back a fixed amount of money (e.g., sender has the choice to either pay back £22 or keep all £40). Thus, the players cannot choose whether to transfer a certain amount of money—between £1 and £10, say— rather, they face the decision whether to transfer the entire amount or nothing. Ermisch et al. argued that this binary trust game is more likely to measure revealed trust and trustworthiness than the standard trust game experiment, in which the possibility of sending "any amount favors the intrusion of other motives such as 'gift giving,' 'let's risk part of it,' 'I like to gamble'" (p. 753). They found that revealed trust in the experiment is more likely if people are older, if they are homeowners, if their financial situation is "comfortable," or if they are divorced or separated. Trustworthiness is lower if a person perceives his or her financial situation as difficult or as "just getting by" compared with those who perceive their own financial situation as "comfortable."

Taken together, these studies demonstrate that there might exist enormous academic benefits from combining experimental studies with representative surveys. First, experiments based on representative samples help to assess potential biases of studies based on student subjects who self-select themselves into the sample. This advances our knowledge of whether and to what extent experimental studies from student samples can be generalized. Second, research measuring both revealed preferences and stated preferences allow researchers to validate their measures. For example, Fehr et al. (2002), Ermisch et al. (2009), and Naef and Schupp (2009) reported that answers to attitudinal questions on trust toward strangers do predict real trusting behavior in the experiment.

Cognitive Tests

In 2006, the GSOEP included cognitive tests in the survey for the first time. We briefly describe three tests here. The aim of the first test (word fluency test) is to measure fluency and declarative knowledge, whereas the second (symbol correspondence test) is aimed at measuring individuals' speed of perception. Both tests last 90 s and are conducted using computer-assisted personal interviewing techniques (CAPI). The rationale for including these two tests in the GSOEP is the perception among psychologists that intellectual skills can be described by two main components. The first component constitutes the cognitive functioning of the brain, and the second describes the pragmatic part of the intellect (Lindenberger, 2002).

In the first test, participants had to name as many animals as possible. Time was measured automatically by the computer, and interviewers entered the number of animals named by respondents into the laptop. The task of the interviewer was to exclude animals that were named more than once and any words that were not clearly identifiable as animal names. If respondents could not name an animal after a considerable time, interviewers were allowed to terminate the test.

The task of the second test—the "symbol correspondence test"—is to assign as many symbols to digits as possible. This test is a revised version of the Symbol Digit Modalities Test developed by Smith (1973). A number of modifications were introduced to ensure that the test could be successfully conducted without requiring special training for interviewers and to minimize sources of error when using the CAPI method. In contrast to the "animal naming" test, participants take this test alone on a laptop. They are informed that the aim of the test is to assign as many symbols to digits as possible. During the test, a correspondence table that shows the mapping between symbols and digits is permanently visible. The first row displays nine different symbols (e.g., +, ⊢), and the second row displays digits from 1 to 9, so that each symbol can be mapped to one particular number. Participants are told that the aim of the test is to map as many symbols to numbers as possible. Prior to the test, they are shown an example on the screen with the correct answers. Because this test involves only numbers and geometric figures, it is relatively culture free and results should be independent of language skills. For further information about reliability and validity of these cognitive tests, see Lang et al. (2007).

The first studies that investigated relationships between these cognitive ability measures and labor market outcomes were Anger and Heineck (in press) and Heineck and Anger (2008). Anger and Heineck used both the word fluency test and the symbol correspondence test to study the relationship between cognitive abilities and labor earnings in Germany. They used data from the 2005 pretest of the GSOEP and found a positive association between symbol correspondence ability scores and earnings but no statistically significant relationship between word fluency test scores and earnings. In a follow-up study, Heineck and Anger focused on the links among personality traits, cognitive ability, and labor earnings. Using data from the main GSOEP survey, they reported a positive significant relationship between cognitive ability and labor earnings for men, but not for women. Their measure of cognitive ability is derived from the symbol correspondence test.

A third measure on cognitive abilities was introduced in 2006 in a questionnaire distributed to all 17-year-old GSOEP participants. Because fluid intelligence is known to be stable from the beginning of adulthood on, cognitive abilities measured at this time point can be used as predictors of later developments in a person's life. Although there are already a large number of established and carefully validated psychological tests of fluid intelligence in adults, none of these is adequate for the survey interviews used for data collection in the GSOEP. Thus, one of the existing tests, the intelligence structure test (Intelligenz-Struktur Test [I-S-T] 2000; Amthauer et al., 2001), was modified to be used in the context of individual panel survey interviews. The test is widely used in Germany and was carefully validated by its authors.

The modifications of the I-S-T 2000 in the GSOEP are described in detail by Solga et al. (2005). The most important modifications were that the test is not described as an intelligence test but with the title "Wanna DJ?", where DJ stands for "Denksport und Jugend [Brainteasers and Youth]." The questionnaires were given a more colorful design. The titles of task groups that sounded quite technical in the original test were replaced by more casual, attention-getting titles, like "Just the right word . . . " or "A good sign . . . " Because of time restrictions, only three subscales of the I-S-T 2000 R were used: (a) Analogies, as a measure of verbal intelligence; (b) Arithmetic Operations, as a measure of numerical intelligence; and (c) Matrices, as a measure of figural intelligence. The total score of all three subscales (IST total) reflects general reasoning abilities as opposed to domain-specific knowledge (Amthauer et al., 2001).

Biomarkers

In household panel studies and most other types of secondary data, health data have usually been collected through self-reported health variables. The three household panels GSOEP, UKHLS, and MESS are currently planning an innovation in this area in the near future: the collection of various physical health measures known as *biomarkers*. Including measured height, weight, waist circumference, blood pressure, saliva samples, heart rate variability, peak flow tests, grip strength, timed walk, balance test, and puff test, biomarkers are considered to provide objective and reliable information about people's physical condition.

In 2006, the GSOEP started collecting a noninvasive health measure, hand grip strength (i.e., the maximum force with which a person can grasp someone's hand), after a successful pretest in 2005. In 2008, a second wave of grip strength was collected. The results of several studies suggest that it is feasible to measure grip strength among survey respondents (Giampaoli et al., 1999), that the participation rate is very high (Hank et al., 2009), and that it is reliable even among physically weak participants.

The measurement of grip strength constitutes a noninvasive health indicator to measure muscular upper body strength and physical functioning. It is measured by using a mechanical dynamometer. It is considered an objective measure because it is less susceptible to response bias than self-reported health variables. In addition, self-reported health measures do not allow researchers to identify health differences among respondents who report no health problems. Several studies have found that grip strength is a significant predictor of future physical disability, morbidity, and mortality among older people (Giampaoli et al., 1999; Metter et al., 2002). If respondents have no limiting health conditions, the grip strength test is performed twice on each hand. Prior to the test, interviewers inform respondents that the grip strength test is not dangerous or harmful and can be conducted at any age, except if respondents have certain clinical conditions such as swelling, inflammation, pain, or if they have had an operation or injury in the last 6 months. If one arm is affected by one of these conditions, grip strength is measured on the healthy arm only. Interviewers are provided with a very detailed description of the test procedure, including several photos showing the correct arm and body positioning when conducting the test. Moreover, interviewers are asked to demonstrate the grip strength test and explain it in detail before respondents are asked to participate in the test themselves. It is crucial for the study that interviewers are well trained in conducting the test accurately and in persuading respondents to participate.

HOUSEHOLD PANEL STUDIES AS REFERENCE DATA

Finally, we point out that household panels can serve as useful reference points for researchers who collect their own data. A recent example is the study by Geyer et al. (2008), who examined whether individuals ages 17 to 45 with operated congenital heart disease have adverse employment chances compared with people without heart problems. Geyer et al. compared their sample of patients ($N = 314$) with a sample drawn from the GSOEP, which served as a comparison group.

The study by Ermisch et al. (2009) also exemplifies how a panel survey can help in accessing the extent to which a particular sample is representative of the general population. Ermisch et al. integrated a new experimental trust design into a former sample of the British population and compared their trust sample with a sample from the BHPS. By using a questionnaire similar to the BHPS, they were able to determine that their trust sample overrepresents women and people who are retired, older, divorced, or separated. A recent article by Siedler et al. (2009) discusses how household panels can serve as reference data for researchers collecting data sets that do not represent the full universe of the population of interest.

RECOMMENDED DATA SETS

The existing data can be used almost free of charge by independent and reputable researchers worldwide. Further information about the various household panel studies can be obtained at the following websites.

- *Panel Study of Income Dynamics*. PSID data can be downloaded at http://psidonline.isr.umich.edu/data/.
- *German Socioeconomic Panel*. GSOEP data cannot be downloaded from the Internet because of German data protection regulations. For further information on data distribution, see http://www.diw.de/english/faq/.
- *British Household Panel Survey* and *United Kingdom Household Longitudinal Study*. Data from the BHPS have been deposited

in the UK Data Archive, which grants data access. More information on the UK Data Archive can be found at http://www.data-archive.ac.uk.

- *Measurement and Experimentation in the Social Sciences*. The MESS is a very new household panel study. Further information can be found at http://www.centerdata.nl/en/TopMenu/Projecten/MESS/.

REFERENCES

Alesina, A., & La Ferrara, E. (2002). Who trusts others? *Journal of Public Economics*, *85*, 207–234. doi:10.1016/S0047-2727(01)00084-6

Amthauer, R., Brocke, B., Liepmann, D., & Beauducel, A. (2001). *Intelligenz-Struktur-Test 2000 R (I-S-T 2000 R)*. Göttingen, the Netherlands: Hogrefe.

Anger, S., & Heineck, G. (in press). Cognitive abilities and earnings—First evidence for Germany. *Applied Economics Letters*.

Bellemare, C., & Kröger, S. (2007). On representative social capital. *European Economic Review*, *51*, 183–202. doi:10.1016/j.euroecorev.2006.03.006

Berg, J., Dickhaut, J., & McCabe, K. (1995). Trust, reciprocity, and social history. *Games and Economic Behavior*, *10*, 122–142. doi:10.1006/game.1995.1027

Camerer, C. (2003). *Behavioral game theory: Experiments in strategic interaction*. Princeton, NJ: Princeton University Press.

Dehne, M., & Schupp, J. (2007). Persönlichkeitsmerkmale im Sozio-oekonomischen Panel (SOEP): Konzept, Umsetzung und empirische Eigenschaften [Personality characteristics in the Socio-Economic Panel (SOEP): Concept, implementation and empirical properties]. *DIW Research Note. 26*. Berlin, Germany: DIW Berlin.

Easterlin, R. A. (2008). Lost in transition: Life satisfaction on the road to capitalism. *IZA Discussion Paper No 3409*. Bonn, Germany: IZA.

Ermisch, J., Francesconi, M., & Siedler, T. (2006). Intergenerational mobility and marital sorting. *The Economic Journal*, *116*, 659–679. doi:10.1111/j.1468-0297.2006.01105.x

Ermisch, J., Gambetta, D., Laurie, H., Siedler, T., & Uhrig, S. C. N. (2009). Measuring people's trust. *Journal of the Royal Statistical Society: Statistics in Society*, *172A*, 749–769.

Fehr, E., Fischbacher, U., von Rosenbladt, B., Schupp, J., & Wagner, G. G. (2002). A nation-wide laboratory: Examining trust and trustworthiness by integrating behavioral experiments into representative surveys. *Schmollers Jahrbuch*, *122*, 1–24.

Francesconi, M., Jenkins, S. P., & Siedler, T. (in press). Childhood family structure and schooling outcomes: Evidence for Germany. *Journal of Population Economics*.

Gerlitz, J.-Y., & Schupp, J. (2005). Zur Erhebung der Big-Five-basierten Persönlichkeits-merkmale im SOEP [The survey of the Big Five personality traits based on SOEP]. *DIW Research Notes 2005: Vol. 4*. Berlin, Germany: DIW Berlin.

Geyer, S., Norozi, K., Buchhorn, R., & Wessel, A. (2008). Chances of employment in a population of women and men after surgery of congenital heart disease: Gender-specific comparisons between patients and the general population. *SOEP Papers on Multidisciplinary Panel Data Research: Vol. 91*. Berlin, Germany: DIW Berlin.

Giampaoli, S., Ferrucci, L., Cecchi, F., Noce, C. L., Poce, A., Dima, F., et al. (1999). Hand-grip strength predicts incident disability in non-disabled older men. *Age and Ageing, 28*, 283–288. doi:10.1093/ageing/28.3.283

Glaeser, E. L., Laibson, D. I., Scheinkman, J. A., & Soutter, C. L. (2000). Measuring trust. *The Quarterly Journal of Economics, 115*, 811–846. doi:10.1162/003355300554926

Gosling, S. D., Rentfrow, P. J., & Swann, W. B., Jr. (2003). A very brief measure of the Big Five personality domains. *Journal of Research in Personality, 37*, 504–528. doi:10.1016/S0092-6566(03)00046-1

Hank, K., Jürges, H., Schupp, J., & Wagner, G. G. (2009). Isometrische Greifkraft und sozialgerontologische Forschung—Ergebnisse und Analysepotentiale des SHARE und SOEP [Isometric grip strength and social gerontology—Research results and analysis potentials of SHARE and SOEP]. *Zeitschrift für Gerontologie und Geriatrie, 42*, 117–126.

Heineck, G., & Anger, S. (2008). The returns to cognitive abilities and personality traits in Germany. *SOEP Papers on Multidisciplinary Panel Data Research: Vol. 124*. Berlin, Germany: DIW Berlin.

John, O. P., & Srivastava, S. (1999). The Big Five trait taxonomy: History, measurement, and theoretical perspectives. In O. P. John & L. A. Pervin (Eds.), *Handbook of personality: Theory and research* (pp. 102–138). New York, NY: Guilford Press.

Lang, F. R., Weiss, D., Stocker, A., & von Rosenbladt, B. (2007). Assessing cognitive capacities in computer-assisted survey research: Two ultra-short tests of intellec-tual ability in the German Socio-Economic Panel (SOEP). *Schmollers Jahrbuch, 127*, 183–192.

Levitt, S. D., & List, J. A. (2008, January 15). Homo economicus evolves. *Science, 319*, 909–910. doi:10.1126/science.1153640

Lindenberger, U. (2002). Erwachsenenalter und Alter [Adulthood and age]. In R. Oerter & L. Montada (Eds..), Entwicklungspsychologie [*Developmental psychology*] (5th ed., pp. 350–391). Weinheim, Germany: Beltz PVU.

Metter, E. J., Talbot, L. A., Schrager, M., & Conwit, R. (2002). Skeletal muscle strength as a predictor of all-cause mortality in healthy men. *Journals of Gerontology: Biological Sciences, 57A*, 359–365.

Naef, M., & Schupp, J. (2009). Measuring trust: Experiments and surveys in contrast and combination. *SOEP Papers on Multidisciplinary Panel Data Research, 167*. Berlin, Germany: DIW Berlin.

Rammstedt, B. (2007). Who worries and who is happy? Explaining individual differences in worries and satisfaction by personality. *Personality and Individual Differens*, *43*, 1626–1634. doi:10.1016/j.paid.2007.04.031

Rammstedt, B., & Schupp, J. (2008). Personality similarities in couples—Only the congruent survive. *Personality and Individual Differences*, *45*, 533–535. doi:10.1016/j.paid.2008.06.007

Rantanen, T., Guralnik, J. M., Foley, D., Masaki, K., Leveille, S., Curb, J. D., & White, L. (1999). Midlife hand grip strength as a predictor of old age disability. *JAMA*, *281*, 558–560. doi:10.1001/jama.281.6.558

Sapienza, P., Toldra, A., & Zingales, L. (2007). Understanding trust. *NBER working Paper 13387*. Cambridge, MA.

Schimmak, U., & Lucas, R. (2007). Marriage matters: Spousal similarity in life satisfaction. *Schmollers Jahrbuch*, *127*, 105–111.

Scott, J., & Alwin, D. (1998). Retrospective versus prospective measurement of life histories in longitudinal research. In J. Z. Giele & G. H. Elder, Jr. (Eds.), *Methods of life course research* (pp. 98–127). Thousand Oaks, CA: Sage.

Siedler, T., Schupp, J., Spiess, C. K., & Wagner, G. G. (2009). The German Socio-Economic Panel as reference data set. *Schmollers Jahrbuch*, *129*, 374–374. doi:10.3790/schm.129.2.367

Smith, A. (1973). *Symbol Digit Modalities Test*. Los Angeles, CA: Western Psychological Services.

Solga, H., Stern, E., Rosenbladt, B. v., Schupp, J., & Wagner, G. G. (2005). *The measurement and importance of general reasoning potentials in schools and labor markets: Pre-test report* (Research note 10). Berlin, Germany: DIW Berlin.

Solon, G. R. (1992). Intergenerational income mobility in the United States. *The American Economic Review*, *82*, 393–408.

Spiess, M., Kroh, M., Pischner, R., & Wagner, G. G. (2008). On the treatment of non-original sample members in the German Household Panel Study (SOEP)—Tracing, weighting, and frequencies. *SOEP Papers on Multidisciplinary Panel Data Research: Vol. 98*. Berlin, Germany: DIW Berlin.

Winkelmann, L., & Winkelmann, R. (2008). Personality, work, and satisfaction: evidence from the German Socio-Economic Panel. *The Journal of Positive Psychology*, *3*, 266–275. doi:10.1080/17439760802399232

II

USING SECONDARY DATA
IN PSYCHOLOGICAL
RESEARCH

7

THE USE OF SECONDARY DATA IN ADULT DEVELOPMENT AND AGING RESEARCH

DANIEL K. MROCZEK, LINDSAY PITZER, LAURA MILLER,
NICK TURIANO, AND KAREN FINGERMAN

One of the forces underlying the increased use of secondary data is a growing division of labor among scholars, a process that has taken place in many other fields. For example, the scientific staff of a particle accelerator includes physicists who vary greatly in skills and specialization. Although the physical sciences were the first to experience a high degree of division of labor, it is now common in the biological and medical sciences as well. For instance, the Human Genome Project was composed of multidisciplinary research teams, as are many clinical trials. More often than not, data from these large-scale projects in physics, genetics, and medicine follow the pattern of one set of scientists collecting data (and perhaps conducting and publishing some initial analyses) and then making these data publicly available, with other sets of scientists engaging in secondary analyses that are often more in-depth and complex. This kind of research is quickly beginning to characterize research in the social and behavioral sciences, and in particular, social scientific research in adult development and aging. In this chapter, we discuss these increasingly important breakdowns of roles and what they mean for adult development and aging research in the social and behavioral sciences.

RESEARCH THAT IS TOO BIG FOR ONE PERSON

Early in the development of a scientific field, it is more common to see individual scientists controlling every aspect of a research project, from planning of data collection through to publication. One pictures Gregor Mendel, hidden away in his monastery, doing all research tasks by himself. The field of genetics has come a long way from the 19th century laboratory of Mendel, and now most genetic research is done in teams with highly differentiated divisions of labor, or in many cases, through the complete separation of the research tasks, with one group collecting molecular data and then handing off to other groups (e.g., bioinformatics specialists) who analyze these data. As scientific fields mature and grow more complex, the jack-of-all-trades begins to disappear and more specialists appear.

Answering scientific questions in adult development and aging research (and in the behavioral and social sciences generally) will require increasingly complex data and study designs. For example, the skills and talents required for the collection of high-quality, large-scale data sets are very different from those needed for high-quality data analysis. Collection of such data demands an ability to manage large staffs and budgets, as well as doctoral-level knowledge of survey sampling, sampling statistics, and particular types of designs. Examples include multiyear longitudinal (multiple occasions over at least 5 to 10 years), large and nationally representative samples, and interdisciplinary data (e.g., psychosocial and biomedical data in the same study). Moreover, the skilled personnel used for data collection are very different from those needed to analyze the resulting data. This is due in part to differences in training but also to differences in talents and abilities.

In adult development and aging research, these points are particularly true. The best studies of adult development and the aging process are long-term longitudinal studies. Many of the important changes associated with aging do not appear quickly. Cognitive declines appear gradually over decades. Personality changes in adulthood typically are observable only over long periods of time (5–10 years or more). Thus, a division of labor and archiving is absolutely necessary because the studies simply take too long. As a result, answers to many of the most important recent questions in adult development and aging have been obtained using secondary data (e.g., Charles, Reynolds, & Gatz, 2001; Lucas, Clark, Georgellis, & Diener, 2003; Small, Fratiglioni, von Strauss, & Backman, 2003; Small, Hertzog, Hultsch, & Dixon, 2003).

In the remainder of the chapter, we focus on secondary social and behavioral research in adult development and aging. Specifically, we give examples of the centrality of secondary data to answer two types of important questions in adult development and aging: (a) questions regarding long-term stability and change, and (b) questions regarding the prediction of physical health outcomes and mortality.

QUESTIONS REGARDING LONG-TERM STABILITY AND CHANGE

Most of the fundamental questions in any area of developmental science, including aging and adulthood, are questions of change. Development implies systematic change over time, although stability of certain functions in certain periods is an important part of development as well (e.g., stability in normal memory function is desirable from late childhood onward). Therefore, questions about development ultimately require longitudinal data. In adult development and aging research, change in key variables often occurs over very long time frames. In research on child development, change in key variables usually occurs over relatively short time frames: Infancy lasts a year or so; children are classified as toddlers for 3 or 4 years; and adolescence lasts 8 to 9 years. However, adulthood lasts at least 50 years for most people, and in the case of centenarians, a minimum of 80 years. Development on this scale demands not only longitudinal data but also long-term longitudinal data. This means that earlier portions of data become archival, even if new waves are continuously being collected.

In this sense, all long-term longitudinal studies are semiarchival in that earlier measurement occasions are archived. It also means that multiple generations of researchers are often involved in the study, either through data collection or analysis, or both. This puts a premium on good mentorship to ensure the smooth passing of the torch. This obviously takes an enormous amount of time and effort, but the questions that are answerable by such valuable long-term data are among the most important in all aging research.

These questions include those on personality change in adulthood, which tends to occur slowly when it does happen. Most studies on personality in midlife or older adulthood have used at least 6 to 10 years worth of data (Mroczek & Spiro, 2003; Small, Hertzog, Hultsch, & Dixon, 2003). Much of the work on change in well-being in adulthood has used longitudinal data spanning 15 to 20 years or longer (Charles, Reynolds, & Gatz, 2001; Griffin, Mroczek, & Spiro, 2006; Lucas et al., 2003, 2004; Mroczek & Spiro, 2005). Some of the best work on stability and change in self-esteem has used secondary data from longitudinal studies that spanned an average of 5 years but has also included some that were as long as 40 years (Trzesniewski, Donnellan, & Robins, 2003). Without archiving and long-term follow-up, these studies would not have been possible.

The data in each of the studies cited here contained multiple measurement occasions per person. More important, none of the lead authors on any of the above articles had a key role in collecting any of their early data. In some cases, the initial measurement occasions (or even all the occasions) were collected so long ago that those original researchers were no longer involved in the study. For example, in the Veterans Affairs (VA) Normative Aging Study (e.g., Mroczek & Spiro, 2003), the original scientists who recruited the panel in the late 1960s were either retired or deceased by the time the more recent analyses were conducted and published. In the next section, we discuss the Terman sample, which has yielded many interesting and important findings in the areas of both child and adult development. Yet, the study founder, Lewis Terman (born in 1877), did not live to read many of the well-known articles that were eventually published on his data. He died in 1956, and some of the most-cited articles using his sample were not published until the 1990s. The maintenance of long-term longitudinal studies is an enterprise that usually requires multiple generations of researchers. The most senior researchers often do not see the ultimate fruits of their labors.

QUESTIONS REGARDING THE PREDICTION OF PHYSICAL HEALTH OUTCOMES AND MORTALITY

Many important questions in aging and adulthood are health-related. Change in physical health is a big part of growing older. The study of such change as well as the prediction of health-related outcomes composes a crucial set of questions in research on aging and adulthood. However, such questions can rarely be answered satisfactorily using short-term studies. Declines in physical health, as well as other aging-related changes, such as memory decline, usually take place over long periods of time.

If researchers want to assess the predictive impact of a behavioral risk factor, such as the quality of one's close relationships, on development of heart disease, they ideally need to measure people on relationship quality and then wait for many years until some develop heart disease. This is the logic behind some of the most famous biomedical longitudinal studies, such as the Framingham Heart Study. The paramount studies of this type recruit and assess participants prior to the onset of disease, when they are still well. Typically, there are analyses that can be done quickly with one measurement occasion, allowing some publications in the early phase of the study. However, many other important research questions require scientists to wait as people slowly develop the major diseases associated with aging.

Studies of mortality in community-dwelling samples are particularly difficult in this regard, as they take a long time. It is next to impossible to conduct a study of mortality using a university's human subject pool or any other kind of short-term convenience sample. Yet, the scientific yield from mortality studies is of high value. The recent burgeoning literature on behavioral and social predictors of mortality has made many researchers think more deeply about the connections between psychosocial and biomedical variables. Behavioral and social variables, such as positive outlook, personality traits, social support, and cognitive functioning, have emerged as key predictors of mortality, with effect sizes that are comparable to those of many biomedical variables such as total blood cholesterol (Deary & Der, 2005; Ferraro & Kelley-Moore, 2001; Friedman et al., 1993; Levy, Slade, Kunkel, & Kasl, 2002; Maier & Smith, 1999; Mroczek & Spiro, 2007; Small & Backman, 1997; Small, Frantiglioni, von Strauss, & Backman, 2003; Sugisawa, Liang & Liu, 1994).

Perhaps the best example of this is Friedman et al.'s (1993) analyses of the Terman data. In 1921, Terman, at Stanford, recruited a sample of gifted children and teenagers from grammar schools and high schools across the state of California. These children were assessed on a number of variables, including intelligence and (teacher-rated) personality. They were followed into their adult years, and eventually, as they began to die, cause of death and age at death were obtained from death certificates. Many people from the 1920s to the 1990s had a role in maintaining the Terman data set and archiving previously collected data. By the early 1990s, the vast majority of the panel had died. It was at this time that Friedman et al. used the teacher-rated childhood personality traits obtained in 1921 to predict survival using proportional hazards (Cox, 1972) models. Despite the 7-decade lag, the childhood personality rating of conscientiousness predicted survival into middle age and older adulthood. As noted above, Terman died in 1956 and missed Friedman's 1993 publication by nearly 40 years, reinforcing our point that the ultimate fruits of long-term longitudinal research are often never seen by the scientists who begin the studies.

CONCLUSION

Terman's willingness to trust is one of our ending messages. Archiving requires trust. The collectors of data must trust that other people might be more capable than they are to use their data and may come to conclusions that they do not necessarily agree with. Likewise, users of data must trust that data they access are of good quality (within limits, of course; data sets that are clearly of low quality should be shunned). Of course, many investigators may not want to share, or entrust to others, data that they have spent a great deal of time, effort, and money to collect. This is understandable, as we are often possessive of things we have labored over intensely for many years. However, the fresh look and new findings provided by secondary data analysts often enhance the status of particular data sets. The researcher who shares data often enjoys a gain in much the same way a small privately held company can increase its value greatly by letting in outside investors. The founder of such a company has to give up 100% ownership and turn over a considerable percentage to outsiders. Yet, the new infusions of money and resources provided by those outsiders can enlarge the company far beyond what the founder could have done on his or her own. It becomes a win–win situation in which both the original owner and outside investors reap the benefits of an enlarged pie. Similarly, researchers who archive and share data with "outsider" secondary data analysts can themselves gain additional accolades and citations that would not have accrued if the data set had been kept in private hands.

There is one other argument for placing data in the public domain. Most high-quality data sets are collected with at least some form of taxpayer funding. We as researchers often benefit from such taxpayer beneficence (our employers usually reward us with raises, promotions, and resources for bringing in such funds), and it is fitting that we give back by making data public for others to use. We should share data because it is generally the right thing to do if we have received significant funding from our fellow citizens.

We conclude with three other points. First, as research questions become clarified over time, statistical techniques are developed to better answer these key questions. The past 4 decades have seen the development of structural equation models, proportional hazards models, item response theory, and multilevel (mixed) models. Each has been important in social science research. Each also was, in part, a response to problems that had arisen in the course of conducting research. Once these statistical models were fully developed, in many instances they were applied to existing data. This led to insights that had not been possible at the time of original data collection. A good example is Lucas's work using the German Socioeconomic Panel Survey (GSOEP), which contains multiple waves of data spanning nearly 2 decades (Lucas, Clark, Georgellis, & Diener 2003, 2004). Lucas et al. (2003, 2004) used multilevel modeling to examine how changes in marital and employment status influence well-being. When the GSOEP was founded in the early 1980s, the development of multilevel models had only recently begun. By the time the GSOEP had over a dozen waves, multilevel models were well developed and widely available in software packages, permitting Lucas et al. (2003, 2004) to capitalize on this large existing data set. In the early 1980s, the founders of the GSOEP could not have foreseen what new statistical techniques would yield important and interesting results from their data 2 decades later, yet by archiving and making their data publically available, they set the stage for future studies. Often, statistical techniques need time to catch up to available data. This is a persuasive argument for archiving and for using archives.

Second, the use of archived data (in aging or other areas) represents value-added on grant dollars already spent. In this time of tight federal research money, grantors are often favorably disposed toward funding secondary data analysis projects. Such projects are typically much less expensive than those that propose new, and often pricey, data collection. For a small fraction of the cost, a grantor can often expect outstanding publications. Sometimes, these secondary analysis articles are more influential than work from the original rounds of data collection. There is simply more "bang for the buck" in secondary analysis.

However, we strongly recommend that researchers applying for funds to do secondary analysis should overtly state the concept of value-added in the grant application itself. The reason is that some reviewers are not favorably disposed to secondary analysis. Although funding agencies might recognize the value of such work, many reviewers may not appreciate it unless the point about value-added is made explicitly.

Third, we also must emphasize that although we are strong advocates of the use of secondary data, doing so presents challenges that are not encountered when collecting one's own data. Often, the exact variables you want may not be available. If you are interested in psychological well-being, you may need to settle for a single-item that asks "how happy you are" in general. Indeed, many constructs may be assessed with single items, as opposed to the multi-item, high–Cronbach's alpha scales that are preferred in the psychological literature. Additionally, some existing data sets may suffer from a lack of good maintenance through the years, or worse, from neglect. Quite a bit of data cleaning and sprucing up may be necessary before any kind of analysis is possible. Some data are in such dire shape that private companies and nonprofits have been created that do nothing other than put such data into usable form. Medicare and Social Security data are notorious for being particularly unfriendly to those (mostly economists and demographers) who wish to analyze them. Yet, the obstacles presented by secondary data are usually outweighed by the benefits.

FINAL THOUGHT: CRONBACH'S "TWO DISCIPLINES"

Despite the advantages of secondary data, especially with respect to research in adult development and aging, there is continued resistance in some quarters. In particular, scholars that promote an experimental perspective on aging tend to discount the use of survey data in general and secondary data in particular (Schwarz, 2006). This remaining lack of acceptance can likely be traced back to the continuing divide identified a half-century ago by Cronbach (1957) in his classic article on the "two disciplines of scientific psychology."

Cronbach pointed out that by the mid-1950s a rift had developed between psychologists who relied mostly on experimentation and those who ventured into the area of nonexperimental methods, including surveys and longitudinal designs. The experimentalists were the vast majority then, and to this day many psychologists are still trained to believe that experimental methods are superior.

Secondary data are almost never experimental (except see Chapter 6, this volume, for recent advances using experimental designs within archived survey studies), and there are many social scientists, especially among psychologists, who fundamentally mistrust any non-experimental data. If an independent variable is not directly manipulated, many of these scholars view the results with suspicion. This lingering doubt presents a challenge for those of us who advocate the use of archives. However, many questions simply cannot be answered with experimentation. As we argued earlier, longitudinal data are perhaps the most valuable type of data in adult development and aging research. Experimental evidence is more often supplementary than primary in answering important questions about change in some of the key aspects of aging, such as cognition, personality, or social behavior. This is not without parallel in other areas of inquiry, such as astronomy or evolutionary theory, where experimentation is very difficult or impossible. Astronomers, for example, are often unable to do experiments because the manipulation of certain key variables is not possible. If astronomers are interested in how the gravitational pull of stars influences the speed of planetary orbits, they cannot manipulate gravitational pull and randomly assign planets to different gravitation groups. They must measure the actual, natural world and draw conclusions as best they can. So it is with many questions in adult development and aging, and indeed, in many areas of the social sciences. It is not possible to assign people to groups that receive varying levels of education and other cognitive stimulation to see who develops early dementia. Similarly, it is not possible and is unethical to assign people to groups that smoke or do not smoke, to determine who gets lung cancer or emphysema. Only long-term data, in which the earliest waves are by definition archival by the time the later waves are collected, can answer these questions.

Books such as the present volume will, we hope, begin to assuage the concerns of those who doubt the usefulness of secondary analysis. We hope that, eventually, the use of secondary data will attain equal status with other techniques within the social scientist's toolkit.

RECOMMENDED DATA SETS

- *National Survey of Midlife Development in the United States Survey (MIDUS)*. The MIDUS contains two waves of data, separated by about a decade. The first wave was collected in 1994–1995, with a sample of over 7,000 Americans, ages 25 to 74. It was funded by the John D. and Catherine T. MacArthur Foundation. In 2002, the National Institute on Aging (NIA) provided a grant to the Institute on Aging at the University of Wisconsin—Madison to carry out a longitudinal follow-up. The second wave was completed in 2004–2008 and includes biomarkers and physiological data in addition to psychosocial information. Both waves are publically available. To access these data, go to http://www.midus.wisc.edu.

- *Health and Retirement Survey (HRS)*. The University of Michigan's HRS surveys more than 22,000 Americans over the age of 50 every 2 years. Like the MIDUS, it is supported by the NIA. These data provide a portrait of how aging trends in the United States are impacting physical and mental health, insurance coverage, financial status, family support systems, labor market status, and retirement planning. All waves are publically available. To access the HRS, go to http://www.hrsonline.isr.umich.edu.

- *National Survey of Families and Households (NSFH)*. The NSFH provides a broad range of information on life course family issues. A considerable amount of life-history information was collected, including the respondent's family living arrangements in childhood; departures from and returns to the parental home; and histories of marriage, cohabitation, education, fertility, and employment. These data allow analyses of past and current living arrangements and other family or marriage experiences, as well as the consequences of earlier family patterns on current psychological states, marital and parenting relationships, kin contact, and economic and psychological well-being. Data were gathered in 1987–1988, 1992–1994, and 2001–2003. The national sample of 13,007 includes a main cross-section of 9,637 households plus an oversampling of Blacks, Puerto Ricans, Mexican Americans, single-parent families, families with stepchildren, cohabiting couples, and recently married persons. To access these data, go to http://www.ssc.wisc.edu/nsfh.

- *Wisconsin Longitudinal Survey (WLS)*. The WLS is a long-term study based on a random sample of 10,317 men and women who graduated from Wisconsin high schools in 1957. The WLS data include information on social background, youthful aspirations, schooling, military service, labor market experiences, family characteristics and events, social participation, psychological characteristics, health and well-being, and retirement. Like the MIDUS and HRS, the WLS is supported by the NIA. To access these data, go to http://www.ssc.wisc.edu/wlsresearch.

- *Integrated Analysis of Longitudinal Studies of Aging (IALSA).* The IALSA is not a publically available data set per se but is rather a research network that provides a collaborative research infrastructure for coordinated interdisciplinary, cross-national investigations aimed at the integrative understanding of within-person aging-related changes in health, personality, and cognition. It is basically a loose consortium of 28 major longitudinal studies of aging, some of which are public. It includes some of the above public-use studies, like the HRS and WLS. Yet, is also contains many other studies that are not officially public. However, almost all of the IALSA studies have standardized collaborative agreements that an investigator can sign to obtain a given data set to answer a circumscribed research question. To learn about the IALSA network, go to http://lifelab.tss.oregonstate.edu/.

In 2005, Richard M. Suzman, of the NIA, wrote a summary of major surveys and databases funded by the NIA. Many of these studies are already listed in this chapter, but others can be found in the following online document: http://www.popcouncil.org/pdfs/PDRSupplements/Vol30_Aging/Suzman_pp239-264.pdf.

FOR FURTHER READING

Charles, S. T., Reynolds, C. A., & Gatz, M. (2001). Age-related differences and change in positive and negative affect over 23 years. *Journal of Personality and Social Psychology, 80,* 136–151.

Friedman, H. S., Tucker, J. S., Tomlinson-Keasey, C., Schwartz, J. E., Wingard, D. L., & Criqui, M. H., (1993). Does childhood personality predict longevity? *Journal of Personality and Social Psychology, 65,* 176–185.

Lucas, R. E., Clark, A. E., Georgellis, Y., & Diener, E. (2004). Unemployment alters the set point for life satisfaction. *Psychological Science, 15,* 8–13.

Mroczek, D. K., & Spiro, A. (2007). Personality change influences mortality in older men. *Psychological Science, 18,* 371–376.

Small, B. J., Hertzog, C., Hultsch, D. F., & Dixon, R. A. (2003). Stability and change in adult personality over 6 years: Findings from the Victoria Longitudinal Study. *Journal of Gerontology: Psychological Sciences, 58B,* 166–176.

Trzesniewski, K. H., Donnellan, M. B., & Robins, R. W. (2003). Stability of self-esteem across the life span. *Journal of Personality and Social Psychology, 84,* 205–220.

REFERENCES

Charles, S. T., Reynolds, C. A., & Gatz, M. (2001). Age-related differences and change in positive and negative affect over 23 years. *Journal of Personality and Social Psychology, 80,* 136–151. doi:10.1037/0022-3514.80.1.136

Cox, D. R. (1972). Regression models and life tables (with discussion). *Journal of the Royal Statistical Society: Methodological, 74B,* 187–220.

Cronbach, L. J. (1957). The two disciplines of scientific psychology. *American Psychologist, 12,* 671–684. doi:10.1037/h0043943

Deary, I. J., & Der, G. (2005). Reaction time explains IQ's association with death. *Psychological Science, 16,* 64–69. doi:10.1111/j.0956-7976.2005.00781.x

Ferraro, K. F., & Kelley-Moore, J. (2001). Self-rated health and mortality among Black and White adults: Examining the dynamic evaluation thesis. *Journal of Gerontology: Social Sciences, 56B,* 195–205.

Friedman, H. S., Tucker, J. S., Tomlinson-Keasey, C., Schwartz, J. E., Wingard, D. L., & Criqui, M. H. (1993). Does childhood personality predict longevity? *Journal of Personality and Social Psychology, 65,* 176–185. doi:10.1037/0022-3514.65.1.176

Griffin, P., Mroczek, D. K., & Spiro, A. (2006). Variability in affective change among aging men: Findings from the VA Normative Aging Study. *Journal of Research in Personality, 40,* 942–965. doi:10.1016/j.jrp.2005.09.011

Levy, B. R., Slade, M., Kunkel, S., & Kasl, S. (2002). Longevity increased by positive self-perceptions of aging. *Journal of Personality and Social Psychology, 83,* 261–270. doi:10.1037/0022-3514.83.2.261

Lucas, R. E., Clark, A. E., Georgellis, Y., & Diener, E. (2003). Reexamining adaptation and the set point model of happiness: Reactions to changes in marital status. *Journal of Personality and Social Psychology, 84,* 527–539. doi:10.1037/0022-3514.84.3.527

Lucas, R. E., Clark, A. E., Georgellis, Y., & Diener, E. (2004). Unemployment alters the set point for life satisfaction. *Psychological Science, 15,* 8–13. doi:10.1111/j.0963-7214.2004.01501002.x

Maier, H., & Smith, J. (1999). Psychological predictors of mortality in old age. *Journal of Gerontology: Social Sciences, 54B,* 44–54.

Mroczek, D. K., & Spiro, A., III. (2003). Modeling intraindividual change in personality traits: Findings from the Normative Aging Study. *Journal of Gerontology: Psychological Sciences, 58B,* 153–165.

Mroczek, D. K., & Spiro, A. (2005). Change in life satisfaction during adulthood: Findings from the Veterans Affairs Normative Aging Study. *Journal of Personality and Social Psychology, 88,* 189–202. doi:10.1037/0022-3514.88.1.189

Mroczek, D. K., & Spiro, A. (2007). Personality change influences mortality in older men. *Psychological Science, 18,* 371–376. doi:10.1111/j.1467-9280.2007.01907.x

Schwarz, N. (2006). Measurement: Aging and the psychology of self-report. In L. L. Carstensen & C. R. Hartel (Eds.), *When I'm 64: Committee on Aging Frontiers in*

Social Psychology, Personality, and Adult Developmental Psychology (pp. 219–230). Washington, DC: National Research Council/The National Academies Press.

Small, B. J., & Backman, L. (1997). Cognitive correlates of mortality: Evidence from a population-based sample of very old adults. *Psychology and Aging, 12,* 309–313. doi:10.1037/0882-7974.12.2.309

Small, B. J., Fratiglioni, L., von Strauss, E., & Backman, L. (2003). Terminal decline and cognitive performance in very old age: Does cause of death matter? *Psychology and Aging, 18,* 193–202. doi:10.1037/0882-7974.18.2.193

Small, B. J., Hertzog, C., Hultsch, D. F., & Dixon, R. A. (2003). Stability and change in adult personality over 6 years: Findings from the Victoria Longitudinal Study. *Journal of Gerontology: Social Sciences, 58B,* 166–176.

Sugisawa, H., Liang, J., & Liu, X. (1994). Social networks, social support, and mortality among older people in Japan. *Journals of Gerontology: Social Sciences, 49,* S3–S13.

Trzesniewski, K. H., Donnellan, M. B., & Robins, R. W. (2003). Stability of self-esteem across the life span. *Journal of Personality and Social Psychology, 84,* 205–220. doi:10.1037/0022-3514.84.1.205

8

USING SECONDARY DATA TO TEST QUESTIONS ABOUT THE GENETIC BASIS OF BEHAVIOR

MICHELLE B. NEISS, CONSTANTINE SEDIKIDES,
AND JIM STEVENSON

Behavioral genetic studies over the past several decades have shown that most human behavior is genetically influenced (Turkheimer, 2000). In general, however, research on genetic factors that influence human behavior becomes more fruitful when investigators move beyond the issue of whether heredity plays a role. Our own work uses behavioral genetic methods to identify the genetically influenced mediators between self-esteem and social behavior. Innate, heritable influences are important in explaining the origins of self-esteem, accounting for approximately 40% of the variance in self-esteem (Neiss, Sedikides, & Stevenson, 2002). Nonetheless, there is probably no "self-esteem gene." Rather, the pathway from DNA to self-esteem involves multiple genes whose expression relates to multiple processes, which in turn are related to multiple behaviors. For example, self-esteem is an affective evaluation of the self and thus may overlap with affective style in general. So it might be the case that the genetic influence on self-esteem reflects positive or negative affective style rather than genetic factors on self-esteem per se. Existing studies often include a wide range of constructs and thus provide an excellent opportunity to investigate genetic links among multiple behaviors. As such, secondary data sets are a useful tool for behavioral genetic research. Perhaps even more pertinently, secondary data sets provide an excellent way for researchers new to behavioural genetics to implement genetically informed methodologies in their own work.

A variety of methodologies can inform whether and how genetic factors influence behavior. Our own work focuses on quantitative genetic analyses of twin data. In this chapter, we present quantitative genetic work that moves beyond identifying the magnitude of genetic influence to provide insight to more substantive questions. Before turning to our work, we describe briefly how adoption and molecular genetic studies provide complementary information about genetic influences on behavior. We present more discussion on twin data using an illustrative study. The purpose of the illustrative study here is to provide nonbehavioral genetic researchers with ideas about how genetically informative secondary data sets could prove useful in their own endeavors. The bulk of our chapter integrates information about the use of secondary twin data sets with an actual application of the approach.

ADOPTION STUDY DATA

Twin data are crucial for investigating genetic influences on behavior but are less suited to identifying shared environmental influences. Data from studies of adopted children are very useful for identifying environmental influences on behavior that operate independently of genetic factors. Resemblances between adopted children and their adoptive parents and nonbiologically related adoptive siblings can arise only through shared environmental effects. Similarly, resemblance between adopted children and their biological parents can arise only through genetic transmission. Both of these assertions are based on the assumption that adoption placements are made at random, and selective placement will undermine this assumption.

Nevertheless, adoption data are a potent adjunct to twin data. The two types of studies are complementary in that the twin design has good power to detect genetic effects on behavior but has less power to detect shared environment effects. The studies of adopted children and their adoptive families are a powerful design to detect shared environment effects but are less suited to examine genetic effects, unless data are available on biological parents (and this is often lacking). In addition, combining information across both types of studies allows for better understanding of more complex gene–environment interplay, such as gene–environment correlations or gene × environment interactions. The strengths and weaknesses of these alternative behavior genetic designs are discussed in Plomin, DeFries, McClearn, and McGuffin (2001).

Twin studies are more prevalent than adoption studies. Consequently, there is less scope for the secondary analysis of existing data from adoption studies. The Colorado Adoption Project (CAP; Plomin, Fulker, Corley, &

DeFries, 1997), a long-running project, is available for secondary data analysis. Details of the CAP can be found at http://ibgwww.colorado.edu/cap/, and the data are available at the Henry A. Murray Research Archive at Harvard University (http://www.murray.harvard.edu/). This study of adoptive children, their biological and adoptive parents, and their siblings has been running for more than 30 years. The study is particularly well suited for research questions that require longitudinal data, as 442 families continue to participate, representing over 90% of the original number enrolled.

MOLECULAR GENETIC DATA

Quantitative genetic analysis of twin and adoption provide significant insights into genetic and environmental influences on behavior. Such data can be used not only to identify which behaviors have strong genetic effects (a prerequisite for molecular genetic studies) but also to examine clues as to the ways different personality characteristics, abilities, and behaviors share genetic and environmental influences. However, such studies do not identify the specific genes involved. For this, molecular genetic data are needed.

The prime questions confronting behavior genetics concern the interplay between genetic and environmental influences (Rutter, Moffitt, & Caspi, 2006). The influences are not independent, and the action of one is highly contingent on the influences of the other. Gene expression is modified by experience, and the impact of life events is moderated by genetic differences between people. The methods for focusing on this joint action of genetic and environmental factors have been systematically reviewed elsewhere (Moffitt, Caspi, & Rutter, 2005). These methods are most insightful if they include molecular genetic data.

A crucial feature of molecular genetic studies of behavior is the need to demonstrate that the results are not sample specific and can be replicated on independent samples. This is necessary in the case of gene–environment interaction studies, in which often a wide range of potential genetic moderators is examined for large sets of environmental measures. Replication is also important. Studies to identify genes implicated in influencing behaviors are now using genome-wide association methods, where 500,000 genetic variants can be tested (e.g., Butcher, Davis, Craig, & Plomin, 2008). In these types of studies, multiple tests of significance may produce false positive result, and replication in an independent sample is highly desirable, if not essential.

Existing and open access databases are particularly valuable when it comes to replication, although there are obvious limitations such as whether the same phenotypic measures are available in the existing data set and whether the same genetic variants (polymorphisms) have been genotyped.

With these constraints in mind, it may be prudent to select some psychological measures for a specific study based on what is known to be available in the established archives.

One such archive that includes genotyping is the National Longitudinal Study of Adolescent Health (Add Health) study (details of which are given in Recommended Data Sets section). The Generation R Study conducted in Holland is also an open access database that includes measures of behavioral and cognitive development, such as maternal and paternal psychopathology, fetal and postnatal brain development, psychopathology and cognition, neuromotor development, and chronic pain (Jaddoe et al., 2007). Investigators enrolled 9,778 mothers, with more detailed information available on a subgroup of 1,232 women and their children. The biological determinants include parental anthropometrics and blood pressure; fetal and postnatal growth characteristics, endocrine and immunological factors; and important for the purposes of this chapter, genetic variants (polymorphisms). The data can be particularly informative, as they include environmental determinants (maternal and childhood diet, parental lifestyle habits including smoking, alcohol consumption, and housing conditions) and social determinants (parental education, employment status and household income, parental marital status, and ethnicity). The inclusion of both biological and social measures means that the data set is well suited for studies of gene–environment interplay. The study accepts requests for collaboration, which are vetted through the Generation R Study Management Team (see http://www.generationr.nl).

ILLUSTRATIVE STUDY

In our own research, we sought to identify behaviors that share genetic factors with self-esteem. Self-esteem correlates with several constructs, such as negative emotionality, depression, and neuroticism (Judge, Erez, Bono, & Thoresen, 2002; Neiss, Stevenson, Legrand, Iacono, & Sedikides, in press). We expected a portion of this correlation to arise from common heritable factors and sought to characterize those heritable factors using twin data. We turned to existing data to investigate the connection between the self and broad affectivity or personality.

ADVANTAGES OF SECONDARY DATA

It is no small undertaking to gather a large, genetically informed sample. Such a sample would include studies of twins, adoptive families, or molecular genetic studies that genotype the participants. Each type of study requires large-scale and expensive recruitment efforts. As some of the existing twin registries have grown to several thousand twin pairs, the standard for twin studies now involves fairly large samples. Adoption studies best assess genetic effects by including both the biological and adoptive families, but that dictates a long-term effort to recruit the multiple informants. These challenges mean that, in most cases, the expense and effort are worthwhile only if a group of investigators wish to carry out an extensive study of participants and follow the participants longitudinally. Such studies usually occur under the aegis of a dedicated research center with considerable administrative support. Many of the larger existing twin registries offer opportunities for collaboration. This route also carries costs, such as substantial charges for data collection and the time involved for the vetting and approval of the research proposal by the associated investigators. For investigators looking for something more immediate and viable on a small scale, existing data sets are an appealing option. In our case, we opted to use the National Survey of Midlife Development in the United States (MIDUS).

A strength of the MIDUS data is that they include a large population-based sample, allowing researchers to contrast phenotypic and genetically informed analyses. Researchers often discuss the potential genetic confound in correlational studies of parenting effects, but few consider shared genetic factors as a potential confound in phenotypic models. Specifically, the apparent causal ordering of the relation between the self and affectivity may be different in phenotypic versus genetic analyses. Given that information on the representativeness of twin samples is rarely available directly, another strength of the MIDUS design is that researchers can verify whether phenotypic relations are similar across the twin and population samples. Researchers also used the large, separate sample of no twin participants to test measurement models for implementation in subsequent behavioral genetic analyses (Neiss et al., 2005).

DISADVANTAGES OF SECONDARY DATA

In dealing with the MIDUS study, we faced challenges common to the use of secondary data. One challenge was finding appropriate measurement scales for our purposes. The original investigators did not directly assess self-esteem, leading us to compile a self-esteem measure from items that assessed personal acceptance and satisfaction with the self.

We intended to look also at broad negative and positive affectivity, conceptualized as general dispositional tendencies to experience either positive or negative mood. Here, we were confronted with another challenge.

Although MIDUS included measures of both positive and negative affect, these did not correspond to the widely accepted Positive Affect and Negative Affect Scales (PANAS; Watson, Clark, & Tillage, 1988). It is important to note that the PANAS is based on the premise that positive and negative affect are relatively independent. Positive and negative affect are, however, inversely correlated in the MIDUS sample (Mroczek & Kolarz, 1998). Hence, we had to cope with a discrepancy between a widely accepted theory about the structure of affect (positive and negative affect are independent) and the empirical findings in the MIDUS sample. This discrepancy could not be reconciled satisfactorily because of the measurement issue. In the end, we chose to focus primarily on negative affectivity. In other words, the use of secondary data required that we modify goals in light of measurement constraints.

However, not all measurement issues are disadvantages. When we combed through the MIDUS variables to construct a scale of mastery or locus of control, we discovered that the survey also assessed primary and secondary control strategies, allowing us to extend our original focus to the broader idea of the executive self. The *executive self* is a broad term that includes such constructs as control beliefs, control strategies, and self-regulation (Baumeister, 1998; Sedikides & Gregg, 2003). The MIDUS survey included items that tap into people's beliefs that they can control many aspects of their lives (*mastery*), possess strategies to change the external world to fit with their own needs (*primary control*), and possess strategies to protect the self in negative situations (*secondary control*). Few studies have assessed directly the executive self, so our operationalization provided a unique addition to the literature.

Accuracy of zygosity determination is one potential issue with twin studies, as self-reported zygosity may be incorrect. The MIDUS investigators included a zygosity questionnaire to assess physical resemblance and attempted to obtain DNA samples from the twin participants to verify zygosity. However, not all existing data sets may have verified the genetic relatedness of sibling pairs and some pairs may be misclassified.

PHENOTYPIC STUDY OVERVIEW

We took advantage of the MIDUS survey by investigating the relations among these three constructs with both (a) phenotypic (i.e., observed) analyses in the population sample (Study 1) and (b) behavioral genetic analyses in the twin sample (Study 3). We also included a short-term longitudinal study to strengthen the phenotypic analyses (Study 2). By using multiple methodologies, we were able to gain a richer understanding of how executive self,

self-esteem, and negative affectivity interrelate. The use of secondary data facilitated this in-depth approach, and in the remainder of this chapter, we describe the analyses drawn from the MIDUS survey.

We examined first the phenotypic relations among these three constructs. In particular, we considered the idea that both the executive self and self-esteem serve as protective factors against psychological distress (Metalsky, Joiner, Hardin, & Abramson, 1993; Pyszczynski, Greenberg, Solomon, Arndt, & Schimel, 2004). We tested two alternative phenotypic models: one in which self-esteem mediates the link between executive self and negative affectivity, and another in which the executive self mediates the link between self-esteem and negative affectivity. The mediational models allowed us to evaluate whether the influence of the self system on negative affectivity operates primarily through one self-aspect (executive self vs. self-esteem). In addition, this study allowed us to validate our composite scales and test the relations among our constructs in a sample independent from that to be used for the behavioral genetic analyses.

In our theory-based construction of composite variables, we combined scales in ways that may not have been foreseen by the original investigators. Preliminary analyses bolstered the case for our constructed measures (Neiss et al., 2005). We then tested the phenotypic relations through a series of hierarchical regression analyses. Specifically, we tested the mediational status of executive self versus self-esteem. Both executive self ($\beta = -.34$, $p < .001$) and self-esteem ($\beta = -.53$, $p < .001$) were related to negative affectivity: People reporting weaker executive self or lower self-esteem also reported higher negative affectivity. Whereas the relation between self-esteem and negative affectivity declined minimally with the addition of executive self, the relation between executive self and negative affectivity was lowered substantially once self-esteem was included in the model. Thus, lowered self-esteem accounted for the majority of the influence of the self system on negative affectivity.

Nevertheless, given that the analyses used nonstandard measures, it is possible that our results were contingent on the specific measures used. We note that we did in fact replicate the phenotypic analyses in another sample using more standard scales (Neiss et al., 2005; Study 2). The use of secondary data encouraged us to pursue multiple methodologies. Although secondary data might require compromises in measurement, replications using smaller-scale studies based on convenience samples can provide important lines of converging evidence. Such a strategy is a compelling scholarly practice that can help build a cumulative science of social and personality psychology. Moreover, behavioral genetic methodologies can provide additional insight into the understanding of psychological mechanisms. We next turned to the behavioral genetic analyses.

TWIN STUDY

A multivariate behavioral genetic approach allowed us to address more complex questions about the relations among executive self, self-esteem, and negative affectivity. Do the three constructs share common genetic antecedents or are genetic influences unique to each? Do environmental effects reflect a common influence on executive self, self-esteem, and negative affectivity, or are environmental effects more specific to each? Such questions help clarify the etiological underpinnings of the constructs.

Behavioral genetic studies seek to identify genetic and environmental sources of variance. Genetic effects include all influences with an origin in genetic differences between people. Environmental sources include shared environmental effects that act to make siblings more alike, and nonshared environmental effects that create differences between siblings. Multivariate behavioral genetic analyses go beyond apportioning the variance of a specific behavior into genetic and environmental components, by identifying the sources of covariance between multiple phenotypes. That is, the covariation between two or more characteristics may be due to common genetic influences or common environmental influences affecting multiple phenotypes. For example, a common genetic factor may influence the executive self, self-esteem, and negative affectivity all together, or each may show a unique and separable genetic influence.

Identifying the source of covariation between phenotypes contributes to the understanding of underlying causal processes. Indeed, we were particularly interested in common genetic etiology as an indicator of an underlying common temperamental "core." Other researchers have suggested that many related personality traits are in fact measures of the same underlying core construct (Judge et al., 2002). For example, Judge et al. (2002) found that self-esteem, locus of control, self-efficacy, and neuroticism were all markers of a higher order construct, which they viewed as broad Neuroticism. It may be that innate, heritable differences account for much of the overlap between the self system and negative affectivity. Furthermore, if this genetically influenced temperamental core is left out of psychological models, researchers may imbue phenotypic correlations (including those found in our own phenotypic analyses) with a misleading causal interpretation.

Our multivariate behavior genetic design apportioned the covariance between executive self, self-esteem, and negative affectivity into genetic and environmental components. We sought to identify both common origins of the different self-aspects and negative affectivity as well as points of uniqueness, where genetic and environmental factors affect primarily one phenotype.

Method

We used the twin sample from the MIDUS survey ($N = 1,914$ individuals). The design allowed multiple twin pairs from the same family to participate; we limited our sample to only one pair per family. Our selection process yielded 878 twin pairs: 344 identical, or monozygotic (MZ), twin pairs (160 female pairs, 184 male pairs), and 534 fraternal, or dizygotic (DZ), twin pairs (189 female pairs, 115 male pairs, 230 mixed-sex pairs). More detail on the sample and methods can be found elsewhere (Neiss et al., 2005).

Results

The phenotypic relations among executive self, self-esteem, and negative affectivity replicated those observed in the nontwin population sample, with self-esteem mediating the relation between executive self and negative affectivity. Next, we used behavioral genetic analyses to identify genetic and environmental connections among the three constructs.

This type of classic twin study relies on the comparison of similarity between MZ twins and DZ twins. MZ twins share all genes that vary between individuals, whereas DZ twins share, on average, half of those genes. The analyses rely on the assumption that DZ twins are treated as similarly to one another as are MZ twins (*equal environment assumption*). Therefore, greater resemblance among MZ twins as compared with DZ twins provides evidence for heritable influences. In our study, the MZ twins resembled each other to a greater degree than did DZ twins, providing cursory evidence of a genetic effect on each of variables. Univariate structural equation modeling confirmed this impression. Genetic influences explained a substantial portion of the differences between individuals in executive self (41%), self-esteem (45%), and negative affect (38%). Shared environmental influences were minimal (0%–4%). Nonshared environmental influences explained the majority of variance in executive self (59%), self-esteem (55%), and negative affect (57%). Thus, environmental influences that make siblings different from one another explained the majority of variance in all three constructs, although this estimate includes measurement error as well.

Our interest, however, lay in identifying the genetic and environmental architecture that underlies the relations among executive self, self-esteem, and negative affect. The logic behind univariate analyses extends to multivariate analyses. Greater MZ as compared with DZ cross-correlations (i.e., the correlation between one twin's score on a variable with the other twin's score on a second variable) implicate common genetic influences. Conversely, if the cross-correlation is similar across MZ and DZ twins, there is evidence for common shared environmental effects. In fact, we found that the MZ cross-correlations were larger than the DZ cross-correlations for our constructs.

We used a Cholesky decomposition to model the genetic and environmental factors underlying the relations among executive self, self-esteem, and negative affectivity. Figure 8.1 illustrates the model for just one member of a twin pair and provides standardized path estimates. The first set of genetic and environmental factors are common to all three variables (a1, c1, e1). The second set of factors underlies only executive self and negative affectivity (a2, c2, e2). The third set of factors represents genetic and environmental influence unique to negative affectivity (a3, c3, e3). Summing all squared path estimates to each construct from a particular source of effects (genetic, shared environment or nonshared environment) provides the total portion of variability ascribed to that source.

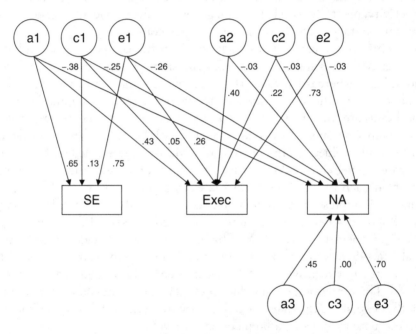

Figure 8.1. Cholesky model of genetic and environmental factors underlying self-esteem (SE), executive self (Exec), and negative affectivity (NA). The Cholesky decomposition models additive genetic factors (a), shared environmental factors (c), and nonshared environmental factors (e). From "Executive Self, Self-Esteem, and Negative Affectivity: Relations at the Phenotypic and Genotypic Level," by M. B. Neiss, J. Stevenson, C. Sedikides, M. Kumashiro, E. J. Finkel, and C. E. Rusbult, 2005, *Journal of Personality and Social Psychology, 89,* p. 602. Copyright 2005 by the American Psychological Association.

The ordering of variables affects the interpretation of a Cholesky model (Loehlin, 1996). The mediational results informed the order chosen: We placed executive self second, to investigate whether genetic and environmental influences explain any modest direct relation between executive self and negative affectivity after accounting for the genetic and environmental influences that also impact self-esteem. The model fit the data well, as evidenced by a nonsignificant chi-square, χ^2 (24, $N = 572$) = 29.34, $p < .21$, a low (.03) root-mean-square error of approximation (RMSEA), and negative Akaike's information criterion (AIC, −18.66).

The genetic factor common to all three variables showed large to moderate genetic loadings (i.e., .43, .65, and −.38 for executive self, self-esteem, and negative affectivity, respectively). The negative loading to negative affectivity reflected the direction of the phenotypic relations: Genetic influences that contributed to higher executive self or self-esteem led to lower negative affectivity. Although the genetic factor on executive self and negative affectivity (second factor) showed a moderate loading to executive self (.40), it had a very low loading on negative affectivity (−.03). In other words, this factor represented genetic effects that were essentially unique to executive self; genetic links between executive self and negative affectivity were carried primarily by the common genetic factor influencing all three variables. Negative affectivity showed moderate unique genetic influence (.45). Overall, the common genetic factor accounted for a large proportion of the genetic influence on executive self and negative affectivity: 53% percent of the genetic variance in executive self and 41% of the genetic variance in negative affectivity. Because of the constraints of the model, genetic influence on self-esteem was modeled entirely through the common factor.

Common shared environmental influences (c1 paths) influenced both self-esteem and negative affect, whereas shared environmental influences on executive self were separable and unique to executive self. However, these results must be interpreted with caution, as shared environmental estimates were small and statistically insignificant. We could drop all six shared environmental paths without reducing significantly model fit, χ^2 (30, $N = 572$) = 29.88, $p < .47$ (AIC = −30.12; RMSEA = .02). In addition, the change in chi-square between the full model and one with no shared environmental influence was not significant, which led us to conclude that shared environmental effects do not explain individual differences in or covariation between executive self, self-esteem, and negative affect.

Each common nonshared environmental factor showed stronger loadings to one particular construct: the first, to self-esteem; the second, to executive self. In addition, nonshared environmental influences on negative affectivity stemmed primarily from the third, specific factor. In other words, nonshared environmental effects were primarily unique to each variable. Any modest overlap stemmed from the common factor underlying all three. These estimates include measurement error.

The multivariate analyses yielded modest links between just executive self and negative affectivity. Therefore, we tested one final model in which we dropped all shared environment paths (as described above) and the remaining direct genetic and nonshared environmental paths between executive self and negative affect (a2 and e2 paths to NA). This reduced model fit well, χ^2 (32, $N = 572$) = 32.52, $p < .44$ (AIC = -31.48; RMSEA = .02). Of note, this model suggests that executive self does not display any genetic or environmental link with negative affect over and above those effects shared with self-esteem.

CONCLUSION

Our aim was to investigate the overlap between aspects of the self system (executive self and self-esteem) and negative affectivity. Using a secondary data set allowed us to compare phenotypic analyses and behavioral genetic analyses involving large samples and complicated study design (twin methodology). Capitalizing on both sets of results, we concluded that self-esteem explained much of the relation between executive self and negative affectivity. The behavioral genetic analyses added the information that the overlap stemmed primarily from common genetic influences. Nonetheless, the behavioral genetic methodology allowed us also to specify distinctions between the self system and negative affectivity, as illustrated by specific genetic and nonshared environmental influences.

The use of secondary data sets permits researchers to use behavioral genetic methods without undergoing the arduous process of actually having to collect genetically informative data. Although behavior genetic methodology can be used to answer theoretically driven questions about psychological phenomena, relatively few psychologists include this method in their toolbox. One obstacle is the difficulty in collecting relevant data—a difficulty that can be overcome by turning to secondary data sets.

RECOMMENDED DATA SETS

Developing and maintaining a large twin registry is expensive and time consuming. The high administrative burden means that investigators must invest substantial funds into collecting and maintaining the data. Thus, it is relatively rare to find genetically informative data that are readily available to other researchers. We note that many twin registries do in fact allow researchers to propose secondary data analyses, collaborate with project directors or principal investigators, or pay for data collection. These are all valuable ways to access genetically informed data sets without setting up independent registries. We encourage researchers to pursue these routes as well. In keeping with the spirit of this book, however, we describe here several archived data sets that are available to researchers. This availability is especially laudable, as the large time and monetary investment in obtaining genetically informative data often encourages proprietary proclivities.

- *National Survey of Midlife Development in the United States (MIDUS)*. Our own research drew from the MIDUS data set, available from Interuniversity Consortium for Political and Social Research (ICPSR; http://www.icpsr.umich.edu). The MIDUS represents an interdisciplinary collaboration to examine the patterns, predictors, and consequences of midlife development in the areas of physical health, psychological well-being, and social responsibility. Respondents provided extensive information on their physical and mental health. Participants also answered questions about their work histories and work-related demands. In addition, they provided information about childhood experiences, such as presence or absence of parents, familial environments, and quality of relationships with siblings and parents. Psychological well-being measures included feelings of accomplishment, desire to learn, sense of control over one's life, broad interests, and hopes for the future. The data include respondents ages 25 to 74 recruited from the general population in a random-digit dialing procedure ($N = 4,244$), siblings of the general population respondents ($N = 950$), and a twin sample ($N = 1,914$). The first data wave was collected in 1995 to 1996 (Brim et al., 2007), and the second in 2004 to 2006 (Ryff et al., 2006).
- *Swedish Adoption/Twin Study on Aging (SATSA)*. Also available from ICPSR are data from SATSA (Pedersen, 1993). SATSA was designed to study the environmental and genetic factors contributing to individual differences in aging. SATSA includes four data waves (sample sizes vary by questionnaire and year, with $N = 1,736$ at 1984). The sample includes twins who were separated at an early age and raised apart as well as a control sample of twins raised together. Respondents answered questions about their personality, attitudes, health status, the way

they were raised, work environment, alcohol consumption, and dietary and smoking habits. A subsample of 150 pairs of twins raised apart and 150 pairs of twins raised together participated in four waves of in-person testing, which included a health examination; interviews; and tests on functional capacity, cognitive abilities, and memory. Identical twins raised apart provide a unique resource for identifying specific nonshared environmental effects.

- *National Longitudinal Study of Adolescent Health (Add Health)*. This study (Harris et al., 2003) surveyed adolescents about health-related behaviors and their outcomes in young adulthood. In-school questionnaires were followed up by in-home interviews approximately 1, 2, and 6 years later. The study assessed adolescent health and sexual behavior, problem behavior, self-efficacy, and feelings. Participants answered questions concerning characteristics of their peer groups, schools, familial relations, familial structure, and communities. Adolescents nominated a social network, members of whom are included in the data set, allowing researchers access to rich detail about peer networks. The study involved 3,139 sibling pairs of varying degrees of genetic relatedness. Specifically, the pairs include identical and fraternal twins, full siblings, half siblings, and unrelated siblings. As such, the sample provides a unique resource for modeling genetic and environmental influences across multiple types of sibling pairs, not just twins. Access to variables concerning genetic relatedness and the molecular genetic data requires completion of a restricted-use data contract (see http://www.cpc.unc.edu/projects/addhealth/data). The application process involves a fee.

FOR FURTHER READING

Caspi, A., Roberts, B. W., Shiner, R. L. (2005). Personality development: Stability and change. *Annual Review of Psychology*, 56, 453–484.

This review summarizes research on personality structure and development, with a section devoted to behavioral genetic approaches to studying personality. This section provides examples of how behavioral genetic approaches can lead to generative lines of research and illuminate the etiology of personality.

Rutter, M. (2002). Nature, nurture, and development: From evangelism through science toward policy and practice. *Child Development, 73*, 1–21.

Rutter presents the strengths of quantitative and molecular genetic research while addressing some of the misleading claims associated with each. His call for greater integration of genetic, developmental, and psychosocial research can be realized with greater use of archival data.

Plomin, R., DeFries, J. C., McClearn, G. E., & McGuffin, P. (2001) *Behavioral genetics* (4th ed.). New York, NY: Worth.

This textbook provides a general introduction to the field of behavioral genetics. Various chapters summarize behavioral genetic research on several specific domains, including intelligence, personality, and psychopathology.

REFERENCES

Baumeister, R. F. (1998). The self. In D. T. Gilbert, S. T. Fiske, & G. Lindzey (Eds.), *The handbook of social psychology* (4th ed., pp. 680–740). Boston, MA: McGraw-Hill.

Brim, O. G., Baltes, P. B., Bumpass, L. L., Cleary, P. D., Featherman, D. L., Hazzard, W. R., et al. (2007). National Survey of Midlife Development in the United States (MIDUS), 1995–1996 [computer file]. ICPSR02760-v4. Ann Arbor, MI: DataStat, Inc./Boston, MA: Harvard Medical School, Department of Health Care Policy [producers]. Ann Arbor, MI: Interuniversity Consortium for Political and Social Research [distributor], 2007-04-16.

Butcher, L. M., Davis, O. S. P., Craig, I. W., & Plomin, R. (2008). Genome-wide quantitative trait locus association scan of general cognitive ability using pooled DNA and 500K single nucleotide polymorphism microarrays. *Genes, Brain and Behavior, 7*, 435–446. doi:10.1111/j.1601-183X.2007.00368.x

Harris, K. M., Florey, F., Tabor, J., Bearman, P. S., Jones, J., & Udry, J. R. (2003). *The National Longitudinal Study of Adolescent Health: Research design.* Retrieved from http://www.cpc.unc.edu/projects/addhealth/design

Jaddoe, V. W. V., Bakker, R., van Duijn, C. M., van der Heijden, A. J., Lindemans, J., Mackenbach, J. P., et al. (2007). The Generation R Study Biobank: A resource for epidemiological studies in children and their parents. *European Journal of Epidemiology, 22*, 917–923. doi:10.1007/s10654-007-9209-z

Judge, T. A., Erez, A., Bono, J. E., & Thoresen, C. J. (2002). Are measures of self-esteem, neuroticism, locus of control, and generalized self-efficacy indicators of a common core construct? *Journal of Personality and Social Psychology, 83*, 693–710. doi:10.1037/0022-3514.83.3.693

Loehlin, J. C. (1996). The Cholesky approach: A cautionary note. *Behavior Genetics, 26*, 65–69. doi:10.1007/BF02361160

Metalsky, G. I., Joiner, T. E., Jr., Hardin, T. S., & Abramson, L. Y. (1993). Depressive reactions to failure in a naturalistic setting: A test of the hopelessness and self-esteem theories of depression. *Journal of Abnormal Psychology, 102*, 101–109. doi:10.1037/0021-843X.102.1.101

Moffitt, T. E., Caspi, A., & Rutter, M. (2005). Strategy for investigating interactions between measured genes and measured environments. *Archives of General Psychiatry, 62*, 473–481. doi:10.1001/archpsyc.62.5.473

Mroczek, D. K., & Kolarz, C. M. (1998). The effect of age on positive and negative affect: A developmental perspective on happiness. *Journal of Personality and Social Psychology, 75*, 1333–1349. doi:10.1037/0022-3514.75.5.1333

Neiss, M. B., Sedikides, C., & Stevenson, J. (2002). Self-esteem: A behavioural genetic perspective. *European Journal of Personality, 16*, 351–367. doi:10.1002/per.456

Neiss, M. B., Stevenson, J., Legrand, L. N., Iacono, W. G., & Sedikides, C. (in press). Self-esteem, negative emotionality, and depression as a common temperamental core: A study of mid-adolescent twin girls. *Journal of Personality.*

Neiss, M. B., Stevenson, J., Sedikides, C., Kumashiro, M., Finkel, E. J., & Rusbult, C. E. (2005). Executive self, self-esteem, and negative affectivity: Relations at the phenotypic and genotypic level. *Journal of Personality and Social Psychology, 89*, 593–606. doi:10.1037/0022-3514.89.4.593

Pedersen, N. L. (1993). Swedish Adoption/Twin Study on Aging (SATSA), 1984, 1987, 1990, and 1993 [computer file]. ICPSR version. Stockholm, Sweden: Karolinska Institutet [producer], 1993. Ann Arbor, MI: Interuniversity Consortium for Political and Social Research [distributor], 2004.

Plomin, R., DeFries, J. C., McClearn, G. E., & McGuffin, P. (2001). *Behavioral genetics.* New York, NY: Worth.

Plomin, R., Fulker, D. W., Corley, R., & DeFries, J. C. (1997). Nature, nurture, and cognitive development from 1–16 years: A parent–offspring adoption study. *Psychological Science, 8*, 442–447. doi:10.1111/j.1467-9280.1997.tb00458.x

Pyszczynski, T., Greenberg, J., Solomon, S., Arndt, J., & Schimel, J. (2004). Why do people need self-esteem? A theoretical and empirical review. *Psychological Bulletin, 130*, 435–468. doi:10.1037/0033-2909.130.3.435

Rutter, M., Moffitt, T. E., & Caspi, A. (2006). Gene–environment interplay: Multiple varieties but real effects. *Journal of Child Psychology and Psychiatry, and Allied Disciplines, 47*, 226–261. doi:10.1111/j.1469-7610.2005.01557.x

Ryff, C. D., Almeida, D. M., Ayanian, J. S., Carr, D. S., Cleary, P. D., Coe, C., et al. (2006). Midlife Developments in the United States (MIDUS2), 2004–2006 [computer file]. ICPSR04652-v1. Madison, WI: University of Wisconsin, Survey Center [producer], 2006. Ann Arbor, MI: Interuniversity Consortium for Political and Social Research [distributor], 2007.

Sedikides, C., & Gregg, A. P. (2003). Portraits of the self. In M. A. Hogg & J. Cooper (Eds.), *Sage handbook of social psychology* (pp. 110–138). London, England: Sage.

Turkheimer, E. (2000). Three laws of behavior genetics and what they mean. *Current Directions in Psychological Science, 9*, 160–164. doi:10.1111/1467-8721.00084

Watson, D., Clark, L. A., & Tellegen, A. (1988). Development and validation of brief measures of positive and negative affect. *Journal of Personality and Social Psychology, 54*, 1063–1070. doi:10.1037/0022-3514.70.3.567

9

SECONDARY DATA ANALYSIS IN PSYCHOPATHOLOGY RESEARCH

NICHOLAS R. EATON AND ROBERT F. KRUEGER

Mental disorders pose huge costs for individuals and societies alike. In addition to the significant economic expenses that arise from caring for affected individuals, the high levels of psychopathology-related impairment and disability are themselves staggering (Lopez & Murray, 1998). Psychological researchers strive to understand the nature of mental disorders, but it is an unfortunate fact that many empirical questions in this area are not very tractable because of limitations on funding, time, availability of study participants, and so on. The presence of large, publicly available data sets provides a means to investigate topics of fundamental importance by leveraging existing resources.

Although straightforward logistical issues highlight the benefits of secondary research, they are by no means the only reason an investigator might decide to use large, public data sets. Sample size can be an issue of major importance to certain research endeavors. Particular topics of study (e.g., low base-rate phenomena) may require large data sets to ensure that an adequate number of cases are observed. Similarly, some multivariate statistical models (e.g., cluster analysis, multidimensional scaling, latent class analysis) are centrally relevant to key questions about mental disorders, but they often require considerable sample sizes. In our own research, which we touch on briefly throughout this chapter, such a scenario has frequently been the case. Indeed, some analyses have required such substantial samples that we have combined across multiple large public data sets.

Throughout this chapter, we address the benefits of using secondary data for psychopathology research. We also discuss the general limitations present in the analysis of existing data sets. In addition, existing studies of mental disorders face their own unique challenges, which are a major focus of our consideration. Finally, resources such as data sets and readings are provided for researchers interested in pursuing the topic further.

WHY USE SECONDARY DATA ANALYSIS
IN PSYCHOPATHOLOGY RESEARCH?

Although there is a litany of practical reasons why psychopathology investigators might turn to large, publicly available data sets, several possibilities are particularly salient. The first is epidemiological. It is not particularly difficult to determine the rate of mental disorders in a given sample. Basic analyses could be conducted on symptom-count data collected by administering diagnostic interviews in 30 neighborhood homes or asking all undergraduates in an introductory psychology course to fill out a cursory screening measure. However, to understand the prevalence or incidence of disorders as they occur in a population, these methods would likely be inadequate. It is extremely unlikely that a truly representative sample of the population of interest (e.g., all individuals 18 and older in a major metropolitan area) could be obtained in such ways. Generalization from the frequencies of mental health problems in these undergraduates to the point prevalence in the population at large would be inappropriate. Calculation of the incidence of disorders in nonrepresentative samples would be equally as futile. Further, some mental disorders are quite rare, and adequate representation of them may require very large samples. For reasons such as these, answering epidemiological questions requires a great deal of methodological rigor, and secondary data sets, which often are designed with strict epidemiologically sound sampling methods, present a reasonable analytic option that is both cost- and time-effective for psychopathology researchers.

Studies of the underlying structure of psychopathology and comorbidity also require large samples. Mental disorders are frequently comorbid, and the observed relations between disorders suggest that they may be linked by latent (i.e., underlying and indirectly observed) constructs. For example, major depression, generalized anxiety, and panic disorder tend to co-occur with each other more frequently than expected by chance, as do drug use, alcohol use, and antisocial behavior (Krueger, 1999; Krueger, Caspi, Moffitt, & Silva, 1998). These relatively high levels of covariation suggest the presence of common latent variables that underlie these disorders and account for these relations. Indeed, our research into this topic has identified two major latent factors when examining these sorts of disorders: an *internalizing* factor, composing depression- and anxiety-related disorders, and an *externalizing* factor, involving substance use, oppositional behaviors, and conduct problems (see Krueger, 1999). The identification of these latent factors required, among other things, large samples. The confirmatory factor analyses involved in uncovering these underlying structures of common mental disorders necessitated a great deal of variation in the symptom count data, which tend to be highly positively skewed and endorsements of certain symptoms can occur somewhat infrequently. The provision of a sufficient number of individuals with psychopathological features as well as an adequate amount of across-disorder symptom covariance was accomplished by using secondary analysis of archival data sets (and sometimes merging these large data sets together; e.g., Krueger & Markon, 2006).

GENERAL CONCERNS OF THE SECONDARY ANALYSIS OF PSYCHOPATHOLOGY DATA SETS AND POSSIBLE SOLUTIONS

We present several concerns regarding the use of secondary psychopathology data sets, and possible solutions, below. The following suggestions summarize many of these solutions and can serve as basic guidelines for researchers interested in using existing data.

1. *Know the data set well.* This step includes knowing the study's method and design, understanding how variable scores were calculated and represented in the data set, and reading all documentation and relevant publications that emerged from the data set.
2. *Think carefully about all data-related decisions.* The researcher's choices (e.g., using symptom counts vs. diagnoses) should be justifiable conceptually and in the context of standard practices in the field of inquiry. Also, decisions that are congruent with those of previous data set users may allow for comparison of findings across published studies.
3. *Keep adequate records of decisions and justifications.* This allows for easier presentation of findings in subsequent reports and helps researchers defend their choices later. Indeed, some data sets have numerous variables representing slightly different conceptualizations of the same disorder (e.g., categorical criterion-based major depression diagnoses made with and without an impairment requirement), and record keeping can be of great benefit, especially if decisions need to be reviewed several years in the future.

One clear consideration in the use of secondary data sets is whether they permit publicly open access. Although we are limiting the present discussion to publicly available data sets, it is important to note that many outstanding proprietary archived data sets exist. One example of such data, from a study on which we collaborate, are those from the Minnesota Center for Twin and Family Research (MCTFR), which encompasses sizeable samples of twins, adoptees, and families followed longitudinally for years (Iacono, McGue, & Krueger, 2006). Proprietary studies often have specific aims, which facilitate certain types of analyses (in the MCTFR, for example, twin and adoption study designs allow researchers to parcel apart genetic and environmental contributions to overt behavior and individual differences). When studies are not publicly available, collaborations with principal investigators are a possibility, and researchers would be remiss in not pursuing them. A researcher need not reinvent the proverbial wheel if adequate data to answer his or her empirical questions are already available in a proprietary data set that is accessible through a collaborative effort or data sharing agreement.

Even when data sets are publicly available, other difficulties must be addressed. One major concern investigators may have, whether warranted or not, regards their lack of control over the data collection. This is a justified concern associated with the use of existing data sets—researchers who use them are at the mercy of the original investigators. There can be no absolute assurance that the procedures of the study were undertaken as they are described. As noted earlier, however, a survey of the large-scale studies that have gone on to become publicly available data sets reveals the competency of the investigators. Indeed, the amount of funding alone required to conduct such large-scale studies indicates the researchers showed a high degree of proficiency (at least in the eyes of the granting agency). Thus, although investigators may be apprehensive about publishing from data collected beyond their purview, this should not prevent them from using the extraordinary resources available in existing data sets. It should also be noted that other fields have embraced the benefits of collaboration by aggregating large data sets collected by multiple research teams, so this issue is not unique to psychopathology research. The study of human genetics is a prime example. Key questions in genetics will require multiple data sets and large-scale cooperation. Collaborative work in this area has yielded promising results (The Wellcome Trust Case Control Consortium, 2007).

Concerns about the integrity of the original data are common to all secondary research projects, regardless of the field, because of the importance of accuracy in scientific inquiry. However, psychopathology research presents unique considerations for prospective users of publicly archived data. Specifically, the investigation of mental disorders can be a difficult endeavor even when all aspects of a study are under the researcher's control; when other investigators made the decisions—often many years prior—psychopathology-related problems may become evident.

One clear example of this is in psychopathology conceptualization. Each successive *Diagnostic and Statistical Manual of Mental Disorders* (DSM) has altered the psychiatric nosology in some way. Although these changes presumably represent positive steps toward a more accurate taxonomy of mental disorders, they pose problems for users of existing data sets. When diagnostic criteria change over the years or, more drastically, when particular mental disorders are added or removed from the classification system, incongruencies may develop between the data in existing resources and current thinking. For example, a researcher interested in the personality disorders as currently conceptualized in the fourth edition of the DSM (*DSM–IV*; American Psychiatric Association, 2000) would have difficulty studying these forms of psychopathology in data sets collected prior to the adoption of the present diagnostic criteria. A similar consideration exists in differences between the *DSM–IV* and the current World Health Organization diagnostic criteria presented in the *International Classification of Diseases* (presently *ICD–10*; World Health Organization, 1992). Researchers need to ensure that the disorders they wish to study were assessed using the most appropriate classification system.

There are other classification-related challenges as well. Although diagnostic criteria may change between the completion of the original study and the use of the resulting data set, another possibility is diagnostic criteria change during the course of the original study. Large longitudinal studies that eventually go on to be secondary data sets run the risk of spanning a major change to the official nosological system. Our MCTFR projects face this difficulty, as one of our studies began following twins when they were children and has continued to do so over the years into adulthood. We have collected mental disorder data resulting from *DSM–III*, *DSM–III–R*, and *DSM–IV* diagnostic criteria. Such multi-*DSM* studies certainly present a hurdle to future users of the data, but this is not overly difficult. Often the importance of findings that could be obtained from longitudinal data overshadows more basic methodological concerns about shifting criterion sets. Depending on the disorder(s) under investigation, these shifts may represent only minor changes to disorder definition. Finally, many studies that span changes to the diagnostic criteria modify their procedures in such a way that older diagnoses continue to be assessed in tandem with revised diagnostic criteria (e.g., assessments will gather information on *DSM–IV* criteria, and a few additional items will ensure congruence of new data with the *DSM–III–R* disorders assessed in previous waves of the study).

The issue of changing diagnostic criteria over time is certainly a complication of using existing secondary data sets. This problem is not insurmountable, however, and several solutions exist. If a researcher is unwilling to settle for outdated diagnostic criteria in a particular data set, the simplest approach is to locate another data set that has the desired information. Although this will not always be possible, several data sets exist using the most recently revised version of the taxonomic system, especially for the most common mental disorders. Researchers whose interests lie in less commonly studied forms of psychopathology (e.g., dissociative identity disorder) may have a very limited group of existing data set options to begin with, and they may have to settle for outdated diagnostic criteria in exchange for the advantages of using existing data.

A second solution to the problem of outdated diagnostic criteria is for the researcher to use these diagnostic criteria anyway. This will certainly not be an adequate solution in all cases, but many psychopathology-related questions do not require data about a specific *DSM* diagnosis. In our own research, for instance, we often use symptom data based on *DSM–III–R* and sometimes even 1980's *DSM–III*. When investigating the structure of common mental disorders, a researcher is concerned with estimating the latent constructs underlying and interconnecting disorders by virtue of symptom counts or covariances between disorders' symptom counts. As long as the symptoms are related to the latent factor(s) under investigation, it is not particularly important whether they appear in the most recent, or any, version of the *DSM*. The results of structural studies of this nature, in fact, support broad underlying factors as underlying psychopathology and leading to significant comorbidity across disorders (Krueger, 1999; Krueger, Caspi, Moffit, & Silva, 1998). The implications of such findings are that focusing on specific diagnoses found in a particular version of the *DSM* may not only be overly confining to researchers but also that important connections between the latent and manifest forms of psychopathology may be missed when investigators are unnecessarily concerned with specific diagnostic criteria from the *DSM* treated verbatim. It seems that positive results can come out of using somewhat outdated criteria in data sets; even data sets compiled almost 30 years ago using *DSM–III* criteria likely contain valuable information for thoughtful and cautious researchers.

Even if investigators are willing to be to be somewhat flexible with regard to how psychopathology was defined at the time of the original study, archived data sets still may not include information about the disorders of greatest interest. For numerous practical reasons, most large-scale studies were unable to probe deeply for the presence of every mental disorder. These holes in the data represent the necessity of selective assessment of disorders by the original investigators. For example, the National Epidemiologic Survey on Alcohol and Related Conditions (NESARC) data set, described in more detail in the Recommended Data Sets section, is an excellent resource for studies of personality pathology because these disorders are not always addressed in major studies that become archived data sets. However, even in NESARC, only a subset of the 10 *DSM–IV* personality disorders was assessed (although a second wave of the study will include the remaining personality disorders). Although such happenstances may initially frustrate the potential user of existing data sets, continued flexibility on the part of the researcher is an asset. These disorder omissions may not allow for a complete analysis of a psychopathology domain, but it is likely that meaningful contributions to the literature can arise from data that are not wholly complete. Even when this is not the case, modern statistical methods—namely, those under the rubric of latent variable modeling—allow researchers to combine information about disorder associations across different studies. For example, assume an investigator is interested in studying the relations between the disorders of the internalizing factor. In one archived data set, she finds symptom counts for major depression, generalized anxiety disorder, and specific phobia. In a second data set, she has access to major depression, generalized anxiety disorder, and panic disorder. In a third data set, she has access to specific phobia and panic disorder data. By modeling the correlations between disorders from the three samples simultaneously, she can estimate an overall association matrix, even though not every study contains every needed correlation. This approach shares some conceptual similarity with more formal meta-analytic methods. An example from our own research demonstrates this point for the interested reader. Markon, Krueger, and Watson (2005) used several data sets to investigate the structure of various normal and abnormal personality traits. Each data set contained only a subset of the personality traits of interest. All pairs of traits, however, were observed together in at least one data set. Thus, some problems that seem insurmountable when dealing with single archived data sets may be rectified by combining data sets.

Assessment of mental disorders also provides another unique concern for secondary researchers interested in psychopathology-related questions. Even when definitive diagnostic criteria are available in the *DSM* or *ICD*, the researcher is faced with the task of how best to determine the presence of these disorders. The decision to use a particular psychopathology measure can be a difficult prospect psychometrically, and the choice is confounded by the often large number of batteries available. Different methods of assessment, such as diagnostic interviews, self-report questionnaires, and so on, represent additional decisions that must be made. In one of our areas of interest, personality pathology, there are at least five major diagnostic interviews and at least as many self-report questionnaires, some of which can also function as informant-report questionnaires (Clark & Harrison, 2001). Although these personality disorder measures typically represent somewhat similar approaches to the *DSM* diagnostic criteria, this is not always the case. Some psychopathology measures are constructed to relate to particular theoretical orientations— orientations to which the user of existing data sets may not subscribe. Also, the increasing application of modern test theory (e.g., item response theory) has led to the creation of more psychometrically sound measures in recent years. On a case-by-case basis, researchers must evaluate the assessment instruments. A reasonable degree of flexibility and psychometric competence allows investigators to take greater advantage of existing resources. We suggest, however, that when researchers have qualms about the assessment tools used in a given data set, they include these reservations in resulting publications.

These points highlight the importance of adequate documentation in secondary data sets. It is imperative that psychopathology-related data sets provide thorough documentation to allow future researchers to use them responsibly. Although the level of documentation varies from study to study, the major existing data sets used for mental disorder research typically do contain detailed information related to data collection methodology, assessment batteries used, treatment of data, explanations of variables included in the data set, and so on. If this information is missing or incomplete, users of these data sets may be able to contact the original researchers or locate answers to their questions in articles or chapters that have resulted from the archived data. However, such avenues may not be possible, and it is conceivable that researchers would be forced to proceed with some amount of uncertainty. Clearly, this is another example in which publications that result from use of the existing data should reflect the author's uncertainty due to any unknown information.

The National Survey of Midlife Development in the United States (MIDUS) studies, discussed in the Recommended Data Sets section, are excellent examples of how readily available study documentation facilitates ease (and confidence) of use by future investigators (Brim, Ryff, & Kessler, 2004). MIDUS includes, along with the data, information about the sampling procedures, recruitment, interviewing, and participant compensation. In addition, all measures used are downloadable, so future researchers can see exactly what questions were asked and in what order. When new variables were coded from other data, algorithms and explanations of this coding are provided. For instance, depression symptoms were assessed individually. The number of symptoms present in each individual was summed to create a continuous variable of depression symptomatology, which was then split into a binary variable whose values indicated whether the number of depression symptoms present met the *DSM* diagnostic threshold. In this way, researchers have several variables available for analysis, some of which arose from other variables. Clear explanations by the original researchers provided in the MIDUS documentation allow new investigators to be certain of how these new variables were created and what they mean. Finally, MIDUS provides references in addition to information about parallel forms used in the original and follow-up assessments.

CONCERNS WITH AGGREGATING ACROSS ARCHIVED PSYCHOPATHOLOGY DATA SETS

Many empirical questions and statistical methods require investigators to aggregate data across several data sets, and this scenario presents additional challenges for the researcher. Often the most salient concern is when the two (or more) data sets do not share diagnostic definitions. It is common for older data sets to have used *DSM–III* or *DSM–III–R*, whereas more recent data sets tend to use *DSM–IV* diagnostic criteria to assess symptoms and evaluate whether each individual should receive a mental disorder diagnosis. There is no hard and fast rule about combining across different versions of the *DSM*, as whether this strategy is acceptable depends on the disorder(s) in question and to what degree diagnostic criteria remained consistent across revisions of the diagnostic manual. In a way, situations such as this require the researcher to conduct a cost–benefit analysis, wherein certain relative strengths and weaknesses must be evaluated: (dis)similarity of the criteria sets, the potential for the resulting study to be informative and impactful, and the potential for the resulting study to obfuscate the research literature. It seems to us that combining diagnostic data resulting from different *DSM* criteria can be a beneficial undertaking, especially when such differences are controlled for statistically (e.g., within a latent variable modeling context), and resulting publications highlight this potential limitation to generalizability. Clearly, the final decision to aggregate data from varying diagnostic criteria rests with the investigator. This problem is not insurmountable, and findings that result from aggregated data can make worthwhile contributions to the literature.

Another complicating factor in aggregating across data sets involves the assessment instruments used in data collection. The impact of this issue depends largely on the question under investigation, but several general issues should be considered. When diagnostic information is assessed through a single method, such as a semistructured interview, this concern may not be as problematic as the use of heteromethod assessments: For example, one existing data set assessed the disorder(s) of interest through a semistructured interview, whereas the other study used a brief self-report questionnaire. If such a scenario arises, again, the researcher must balance strengths and weaknesses of each approach. Also, the investigator may find it helpful to understand the psychometric properties of, and research related to, each instrument used. Of particular interest may be a comparison of the reliabilities of each assessment device as well as any studies that have compared the performance of the diagnostic measures in classifying the same group of individuals. If such data are not present, another, less informative, approach would be to compare the disorder base rate each battery indicates exists in similar populations.

It should be noted that particular assessment devices treat diagnostic criteria in different ways. Whereas some measures ask only whether a particular symptom is present (a binary, yes–no decision), others may have individuals rate the presence of a particular symptom on a Likert-type scale (e.g., *never present* to *always present*). To complicate matters further, many secondary data sets of psychopathology use different time frames for the appearance of symptomatology. For instance, one study may ask individuals about the lifetime prevalence of a given symptom, whereas another study may require the symptom to have been present in the past 3 to 6 months. A related issue is the use of skip-out rules. *Skip-out rules* are algorithms that determine whether an individual meets diagnostic criteria by the administration of a subset of symptoms. For example, a researcher might determine that individuals who fail to endorse the first three symptoms of a disorder will likely not meet full diagnostic criteria and thus the assessment protocol will "skip out" of assessing the disorder's remaining symptoms in the interests of time. Such an approach may result in nonignorable missing symptom data for many participants. The only recourse for individuals wishing to aggregate two psychopathology-related data sets is to familiarize themselves with the temporal requirements and skip-out rules for the symptoms used in each study and to attempt to rectify any differences. Aggregation of data sets with widely divergent temporal requirements (e.g., past 3 months vs. lifetime) or skip-out rules may not be warranted. Moreover, the use of skip-outs prevents symptom-level analysis unless the researcher makes the tenuous assumption that participants who failed to endorse the screening symptoms would not have endorsed the remaining symptoms.

Even when disorders are defined similarly and assessment batteries used are congruent across multiple secondary data sets, differential sampling methodologies must be considered. Studies typically have somewhat different recruitment strategies, whether through random phone number digit dialing or by placing study advertisements in local newspapers. Aggregating representative with nonrepresentative samples may not be a sound practice. Indeed, one of the greatest advantages of using secondary data sets for many research questions is the sampling strategies used for many data sets. The potential loss of this advantage by combining several data sets should be of primary importance to researchers considering aggregation.

Once individuals are recruited, they must often pass additional barriers to become participants in the study. Often, psychopathology screening devices are used to determine whether individuals are or are not members of certain disorder-related populations. A difficulty arises when aggregating one data set that used a screening device for inclusion in the study with one or more additional data sets that admitted individuals for participation without such a screen. Screening devices themselves can vary, and users of aggregated data sets must understand what criteria were used for each screen to determine study inclusion–exclusion rules.

A related issue to that of screening is of general inclusion and exclusion criteria studies incorporate into their designs. For instance, there is a notable difference if one study admitted participants age 18 versus age 21, although this issue is likely immaterial to many empirical questions. Issues relating to psychopathology itself may be more problematic, however. One common exclusion criteria is to screen out individuals who show mental retardation (MR), pervasive developmental disorders (PDDs), or psychosis (although, clearly, the inclusion and exclusion criteria used depends on the question of interest for a given study). If one of the studies in an aggregated data set created by a researcher was representative of a major metropolitan district X, minus individuals who were screened out because of MR, PDDs, and psychosis, this sample does not overlap completely with another data set whose sample was representative of all individuals who live in district X. Although such overlap may not be of great importance to the research inquiries of the investigator using the aggregated data set, such incongruencies in inclusion–exclusion criteria should still be noted in resulting publications.

A final concern that commonly arises with large psychopathology data sets involves the way in which mental disorders are coded. As mentioned previously, one can code a particular disorder on the basis of either the number of symptoms an individual endorses or by an algorithm that outputs a binary variable: a yes–no indication of whether a given disorder is present. We refer to the former as "Study A" and the latter as "Study B." There are at least two approaches that researchers can adopt when faced with differentially coded psychopathology variables in aggregated data sets. The first is simple: One can dichotomize the symptom-count variable in Study A using the algorithm to create the binary variable in Study B. However, this algorithm may not always be available to the researcher. A second approach would be to use statistical methods that allow binary variables to be treated as continuous (e.g., symptom counts), such as a tetrachoric correlation. Space limitations prevent in-depth discussion of such methods, but the user of aggregated data sets who faces this variable coding problem may find it helpful to investigate possible statistical means of addressing the differences in variable coding.

SUMMARY

Secondary analysis of large data sets presents myriad opportunities for psychopathology researchers and researchers in general. Many questions related to mental disorders raise complex sampling and assessment considerations, which can require a great deal of resources and methodological expertise to address. Although there are particular concerns associated with conducting secondary analysis of data sets of mental disorder, these issues are generally surmountable and outweighed by the benefits of secondary analysis. When conducted responsibly, secondary analysis permits researchers to address questions of interest that might otherwise be intractable and thus represents an important part of psychopathology research.

RECOMMENDED DATA SETS

The following are brief descriptions of some major existing data sets frequently used in psychopathology research. This list is by no means exhaustive, but these studies represent excellent resources for individuals interested in studying mental disorders through the secondary analysis of existing resources.

- *Epidemiologic Catchment Area (ECA)*. The ECA study emerged in the early 1980s as a major epidemiological study of psychopathology. Conducted in several sites across the United States, the ECA consisted of over 20,000 participants assessed over two waves of data collection. A broad array of disorders was screened for in the ECA study, including mood, anxiety, psychosis, and substance use. For ECA study information and data, visit the Interuniversity Consortium for Political and Social Research (ICPSR) at http://www.icpsr.umich.edu/.
- *Midlife in the United States (MIDUS)*. The MIDUS study, which began around 1994, concerned midlife development in the United States. A large national probability sample of 3,485 individuals included oversamples of metropolitan areas, a twin sample, and a sibling sample. Approximately a decade later, a second wave of data collection, MIDUS-II, recontacted many of the original participants, making this an excellent longitudinal resource. In addition to broad psychopathological variables, the sample also includes a broad range of diversity, including older adults. Overall, the MIDUS documentation is excellent, making it an ideal place for researchers to begin using secondary data sets. For more information, see http://midus.wisc.edu. The MIDUS data are also available through the ICPSR.
- *National Comorbidity Survey (NCS)*. The NCS study, conducted in the early 1990s, was a nationally representative study of mental health in the United States. A second wave of data collection, NCS-2, followed up the original participants approximately a decade later. Another sample of 10,000 individuals (NCS-R) was

collected as a replication sample of the original NCS. This study is an excellent resource for epidemiological information, especially because of its use of a structured diagnostic interview. For more information, see http://www.hcp.med.harvard.edu/ncs. Data are also available through the ICPSR, and an aggregated data set of three nationally representative data sets is available at http://www.icpsr.umich.edu/CPES.

■ *National Epidemiologic Survey on Alcohol and Related Conditions (NESARC).* The NESARC began around 2001 with its first of two waves of data collection. This study has a sample size of 43,093 individuals and is a representative sample of the U.S. population. These data focus on alcohol and substance use, although the survey assesses some other mental disorders as well. For information, documentation, and data, visit http://niaaa.census.gov.

FOR FURTHER READING

The interested researcher might find it helpful to read a few studies that addressed psychopathological questions through the analysis of existing data sets. The articles below are only a few of the possible choices of readings; many of the websites listed in Recommended Data Sets have links to studies emerging from their data sets, and a literature search for a particular data set should yield additional studies.

Krueger, R. F., Chentsova-Dutton, Y. E., Markon, K. E., Goldberg, D., & Ormel, J. (2003). A cross-cultural study of the structure of comorbidity among common psychopathological syndromes in the general health care setting. *Journal of Abnormal Psychology, 112,* 437–447. doi:10.1037/0021-843X.112.3.437

Krueger et al. discuss how a large World Health Organization data set was used to confirm previous findings about a two-factor model of psychopathology, this time in 14 countries around the globe. This data set was accessible to Goldberg and Ormel because of their involvement with the data collection.

Kessler, R. C., DuPont, R. L., Berglund, P., & Wittchen, H. (1999). Impairment in pure and comorbid generalized anxiety disorder and major depression at 12 months in two national surveys. *The American Journal of Psychiatry, 156,* 1915–1923.

Kessler et al. used data from the NCS and MIDUS archives to determine whether generalized anxiety disorder was due to depression (or other comorbid disorders) and to explore the level of impairment seen in independently occurring cases of generalized anxiety disorder.

Krueger, R. F. (1999). The structure of common mental disorders. *Archives of General Psychiatry, 56,* 921–926. doi:10.1001/archpsyc.56.10.921

Krueger used the NCS data set (publicly available on the web) to explore how 10 mental disorders fit into two- and three-factor models of psychopathology.

Krueger, R. F., & Markon, K. E. (2006). Reinterpreting comorbidity: A model-based approach to understanding and classifying psychopathology. *Annual Review of Clinical Psychology, 2,* 111–133. doi:10.1146/annurev.clinpsy.2.022305.095213

Krueger and Markon conducted a meta-analysis of studies published on major data sets (e.g., NCS, NCS-R, Virginia Twin Registry). The data for this analysis (correlation matrices) were taken from published reports.

REFERENCES

American Psychiatric Association. (2000). *Diagnostic and statistical manual of mental disorders* (4th ed., text rev.). Washington, DC: Author.

Brim, O. G., Ryff, C. D., & Kessler, R. C. (Eds.). (2004). *How healthy are we? A national study of well-being at midlife.* Chicago, IL: University of Chicago Press.

Clark, L. A., & Harrison, J. A. (2001). Assessment instruments. In W. J. Livesley (Ed.), *Handbook of personality disorders: Theory, research, and treatment* (pp. 277–306). New York, NY: Guilford Press.

Iacono, W. G., McGue, M., & Krueger, R. F. (2006). Minnesota Center for Twin and Family Research. *Twin Research and Human Genetics, 9,* 978–984.

Krueger, R. F. (1999). The structure of common mental disorders. *Archives of General Psychiatry, 56,* 921–926. doi:10.1001/archpsyc.56.10.921

Krueger, R. F., Caspi, A., Moffitt, T. E., & Silva, P. A. (1998). The structure and stability of common mental disorders (*DSM–III–R*): A longitudinal-epidemiological study. *Journal of Abnormal Psychology, 107,* 216–227. doi:10.1037/0021-843X.107.2.216

Krueger, R. F., & Markon, K. E. (2006). Reinterpreting comorbidity: A model-based approach to understanding and classifying psychopathology. *Annual Review of Clinical Psychology, 2,* 111–133. doi:10.1146/annurev.clinpsy.2.022305.095213

Lopez, A. D., & Murray, C. C. J. L. (1998). The global burden of disease, 1990–2020. *Nature Medicine, 4,* 1241–1243. doi:10.1038/3218

Markon, K. E., Krueger, R. F., & Watson, D. (2005). Delineating the structure of normal and abnormal personality: An integrative hierarchical approach. *Journal of Personality and Social Psychology, 88,* 139–157. doi:10.1037/0022-3514.88.1.139

The Wellcome Trust Case Control Consortium. (2007, April 1). Genome-wide association study of 14,000 cases of seven common diseases and 3,000 shared controls. *Nature, 447,* 678–683. doi:10.1038/nature05911

World Health Organization. (1992). *International classification of diseases (10th rev.).* Geneva, Switzerland: Author.

10

USING SECONDARY DATA
TO STUDY ADOLESCENCE AND
ADOLESCENT DEVELOPMENT

STEPHEN T. RUSSELL AND EVA MATTHEWS

Development during adolescence is unique among stages in the human life span. It is positioned between adulthood and the stages of infant and child development that take place during the first decade of life; its culmination prepares the individual for adult roles and responsibilities. Dramatic biological, cognitive, and social changes characterize development during adolescence. In recent decades, there has been growing interest in the life stage of adolescence and in the study of human development over the course of the adolescent years; this interest has been seen in multiple disciplines and fields of science. These bodies of research focus on understanding changes in biological, cognitive, and social domains during adolescence, interactions among these domains, and their influences on individual adjustment and optimal development; in addition, the study of this life stage has been shaped by analyses of differences in the adolescent experience across historical time and across cultures. The use of secondary data has been important in the development of the broad field of adolescence studies, and there are a growing number of existing data sets that may be used to better understand adolescence and adolescent development from multiple disciplinary perspectives.

When considering data sources for the study of adolescence and adolescent development, most researchers have focused their attention on large-scale survey questionnaires of adolescents. However, multiple types of preexisting data have influenced the study of adolescence; several early studies based on archival research that included surveys, ethnographic case studies, and demographic data launched the field. Elder's (1974) *Children of the Great Depression,* which made use of a longitudinal historical archive of questionnaires, interviews, and psychological inventories from 167 children, demonstrated the ways that historical change could dramatically shape adolescence, and through the adolescent experience, alter the adult life course. Nearly 20 years later, analyses of archives of multiple anthropological ethnographic studies led to the influential text that provided the first comprehensive, cross-cultural analysis and description of adolescence in preindustrial societies: *Adolescence: An Anthropological Inquiry* (Schlegel & Barry, 1991). Another influential text published in the same year used administrative data, public records, and demographic archives to understand how adolescence has changed over the course of recent generations: *Into One's Own: From Youth to Adulthood in the United States, 1920–1975* (Modell, 1991). Modell demonstrated that the distinctiveness of the adolescent cohorts of the late 20th century was characterized by the degree to which they shared historically unique agency in constructing their life courses, coupled with strong collective norms for the timing and sequencing of transitions into adulthood. Grounded in diverse disciplines (sociology, psychology, anthropology, and history), the studies of Elder (1974), Schlegel and Barry (1991), and Modell (1991) each drew from diverse sources of archival data. They provide rich examples for comparative and historical research, and each has had a significant influence on the field of adolescence studies.

In this chapter, we briefly discuss the uses of secondary data as relevant for the study of adolescence and adolescent development. We focus on survey questionnaire data because they are a primary source of existing data; however, we note that because questionnaires typically cannot provide rich descriptive data on the subjective meanings of the adolescent experience, archives that include qualitative data (e.g., interviews, photographs, personal narrative) offer a unique lens for the study of adolescence. We identify advantages of, and challenges involved in, secondary data analysis for studying adolescence. In our discussion, we include examples drawn from our experiences as well as the experience of others. These examples are used to illustrate both the challenges of working with secondary data sources and the distinct contributions that can come from such research. We refer to multiple existing data sets based on samples that have been collected over the past 40 years; several prominent data sources are reviewed in the section Recommended Data Sets. We conclude that the analysis of existing data sets hold great promise for advancing the scientific study of adolescence.

ADVANTAGES

Several important advantages pertaining to many existing survey data sets are worthy of mention but are not necessarily exclusive to the study of adolescent development: large sample sizes, population-representative data, longitudinal data, data from multiple reporters, insights about multiple contexts of development, and the ability to conduct cross-historical or cross-national comparisons. In addition, the use of secondary data has important logistical advantages.

First, such data sets are often characterized by large sample sizes, which provide several related advantages. Large samples provide statistical power to test complex multivariate analyses. Large samples also provide the opportunity to investigate low prevalence behaviors among adolescents. For example, analyses of the National Longitudinal Study of Adolescent Health (Add Health) data have allowed for unique contributions to the study of adolescent suicide behaviors, which have a low prevalence in the general population. Bearman and Moody (2004) made use of the friendship data available in Add Health and found that suicide attempts are higher among adolescents who reported that a friend had committed suicide. Russell and Joyner (2001) showed that the risk of suicide is higher among same-sex-attracted adolescents compared with those with heterosexual attractions. The issue of suicide was compounded by the low prevalence of suicide within friendship networks, and by the small numbers of same-sex-attracted adolescents; the Add Health study was historically unique in offering a representative sample large enough to address these questions. Each of these studies examined research questions about topics crucial to adolescent health that had not been documented with representative data.

As the above illustration suggests, large samples also provide the opportunity to investigate small population subgroups that are typically understudied. Analyses of the Add Health study data have provided important new information about adolescent who were adopted (Miller, Fan, Christensen, Grotevant, & van Dulmen, 2000), who were from understudied ethnic subgroups (Russell, Crockett, Shen, & Lee, 2008), or who had same-sex romantic attractions (Russell & Joyner, 2001). Most prior research on these small subpopulations had been drawn from community-based samples of convenience; the large size of the Add Health study has allowed nationally generalizable results of research on these subpopulations that was never possible before.

A second advantage of using existing surveys is that many are designed to be representative at local, state, or national levels. The obvious, yet critically important, advantage is the possibility for generalizability of research findings to broad populations of adolescents. This advantage may be especially significant for policy research, for which a typical goal is to provide findings specifically applicable to a target policy audience. For example, analyses of the California Health Kids Survey, a representative survey of more than 230,000 California public school students in Grades 7, 9, and 11 in the 2001–2002 school year, were used to advocate for school safety legislation in the state of California. The *Safe Place to Learn* report (O'Shaughnessy, Russell, Heck, Calhoun, & Laub, 2004) highlighted the deleterious consequences of harassment based on sexual orientation and gender identity, and led to the enactment of California Assembly Bill 394, the Safe Place to Learn Act of 2007, a law that provides clarification and guidance to school districts to ensure that school safety standards are implemented. Central to the success of the legislative advocacy was the availability of state-level representative data to document to prevalence and negative outcomes associated with harassment by adolescents in California schools.

An additional advantage is that many secondary data sources include information from multiple reporters. The importance of multiple reporters in developmental research is clear: Multiple perspectives allow for estimates of reliability and consistency in reporting. The challenges of reporter bias may be particularly relevant during the adolescent years, when the influence of social desirability is strong; this is especially true for the reporting of sensitive information from adolescents (e.g., emotional health, risk behavior, delinquency, sexual behavior). In answer to these challenges, large-scale surveys have included parents, siblings, peers, and teachers as respondents in surveys designed to assess adolescent development. For example, recent research on aggression in adolescence highlights the importance of independent reports from adolescents, their siblings, and their parents. Using longitudinal survey data from the Iowa Youth and Families Project, Williams, Conger, and Blozis (2007) showed that adolescents' interpersonal aggression can be predicted by independent reports by their siblings of the siblings' own aggression.

Access to data about multiple contexts of adolescents' lives is an additional advantage of many existing data sources and is increasingly important in developmental research that seeks to situate the study of adolescence within the broader contexts that guide and shape development (Schulenberg, 2006). Adolescent survey data may include intrapersonal questions about the adolescent: physical development; physical and emotional health; risk-taking and health-promoting behaviors; and attitudes, beliefs, values, and goals. Surveys may also include questions about interpersonal relationships (relationships between adolescents and their parents, siblings, and peers), the school environment (school characteristics, and adolescents' attitudes and beliefs about their school), peers and friendships, and religion. The field of adolescence studies has been strongly influenced by notions of developmental contextualism (Lerner, 1986), which emphasizes the changing and interactive nature of the relationship between adolescents and their evolving social and environmental contexts; these secondary data sets allow for direct study of overlapping and mutually influencing developmental contexts.

Many secondary data sources on adolescents are longitudinal; this is a distinct advantage, particularly when the topic of interest is on developmental change across time. Multiple cohort studies in Great Britain have followed subjects from birth through adulthood; similar long-term cohort studies have been conducted in New Zealand (see the Recommended Data Sets section). There are multiple relatively contemporary longitudinal studies in the United States that include the adolescent years and therefore are relevant for the study of adolescent development. The much-anticipated National Children's Study will begin in childhood and continue through adolescence and into young adulthood. Add Health and other longitudinal studies (National Education Longitudinal Study [NELS], National Longitudinal Study of Youth [NLSY], High School and Beyond) began in adolescence or early adolescence and continued into young adulthood. Analyses of existing and publically available longitudinal data have advanced understanding of the child developmental precursors of adolescent health and well-being (e.g., Russell, 2002), growth and development across the course of the adolescent years (e.g., Grimm, 2007), and the links between adolescent and young adult health and adjustment (e.g., Lynam, Caspi, Moffitt, Loeber, & Stouthamer-Loeber, 2007).

Finally, the discussion of longitudinal studies suggests other important possibilities that existing data offer for the study of adolescence: cross-national and historical understandings of adolescence and adolescent development. With multiple longitudinal studies from multiple continents over the course of recent decades, it is possible to consider comparative and historical analyses of adolescent development. For example, Schoon (2006) used two British birth cohort studies, 12 years apart, to study historical changes in developmental pathways of risk and resilience through adolescence.

Alongside these scientific and methodological advantages are equally important logistical considerations that can influence the feasibility and integrity of research. One of the primary challenges of studying adolescents is balancing the scientific and public health need for data on adolescents (who are considered a vulnerable population) with protection for human subjects. Although the U.S. Department of Health and Human Services Office for Human Research Protections (n.d.) offers guidance with regard to conducting research with minors, there is inconsistency across U.S. academic institutions with regard to the interpretation and application of guidelines for conducting research on minors and on obtaining parental consent. Each institutional review board (IRB) has the ability to determine what constitutes risk, and it is the institutional definition of risk that dictates decisions regarding parental consent, in addition to child assent. Inevitably, some institutions are more sensitive to adolescent participation in social and behavioral research than are others, and there are ongoing discussions in the field of adolescence studies about challenges in balancing concerns for the collection of research data with the protection of adolescent research participants. Although these challenges should not discourage researchers from pursuing original studies with adolescents, they highlight some additional benefits of using existing data to study adolescents. Secondary data sources have the unique advantage of having been properly vetted by the originating IRB and represent no or few new risks to participants (the risk of deductive disclosure of the identity of adolescent participants is possible given the breadth of information included in some studies, and methods to mitigate that risk have been used in some studies; see Udry & Bearman, 1998). Further, the ease of access to secondary data, compared with collecting new data, can facilitate the rapid turnaround of research findings, potentially moving the science of adolescent development forward more efficiently.

Finally, the cost of using secondary data sets to study adolescence is lower in comparison with conducting individual, even smaller scaled studies. Although this advantage may seem insignificant in comparison with others listed here, it speaks to the feasibility of conducting research on adolescent development. The wide availability and relative ease of access to this type of data allow for far more research questions to be addressed than would otherwise be possible. Given the finite (and often dwindling) resources available through both public and private funders, use of secondary data is scientifically strategic because it is financially practical. This may be particularly true for young scholars, for whom secondary data may afford an opportunity to make contributions to the field earlier in their careers than might be possible were they to conduct studies that require data collection.

CHALLENGES

Working with secondary data is not without challenges, especially when studying adolescent development. One significant issue is that most large-scale surveys of adolescents are conducted in school-based settings; findings from analyses of such data sets have limited generalizability to adolescents who are not in school. Adolescents not enrolled in school tend to engage in more health risk behaviors than those who are in school. Results from both the Add Health study and the NELS, for example, cannot yield information about youth who are homeschooled or who are homeless and not in school. Both are growing populations in the United States and have distinct needs from an adolescent health perspective: The large, school-based surveys omit these adolescents.

Remaining challenges that we have identified each have to do with survey measurement. As in all survey research, there are persistent concerns about the valid assessment of measures, particularly of sensitive behaviors. There is strong evidence that adolescents provide valid responses to survey questions about sensitive topics (e.g., Akers, Massey, & Clarke, 1983); nevertheless, concerns about survey item validity will remain. On the positive side, some surveys now use interview methods that ameliorate questions of response validity. Audio computer-assisted self-interview is a method that allows the adolescent respondent to listen to survey questions through headphones and respond to interview items on a touch-screen computer; only the response set appears on the screen. The method was developed as a way to assure adolescents that not even a person present in the room would know their responses to survey questions. This method has been used in several large-scale surveys of adolescent health and behavior and elicits more reports of sensitive information (risk behavior, delinquency, sexual behavior) from adolescents than traditional paper surveys (Supple, Aquilino, & Wright, 1999; Turner et al., 1998).

In addition to measure validity, there may be significant challenges with measurement content when using existing data sets (see Chapter 3). Because the study was designed by others, it is unlikely that the full battery of measures required to test a research question will necessarily be present. Researchers have to make creative use of existing data, and assess the degree to which crucial constructs can or cannot be measured with the data at hand. For example, the first waves of the Add Health data included questions about same-sex romantic attractions and relationships but not about self-identity as gay or lesbian, which had been the focus of prior research on adolescent sexual orientation. In the early publications using those data, a justification was necessary to explain the use of romantic attraction as a measure of sexual orientation. Although the lack of data on sexual self-identity was initially seen as a limitation to the use of the Add Health data, an unintended benefit resulted from those studies. Prior research had been based on self-identified gay and lesbian adolescents: Sexual orientation development was viewed as a simple dichotomy between "heterosexual" and "gay." Results from the Add Health study encouraged researchers to include same-sex desire, attraction, and relationships as meaningful indicators of same-sex sexuality in adolescence (Russell, 2006).

Measurement challenges may be compounded by disciplinary differences in approaches toward measurement. Because they are focused on broad populations, many of the large-scale existing data sources were (at least historically) developed by economists and sociologists; psychologists may be dismayed that standard measures typical in psychological research are unavailable in many of the large-scale existing data sources. For example, the Add Health study does not include "standard" measures of self-esteem (Rosenberg, 1979) or depression (Radloff, 1991); several researchers have developed measures that approximate the constructs familiar in the field of psychology (Crockett, Randall, Shen, Russell, & Driscoll, 2005; Russell et al., 2008), but they are not identical. In addition to this basic challenge of what is (or is not) measured, researchers using archives from several decades ago must be aware of changes in measurement convention; many of the data sets predate the measures that are now taken as standard (e.g., self-esteem, depression) or were conducted in different cultural settings and make use of different measures for key constructs.

Finally, it is critical to keep in mind that survey measures will always leave the scientist asking the question, What did the adolescent think this question meant? To better understand adolescent development, researchers must have some grasp of adolescents' experiences and their understandings of the phenomenon about which researchers ask. It is rare to be able to examine the deeper meanings of developmental processes using questionnaire data; a deep level of understanding of adolescents' perspectives is simply not possible through closed-ended survey questionnaires. Although it is not uncommon for large-scale studies to include, for example, open-ended questions that might yield further insight into the individual experience of adolescent development, such data are rarely used; the labor to code them would be significant, with uncertain benefit. Another strategy is to combine existing survey data with original qualitative data collection. For example, a recent study uses focus group data to better understand adolescents' responses to questionnaires; adolescents from specific ethnic groups were asked to reflect on Add Health measures to better understand the degree to which cultural differences may influence adolescents' understandings of the survey items (Crockett, Brown, Russell, & Shen, 2007).

CONCLUSION

Several key advantages of existing survey data sets have been discussed in this chapter: large sample sizes, population representative data, longitudinal data, data from multiple reporters, insights about multiple contexts of development, and the ability to conduct cross-historical or cross-national comparisons. Although these advantages may not be unique to scholars interested in issues of adolescence, it is critical to note that scholars who seek to study sensitive issues such as adolescent sexuality, substance use, and peer victimization face unique logistical challenges in collecting primary data. Thus, the availability of secondary data that assesses such topics has created opportunities for scientists to study these topics, and for public health programs to meet the needs of this often vulnerable population.

Analysis of secondary data has advanced the scientific investigation of adolescence and adolescent development in meaningful ways, as numerous scholars from diverse disciplinary perspectives have come together to study common issues of adolescence. For example, in the study of peer victimization, scientists from a variety of fields, including public health (e.g., Spriggs, Halpern, Herring, & Schoenbach, 2009), psychology (e.g., Aceves & Cookston, 2007), and criminology (e.g., Haynie & Piquero, 2006) have published work derived from analysis of the Add Health data set. In the development of policy and programming aimed to improve the lives of young people, the existence of a comprehensive, multidisciplinary body of literature around a single topic can be invaluable.

Several recommended data sets are outlined next; included are references to relevant readings that provide a summary of the data sources. In spite of the cautions, it is clear that existing data sources provide unique opportunities for the study of adolescents and their development, as well as for comparative and historical analyses of adolescent life.

RECOMMENDED DATA SETS

A number of existing data sets are currently available to researchers. Large repositories of archived data sets such as those housed in the Henry A. Murray Research Archive at Harvard University (http://www.murray.harvard.edu/frontpage) and by the Interuniversity Consortium for Political and Social Research (http://www.icpsr.umich.edu/ICPSR/) contain a wealth of data relevant for adolescent researchers. In addition, a growing number of data sets are becoming available as a result of the National Institutes of Health (2003) data sharing policy, which requires final research data sets from large grants (i.e., $500,000 or more in direct costs in any project year) to be made publicly available. Also of note is that the ongoing data collection that is occurring in studies that originated in childhood (e.g., the National Institute of Child Health and Human Development Study of Early Child Care and Youth Development) now has adolescent data available.

Although an exhaustive list of available data sets is beyond the scope of this section, the data sets listed here have been extensively used and have methodological strengths that provide substantial opportunity for further inquiry. We include references to recommended readings that summarize the methods and content of the data archive where relevant.

- *National Children's Study.* This study examines environmental influences on the health and development of more than 100,000 children in the United States. Study children will be followed from before birth until age 21. First study results are anticipated in 2010. See http://www.nationalchildrensstudy.gov/.

- *Longitudinal studies in New Zealand.* The Families Commission of the government of New Zealand summarized and reviewed these studies in a report on nine longitudinal studies. See http://www.familiescommission.govt.nz/research/family-relationships/review-of-new-zealand-longitudinal-studies.
- *Centre for Longitudinal Studies in the Institution of Education at the University of London.* The centre houses three internationally renowned birth cohort studies: the 1958 National Child Development Study, the 1970 British Cohort Study, and the Millennium Cohort Study. See http://www.cls.ioe.ac.uk/.
- *National Longitudinal Study of Youth.* This study includes two nationally representative panels of U.S. youth. The NLSY79 included 12,686 youth ages 14 to 22 when they were first surveyed in 1979; they were interviewed annually through 1994; since 1994, they have been interviewed on a biennial basis. The NLSY97 included approximately 9,000 youth ages 12 to 16 as of December 31, 1996. Round 1 of the survey took place in 1997, during which the eligible youth and one parent participated in personal interviews; the youth have been interviewed annually since the first round. See http://www.bls.gov/nls/.
- *Add Health.* Data for this nationally representative study of health-related behaviors of U.S. adolescents were initially obtained through school-based samples, and subsequent in-home interviews were conducted. Respondents were in Grades 7 through 12 at the time of the first interview (1994–1995); a majority of participants had one parent who completed a questionnaire at this wave. Respondents were interviewed 1 year later, and then again in young adulthood (2001–2002; Resnick, et al., 1997). See http://www.cpc.unc.edu/addhealth/data.
- *National Education Longitudinal Study.* Starting in 1988, this nationally representative school-based study of topics related to school, work, and home experiences of school-aged students also assessed limited health related behaviors (smoking, alcohol, and drug use). Baseline data as well as three additional waves of data were collected. The initial sample included eighth graders in spring 1988, with follow-up of a subsample in 1990, 1992, 1994, and 2000. Surveys were also administered to students' teachers, parents, and school administrators, and some archival academic data are available in the data set as well (Berkner, 2000). See http://nces.ed.gov/surveys/nels88/.
- *High School and Beyond.* This survey included two nationally representative cohorts: the 1980 senior class and the 1980 soph-

omore class. Both cohorts were surveyed every 2 years through 1986, and the 1980 sophomore class was also surveyed again in 1992. See http://nces.ed.gov/surveys/hsb/.

- *Monitoring the Future.* This is an ongoing, nationally representative study of behaviors, attitudes, and values of secondary school students, college students, and young adults. Each year, a total of approximately 50,000 8th-, 10th-, and 12th-grade students are surveyed. Annual follow-up questionnaires are mailed to a sample of each graduating class for a number of years after their initial participation. See http://www.monitoringthe future.org/ and http://www.icpsr.umich.edu/SAMHDA/.

- *National Survey of Family Growth.* For this ongoing study of family life, fertility, and health, data were collected from nationally representative samples of women, ages 15 to 44 years, in the first five cycles of the survey (1973, 1976, 1982, 1988, and 1995). National samples of both men and women have been collected in subsequent survey administrations (2002 and 2006). See http:// www.cdc.gov/nchs/nsfg.htm.

- *Youth Risk Behavior Surveillance System.* This includes a national school-based survey, as well as state and local school-based surveys that have been conducted biennially since 1991. The Youth Risk Behavior Survey (the portion administered in schools) assesses health risk behaviors ranging from unintentional injury to substance use, sexual behavior, and physical activity (Kann, 2001). See http://www.cdc.gov/healthyyouth/ yrbs/data/index.htm.

- *National Youth Tobacco Survey.* This nationally representative study of middle and high school students' tobacco related beliefs, behaviors, and attitudes also assesses exposure to media messages. Data are collected from school-based samples, and waves from surveys administered in 1999, 2000, 2002, and 2004 are currently available for research purposes (Centers for Disease Control and Prevention, 2004). See http://www.cdc.gov/tobacco/ data_statistics/surveys/NYTS/index.htm.

REFERENCES

Aceves, M., & Cookston, J. (2007). Violent victimization, aggression, and parent–adolescent relations: Quality parenting as a buffer for violently victimized youth. *Journal of Youth and Adolescence, 36,* 635–647. doi:10.1007/s10964-006-9131-9

Akers, R. L., Massey, J., & Clarke, W. (1983). Are self-reports of adolescent deviance valid? Biochemical measures, randomized response, and the bogus pipeline in smoking behavior. *Social Forces, 62*, 234–251. doi:10.2307/2578357

Bearman, P. S., & Moody, J. (2004). Suicide and friendships among American adolescents. *American Journal of Public Health, 94*, 89–95. doi:10.2105/AJPH.94.1.89

Berkner, L. (2000). Using National Educational Longitudinal Study data to examine the transition to college. *New Directions for Institutional Research, 2000*, 103–107. doi:10.1002/ir.10707

Centers for Disease Control and Prevention. (2004). *National Youth Tobacco Survey methodology report.* Retrieved from http://www.cdc.gov/tobacco/NYTS/nyts2004.htm

Crockett, L. J., Brown, J., Russell, S. T., & Shen, Y.-L. (2007). The meaning of good parent–child relationships for Mexican American adolescents. *Journal of Research on Adolescence, 17*, 639–668.

Crockett, L. J., Randall, B. A., Shen, Y., Russell, S. T., & Driscoll, A. K. (2005). Measurement equivalence of the Center for Epidemiological Studies Depression Scale for Latino and Anglo adolescents: A national study. *Journal of Consulting and Clinical Psychology, 73*, 47–58. doi:10.1037/0022-006X.73.1.47

Elder, G. H., Jr. (1974). *Children of the Great Depression.* Chicago, IL: University of Chicago Press.

Grimm, K. J. (2007). Multivariate longitudinal methods for studying developmental relationships between depression and academic achievement. *International Journal of Behavioral Development, 31*, 328–339. doi:10.1177/0165025407077754

Haynie, D. L., & Piquero, A. R. (2006). Pubertal development and physical victimization in adolescence. *Journal of Research in Crime and Delinquency, 43*, 3–35. doi:10.1177/0022427805280069

Kann, L. (2001). The Youth Risk Behavior Surveillance System: Measuring health-risk behaviors. *American Journal of Health Behavior, 25*, 272–277.

Lerner, R. M. (1986). *Concepts and theories of human development* (2nd ed.). New York, NY: Random House.

Lynam, D. R., Caspi, A., Moffitt, T. E., Loeber, R., & Stouthamer-Loeber, M. (2007). Longitudinal evidence that psychopathy scores in early adolescence predict adult psychopathy. *Journal of Abnormal Psychology, 116*, 155–165. doi:10.1037/0021-843X.116.1.155

Miller, B. C., Fan, X., Christensen, M., Grotevant, H. D., & van Dulmen, M. (2000). Comparisons of adopted and non-adopted adolescents in a large, nationally representative sample. *Child Development, 71*, 1458–1473. doi:10.1111/1467-8624.00239

Modell, J. (1991). *Into one's own: From youth to adulthood in the United States, 1920–1975.* Berkeley, CA: University of California Press.

National Institutes of Health. (2003). *NIH data sharing policy and implementation guidance.* Retrieved from the National Institutes of Health, Office of Extramural Research: http://grants.nih.gov/grants/policy/data_sharing/data_sharing_guidance.htm

O'Shaughnessy, M., Russell, S. T., Heck, K., Calhoun, C., & Laub, C. (2004). *Safe place to learn: Consequences of harassment based on actual or perceived sexual orientation and gender nonconformity and steps for making schools safer*. San Francisco, CA: California Safe Schools Coalition.

Radloff, L. S. (1991). The use of the Center for Epidemiologic Studies Depression Scale in adolescents and young adults. *Journal of Youth and Adolescence, 20*, 149–166. doi:10.1007/BF01537606

Resnick, M. D., Bearman, P., Blum, R. W., Bauman, K. E., Harris, K. M., Jones, J., . . . Udry, J. R. (1997). Protecting adolescents from harm: Findings from the National Longitudinal Study of Adolescent Health. *JAMA, 278*, 823–832. doi:10.1001/jama.278.10.823

Rosenberg, M. (1979). *Conceiving the self*. New York, NY: Basic Books.

Russell, S. T. (2002). Childhood developmental risk for teen childbearing in Britain. *Journal of Research on Adolescence, 12*, 305–324. doi:10.1111/1532-7795.00035

Russell, S. T. (2006). Substance use and abuse and mental health among sexual minority youth: Evidence from Add Health. In A. Omoto & H. Kurtzman (Eds.), *Sexual orientation and mental health: Examining identity and development in lesbian, gay, and bisexual people* (pp. 13–35). Washington, DC: American Psychological Association. doi:10.1037/11261-001

Russell, S. T., Crockett, L. J., Shen, Y.-L., & Lee, S.-A. (2008). Cross-ethnic invariance of self-esteem and depression measures for Chinese, Filipino, and European American adolescents. *Journal of Youth and Adolescence, 37*, 50–61. doi:10.1007/s10964-007-9231-1

Russell, S. T., & Joyner, K. (2001). Adolescent sexual orientation and suicide risk: Evidence from a national study. *American Journal of Public Health, 91*, 1276–1281. doi:10.2105/AJPH.91.8.1276

Safe Place to Learn Act, California AB 394 (2007).

Schlegel, A., & Barry, H., III. (1991). *Adolescence: An anthropological inquiry*. New York, NY: The Free Press.

Schoon, I. (2006). *Risk and resilience: Adaptations to changing times*. Cambridge, England: Cambridge University Press. doi:10.1017/CBO9780511490132

Schulenberg, J. E. (2006). Understanding the multiple contexts of adolescent risky behavior and positive development: Advances and future directions. *Applied Developmental Science, 10*, 107–113. doi:10.1207/s1532480xads1002_6

Spriggs, A. L., Halpern, C. T., Herring, A. H., & Schoenbach, V. J. (2009). Family and school socioeconomic disadvantage: Interactive influences on adolescent dating violence victimization. *Social Science & Medicine, 68*, 1956–1965. doi:10.1016/j.socscimed.2009.03.015

Supple, A., Aquilino, W., & Wright, D. (1999). Collecting sensitive self-report data with laptop computers: Impact on the response tendencies of adolescents in a home interview. *Journal of Research on Adolescence, 9*, 467–488. doi:10.1207/s15327795jra0904_5

Turner, C. F., Ku, L., Rogers, S. M., Lindberg, L. D., Pleck, J. H., & Sonenstein, F. L. (1998, May 8). Adolescent sexual behavior, drug use, and violence: Increased reporting with computer survey technology. *Science, 280*, 867–873. doi:10.1126/science.280.5365.867

Udry, J. R., & Bearman, P. S. (1998). New methods for new research on adolescent sexual behavior. In R. Jessor (Ed.), *New perspectives on adolescent risk behavior* (pp. 241–269). Cambridge, England: Cambridge University Press.

U.S. Department of Health and Human Services, Office for Human Research Protections. (n.d.) *Special protections for children as research subjects*. Retrieved from http://www.hhs.gov/ohrp/children/

Williams, S. T., Conger, K. J., & Blozis, S. A. (2007). The development of interpersonal aggression during adolescence: The importance of parents, siblings, and family economics. *Child Development, 78*, 1526–1542

11

USING SECONDARY DATA TO ADVANCE CROSS-CULTURAL PSYCHOLOGY

EVERT VAN DE VLIERT

Archives are echos of culture. If this statement calls for clarification, I would like to add the part played by language: No language, no culture, no archives. Oral and written languages, such as Arabic, Chinese, and Dutch, are tools to create, send, and receive cultural values, beliefs, and behaviors. Accordingly, cross-cultural psychologists often compare cultures on the basis of responses to interviews and questionnaires, and observations of behaviors, not infrequently turning their findings into data sets for further use. For laypeople and scholars alike, languages are also tools to save and store information about cultural values, beliefs, and behaviors in archives. Thus, archival data are rich sources for the researcher looking for how culture is revealed or displayed (*manifestations*); how culture comes about (*antecedents*); and how culture influences people's comings, doings, and goings (*consequences*), as the following examples illustrate.

MANIFESTATIONS

In a book about culture-based conflict in preindustrial societies around the globe, Ross (1993) mapped and interrelated violence within ethnic groups and warfare with outsiders. He used the Human Relations Area Files, a large archive of ethnographic reports of anthropologists, missionaries, and travelers, carefully coded for hundreds of variables, including the acceptability, frequency, and intensity of internal conflict and violence, and external conflict and warfare. Although conflicts were found in all societies, some communities were especially prone to aggressive conflict management, whereas others were more peaceful. The data best supported a dichotomy of *generalizing societies* with roughly the same levels of internal and external conflict, and *differentiating societies* with much more internal than external conflict or the other way round. For example, the Jivaro (much conflict) and the Mbuti (little conflict) had generalizing cultures, whereas the Ifugao (much more internal than external conflict) and the Timbira (much less internal than external conflict) had differentiating cultures.

ANTECEDENTS

In a classic piece of research, McClelland (1961) classified 52 preliterate societies on the basis of available long-term weather recordings of their residential area (climate: cold, temperate, hot) and codings of the density of need for achievement in their folktale texts. Cultures of societies in temperate climates appeared to be more achievement oriented than cultures of societies in either colder-than-temperate or hotter-than-temperate climates. A major problem with this observation is that no distinction was made between competitors and improvers. No distinction was made between the degree to which workers want to do better than comparable others, irrespective of how well they themselves are doing (competition-oriented workforces in, e.g., Bangladesh and Iraq), or better than they did before, irrespective of how well comparable others are doing (improvement-oriented workforces in, e.g., Argentina and Venezuela; Van de Vliert & Janssen, 2002).

CONSEQUENCES

Vandello and Cohen (1999) used secondary data to rank the 50 states of the United States on consequences of culture, ranging from most collectivistic (Hawaii, Louisiana, and South Carolina) to most individualistic (Nebraska, Oregon, and Montana). The more individualistic the state's citizens, the more likely they were to live alone or at least in households with no grandchildren, be divorced, have no religious affiliation, vote for the Libertarian party, and be self-employed. For the same reason, carpooling to work compared with driving alone was found more in the Deep South than in the Mountain West and Great Plains. It is not surprising that this 50-state collectivism–individualism index as a metaform of secondary data is of further use to scholars seeking a construct to account for unique regional variation within the predominantly individualistic culture of the United States (e.g., Kemmelmeier, Jambor, & Letner, 2006).

WHY SECONDARY DATA?

The preceding illustrations exemplify cross-cultural psychologists' interest in culture-level variables that affect basic psychological processes. They compare societal values, beliefs, behaviors, and their interrelations across time (*longitudinal comparisons*), across place (*cross-sectional comparisons*), or both (*diagonal comparisons*). Given the long-wave change in culture, longitudinal comparisons of values and beliefs are virtually impossible without making use of archived data. For example, the following finding rests on comparisons of analysis-ready data sets covering 38 nations during the 1980–2000 period. Inhabitants of countries in more demanding climates changed from emphasizing quality of life and self-actualization toward emphasizing physical and financial security, to the extent that they faced economic recession, as was the case in Soviet successor states after the collapse of the Soviet Union in 1990–1991 (Van de Vliert, 2007b).

The much easier approach of cross-sectional comparisons of cultures at approximately the same point in time can make fruitful use of an abundance of information routinely gathered by United Nations agencies, the World Economic Forum, multinational business organizations, and the like. A worldwide consortium of researchers, for instance, used low discrimination against women and proportion of women in earned income as validation criteria for gender egalitarianism in 62 cultures (Gupta, Sully de Luque, & House, 2004). Likewise, they used high use of fax machines per capita, indicating high emphasis on information processing and need for security, as a validation criterion for uncertainty avoidance in the same 62 cultures.

At first sight, a diagonal comparison between, for example, the Viking pirates in the 8th to 10th centuries and the Somali pirates today, seems an unwise and unscientific research approach, as it is unclear how differences must be attributed to the millennium gap, the geographic gap, or their interaction. On closer consideration, however, such a prejudiced rejection of comparative studies of different time–place niches of culture comes at a high price. It would mean that the Human Relations Area Files, mentioned previously, which contain a quarter million pages of detailed ethnographic information on 863 societies in distinct time–place niches of culture, have to be banned from future analyses.

ADVANTAGES AND DISADVANTAGES

Compared with studies using surveys, observations, and experiments, secondary data analysis has some clear strengths and weaknesses. This section reviews three advantageous strengths all having to do with the accessibility of the data, and three disadvantageous weaknesses all having to do with inaccurate measurement.

Advantages

Compared with studies using surveys, observations, and experiments, secondary data analysis has some clear virtues. First, unlike historians, archeologists, and palynologists, cross-cultural psychologists are short of vehicles for moving across time, with archival data-mining searches as a notable exception. Take the mystery of the collapse of the Norse society in medieval Greenland around 1450. Church documents, travel reports, proofs of payment, and sagas show that the Norse shared the shores of iceberg-strewn fjords with the Inuit; that the Norse had a sedentary and agricultural lifestyle; that the Inuit had a nomadic and aquacultural lifestyle; and that the Norse saw the Inuit as despicable and mean people, calling them *skraeling,* that is, "wretches" (Diamond, 2005). No wonder, then, that the Norse did not learn from the Inuit how to use blubber for heating and lighting, how to build fast kayaks by stretching sealskins over frameworks, how to make harpoons and other whale-hunting equipment, and so forth. Indeed, archives produce the information needed to conclude that discrimination toward the "inferior" Inuit pushed the "superior" Norse on a slippery slope toward extinction.

Second, the most frequently used method for examining cross-cultural questions is to simply conduct field studies or lab experiments in a few countries and determine whether national culture moderates the observed effects. Self-evidently, the questions that can be addressed with comparisons between participants from a few countries are limited and may lead to inaccurate conclusions, certainly when only students are investigated. Therefore, analysis of existing large-scale data sets often provides the best way to overcome problems of size and representativeness of cross-cultural samples. Vandello and Cohen's (1999) study of collectivist versus individualist tendencies in all 50 states of the United States is an elegant case in point.

Finally, more so than subjective answers, systematic observations, and reactions of participants to experimental conditions, secondary data are publicly accessible and recodable, with the consequence that the research is accurately reproducible and verifiable. This is not to say that information retrieved from archives is more reliable and is more validly measuring the right thing, as I discuss next.

Disadvantages

If documents or data compilations to be compared are available in the languages of the places of origin, a Babel-like confusion of tongues results. Linguistic equivalence requires that the original documents or data sets are translated into a target language by a first interpreter and back-translated into the source language by a second interpreter. Next, the accuracy of the translation is evaluated and improved by comparing the original and back-translated versions. Yet, this procedure

> puts a premium on literal translations, and such translations can yield a stilted language that does not approach the naturalness of the text in the original version. A translation–backtranslation procedure pays more attention to the semantics and less to connotations, naturalness, and comprehensibility. (Van de Vijver & Leung, 1997, p. 39)

If linguistic equivalence is achieved, secondary indices have the remaining drawback of being proxy measures of the theoretical construct projected onto the data at best. Granted, participants' responses, observers' responses, and secondary codings are always proxy measures. But this problem is particularly relevant to research in the records, given that the selection, interpretation, and codification of the records is more than a couple steps removed from the actual construct of interest. For example, on the one hand, prevalence of carpooling to work may insufficiently tap into the subtle collectivistic pattern of closely linked individuals who define themselves as interdependent members of a collective (e.g., family, work team, compatriots). On the other hand, carpooling to work may to a large extent reflect considerations of convenience, or financial motives for not driving alone. Moreover, carpooling may have a different meaning in regions with differing population densities or differing ethnic compositions, so that apples and oranges are compared. As a consequence, the nomological networks of secondary indices in the cultures investigated should be compared to demonstrate construct equivalence (for details, see Van de Vijver & Leung, 1997).

Last but not least, archives are all-too-global echos of culture. Secondary information virtually always misses necessary individual-level or dyad-level specifications to identify and help explain processes that underlie cultural differences of psychological interest. Only when archives have been created with cross-cultural research in mind may more advanced psychological questions be successfully addressed. For example, a 33-nation, multilevel analysis of archived scores of individual-level motives for doing unpaid voluntary work (Van de Vliert, Huang, & Levine, 2004) yielded the following results. In poorer countries with demanding, cold climates, such as the Baltic states, voluntary workers had either predominantly altruistic or predominantly egoistic motives for volunteering. In countries with temperate climates, including those in southern Europe, altruistic and egoistic reasons for volunteering were unrelated. And in richer countries with demanding, cold climates, such as Norway and Sweden, voluntary workers mingled altruistic and egoistic motives into cooperation. All of these tendencies held true for both men and women.

ILLUSTRATION: THEORY AND METHOD

For more than 40 years, cross-cultural psychologists have thoroughly and fruitfully investigated manifestations and consequences rather than causes of culture. Now the time seems to be ripe for a paradigm shift from the fruits of culture to the roots of culture. The most fundamental explanations of culture have foundations in two clearly distinguishable types of survival: genetic survival over time (for an overview, see Buss, 2004) and climatic survival in a particular place (for an overview, see Van de Vliert, 2007a).

On the one hand, culture has been traced back to human reproduction represented by, for example, the "selfish gene" (Dawkins, 1989), menstruation (Knight, 1991), son–daughter preferences (Kanazawa, 2006), and parental investment (Buss, 2004). On the other hand, through the ages, Hippocrates, Ibn Khaldun, Montesquieu, Quetelet, and Huntington, to mention but a handful of classic scientists, have all tried in vain to relate culture to climate. At the beginning of the 20th century, the proponents of the so-called geographical school also argued that climate matters for all sorts of psychosocial phenomena (for an overview, see Sorokin, 1928). But the geographical school, too, failed to demonstrate and clarify convincingly how climatic effects come about and link up to values and practices. As a result, genetic roots of culture have received much more attention than climatic roots of culture, which is unfortunate because climatic survival is more basic than genetic survival. Genetic survival is impossible without climatic survival simply because people die in arctic environments with temperatures below minus 60°C as well as in desert environments with temperatures above 60°C.

To my own surprise, I have discovered why Hippocrates and all the other scientific ancestors failed to successfully relate climate to culture (for details, see Van de Vliert, 2009). The first mistake in this line of research was that they measured climatic temperature on Celsius or Fahrenheit scales, with an arbitrary zero point of reference. But for humans, as a warm-blooded species, a temperature scale with a comfortability optimum as the point of reference is more appropriate. Both colder-than-temperate and hotter-than-temperate climates are more demanding and call for more cultural adaptation in the longer run. The second mistake was that climate–culture researchers, including the younger me, overlooked the complicating role of money. A valid analysis of cultural adaptation to climate should take into account how much cash (ready money) and capital (unready money) a society has available to cope with bitter winters, scorching summers, or both. We need to search for climato-economic origins of culture.

Theory

Of course, a society may adapt its cultural values, beliefs, and practices to its climatic environment (e.g., House, Hanges, Javidan, Dorfman, & Gupta, 2004), its economic environment (e.g., Inglehart & Baker, 2000), both in a parallel fashion (e.g., Nolan & Lenski, 1999), or both in a sequential fashion (e.g., Hofstede, 2001). But all of these viewpoints neglect the equally obvious viewpoint that the climatic and economic impacts on culture may influence each other. A more accurate understanding of culture may unfold when one thinks of the environment as an integrated climato-economic habitat requiring integrated cultural responses. Hence, my emphasis on the hypothesis that the interaction of climatic demands and collective income matters most to culture. Demanding colder-than-temperate and hotter-than-temperate climates make income resources more useful. Income resources make harsher climates less threatening and often more challenging.

Psychologists will have little trouble adopting the general idea that resources can make up for demands; this line of reasoning is familiar to them (e.g., Bandura, 1997; Karasek, 1979; Lazarus & Folkman, 1984). Greater demands mismatched by unavailable or inadequate resources to meet the demands impair psychological functioning, as the actors cannot control the threatening and stressful situation. By contrast, greater demands matched by personal or societal resources to meet the demands improve psychological functioning, as the actors can control the situation, can turn threats into opportunities, and can experience relief and pleasure instead of disappointment and pain. If the demands are negligible, resources do not serve a useful purpose, with the consequence that no joint impact of demands and resources on psychological functioning surfaces.

Using secondary data, recent research demonstrated that these demands–resources explanations of human functioning are generalizable to (mis)matches of climatic demands and income resources as origins of aspects of culture. Greater climatic demands mismatched by collective poverty produce more life stress and mortality salience, and increase one's quest for certainty and one's inclination to show favor to "us" above "them." These threatening climato-economic niches led to more encouragement of selfishness in children, more rule-and-role taking in organizations (Van de Vliert, 2009), and more familism and nepotism—the advantageous treatment of relatives compared with nonrelatives (Van de Vliert, in press). Greater climatic demands matched by collective wealth, however, produce more life satisfaction and life challenges, and increase one's open-mindedness and creativity. These climato-economic niches produced more encouragement of cooperativeness in children, more rule-and-role making in organizations, and more egalitarianism and professionalism in treating others. In temperate climates, where climatic demands and money resources are less crucial, in-between profiles of child enculturation, organization, and favoritism–egalitarianism surfaced irrespective of the inhabitants' income per head.

This rather complex pattern of findings has been simplified (Van de Vliert, 2009), using the survival versus self-expression dimension from the World Values Surveys (Inglehart, Basáñez, Díez-Medrano, Halman, & Luijkx, 2004). That bipolar dimension ranges from the importance of security, prejudice, and social mistrust (*survival culture*) to the importance of self-realization, tolerance, and social trust (*self-expression culture*). Survival cultures, as an umbrella of selfish enculturation, rule-and-role making, and favoritism, appeared to thrive better in poorer societies in more demanding climates. Self-expression cultures, as an umbrella of co-operative enculturation, rule-and role making, and egalitarianism, appeared to thrive better in richer societies in more demanding climates.

Extending this line of research to leadership, one may hypothesize that autocratic leadership thrives better in poorer countries with more demanding climates and survival cultures, that democratic leadership thrives better in richer countries with more demanding climates and self-expression cultures, and that mixtures of autocratic and democratic leadership thrive better in countries with temperate climates, irrespective of their income per head. This interaction hypothesis was tested with existing nation-level indicators of climatic demands and collective income, and previously published indicators of leadership culture in some 60 nations.

Level of Analysis

Collective leadership values, beliefs, or practices can best be operationalized and analyzed at the national level for pragmatic, methodological, and theoretical reasons. The pragmatic reason is that nations have country-level archives and domestic indicators available for research. The methodological reason has been provided by Shalom Schwartz (2004). He used various national subsamples (male vs. female, young vs. old, student vs. teacher), to demonstrate that these subsamples produce highly similar orders of nations on seven cultural dimensions and to therefore conclude that nations are indeed meaningful units of cross-cultural analysis.

A descriptive theoretical reason is that two-dimensional pictures that interrelate differences in leadership culture across clearly locatable nations have at least as much scientific merit as geographic maps and astronomic charts. The most important theoretical reason is that nations generate cultures. Although national borders are seldom cultural boundaries, it still makes sense to use nations as units of measurement and explanators of culture: "Nations are political units with distinctive ecological, historical, political, educational, legal, regulatory, social, and economic characteristics. As such, they constitute systems and have cultures" (Smith, Bond, & Kağitçibaşi, 2006, p. 77).

Secondary Data: Leadership Culture

This study was a secondary analysis of survey data gathered by over 170 researchers of Global Leadership and Organizational Behavior Effectiveness (GLOBE; House et al., 2004, pp. 713–714; for research details, see House & Hanges, 2004). The GLOBE group gathered data in 62 cultures from 59 countries, representing all major regions of the world. In three multicultural countries, more than one culture was sampled (East and West Germans, German-speaking and French-speaking Swiss, and White and Black South Africans). Within each culture, middle managers from domestic organizations were sampled ($N = 17,370$; range $= 27–1,790$ per culture; $M = 285$, $SD = 237$; the Czech Republic had to be removed because of substantial and pervasive response bias).

The managers rated how important each of about 100 characteristics and behaviors is for a leader to be "exceptionally skilled at motivating, influencing, or enabling you, others, or groups to contribute to the success of the organization or task." The rating scale ranged from 1 (*greatly inhibits a person from being an outstanding leader*) to 7 (*contributes greatly to a person being an outstanding leader*). Confirmatory factor analysis resulted in indices of autocratic, self-protective, autonomous, humane-oriented, team-oriented, and charismatic leadership ideals in a country's organizations. For each of these six leadership scores, coefficients for reliability, individual-to-nation aggregation, construct equivalence across cultures, and cross-cultural validity were good to excellent (for details, see Hanges & Dickson, 2004, pp. 132–137, 147–148).

To eliminate cross-cultural response bias in scale use, the six leadership factors were centered on their mean score within each of the 61 cultures. Second-order factor analysis produced a bipolar dimension that predicted 77% of the variance in four of the six leadership ideals. Autocratic leadership ($-.87$) and self-protective leadership ($-.83$) loaded on the autocratic pole of this dimension, team-oriented leadership ($.85$) and charismatic leadership ($.96$) ideals loaded on the opposite democratic pole. After removal of an outlier (Qatar $= -3.20$), the standardized autocratic versus democratic leadership index ranged from −1.80 in Egypt (strongly autocratic) to +1.61 in Finland (strongly democratic).

Secondary Data: Climatic Demands

Thermal climates, generally expressed in average monthly degrees Celsius across a country's major cities, are more demanding to the extent that winters are colder-than-temperate, summers are hotter-than-temperate, or both. The point of reference for temperateness in this line of research is 22°C (about 72°F) because it is the approximate midpoint of the range of comfortable temperatures, and it happens to be the highest world temperature in the coldest month (July on the Marshall Islands) as well as the lowest world temperature in the hottest month (July on the Faroe Islands). Specifically, climatic demands were operationalized as the sum of the absolute deviations from 22°C for the average lowest and highest temperatures in the coldest and in the hottest month (Parker, 1997; somewhat lower or higher reference points than 22°C yield almost identical research results).

The scores for climatic demands ranged from 29 in Singapore to 105 in Canada ($M = 64$, $SD = 20$). Weighted regression analysis was used to address the potential problem of temperature variations in countries spanning multiple latitudes. However, giving countries with shorter latitude ranges higher weights produced more rather than less support for the hypothesis, so that it is unproblematic to report unweighted results.

Secondary Data: Collective Income

To reduce the skewness of its distribution, the index of the available money resources had to be log transformed. The natural logarithm of gross domestic product per capita in 1995 (purchasing power parity in U.S. dollars; United Nations Development Programme, 1998) ranged from 6.89 in Zambia to 8.74 in Switzerland ($M = 8.46$, $SD = .46$). Collective income was weakly related to climatic demands ($r = .26$, $N = 60$, $p < .05$).

ILLUSTRATION: RESULTS AND CONCLUSIONS

As reported in detail elsewhere (Van de Vliert, 2009, pp. 154–155, 161–162), climatic demands ($\Delta R^2 = 4\%$), collective income ($\Delta R^2 = 13\%$), and climatic demands and collective income in concert ($\Delta R^2 = 14\%$) accounted for 31% of the variation in autocratic versus democratic leadership culture. Figure 11.1 gives the computer-generated positions, in a two-dimensional space, of 56 countries on the three dimensions of temperate versus harsh cli-

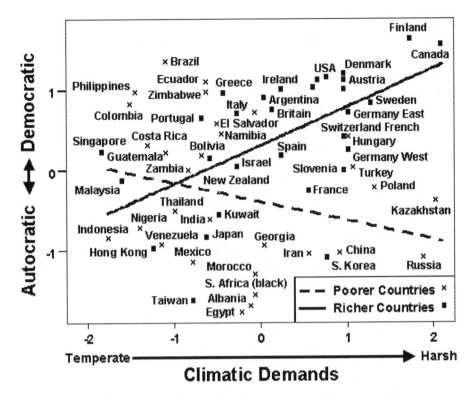

Figure 11.1. Effect of more demanding cold or hot climates on autocratic versus democratic leadership ideals, broken down for poorer and richer countries.

mate, low versus high collective income, and autocratic versus democratic leadership culture (because of space restrictions, the positions of Australians, Dutch, German-speaking Swiss, and White South Africans could not be labeled).

In support of the hypothesis, Figure 11.1 shows a downward sloping regression line for the poorer countries, $r(30) = -.26, p < .08$; an upward sloping regression line for the richer countries, $r(30) = .56, p < .001$; negligible differences between poorer and richer countries in temperate climates at the left, $r(30) = .01$, *ns*; and significant differences between poorer and richer countries in harsher climates at the right, $r(30) = .65, p < .001$. The downward sloping line confirms the proposition that more threatening mismatches of climatic demands and income resources impair psychological functioning by generating more autocratic leadership ideals. The upward sloping line confirms the proposition that more challenging matches of climatic demands and income resources improve psychological functioning by generating more democratic leadership ideals.

This pattern of results survived many attacks by rival predictors. Notably, main and interactive effects of climatic precipitation could not account for, or qualify, the joint impact of thermal climate and income per head. Likewise, main and interactive effects of income inequality could not destroy the picture either. As expected, only when I controlled for the above-mentioned World Values Surveys' dimension of survival culture versus self-expression culture (Inglehart et al., 2004), did the climato-economic regression coefficients fail to reach significance anymore. Variation in survival versus self-expression culture, accounting for 41% of the variation in autocratic versus democratic leadership culture, appeared once again to function as an overarching cultural umbrella of values, beliefs, and practices. Climato-economic niches of survival culture, including autocratic leadership ideals, contrast with climato-economic niches of self-expression culture, including democratic leadership ideals.

Together with previous findings in this strand of research (Van de Vliert, 2009), the present pattern of results reflects consistency, parsimony, and accuracy, and inspires confidence in the following interpretation of Figure 11.1.

- More autocratic and relatively selfish leaders thrive in survival cultures that evolve in poorer countries with harsher climates, as represented by China, Kazakhstan, and Russia in the lower right corner.
- Leaders who embrace neither autocratic nor democratic approaches thrive in countries with temperate climates irrespective of the inhabitants' income per head (e.g., Malaysia and Zambia, in the middle at the left).
- More democractic and relatively cooperative leaders thrive in self-expression cultures that evolve in richer countries with harsher climates, as represented by Austria, Denmark, and Finland in the upper right corner.

This set of conclusions supports the impression that leaders are products rather than producers of culture. Indeed, rather than shaping climato-economic niches, the results indicate that leadership cultures are shaped by their environment, just as world citizens adapt their values, beliefs, and practices to the climate of their residential area using the money they have and hold available to cope with that climate. Everyone, everyday, everywhere has to satisfy climate-based needs for thermal comfort, nutrition, and health with the help of money resources. Corresponding values, beliefs, and practices have been learned with the greatest of ease, without awareness of their age-long evolution, and with next to no recollection of survival as their ultimate objective. As a consequence, archived cultural remnants of the climato-economic past are silently waiting to be discovered as companions of the climato-economic present.

RECOMMENDED DATA SETS

Predominantly climato-economic sources:

- http://faculty.insead.edu/parker/resume/personal.htm
- *Human Development Report:* http://www.undp.org/publications/annualreport
- *World Economic Forum:* http://www.weforum.org/en/initiatives/gcp/index.htm

Predominantly sociological sources:

- *Political democracy:* http://www.freedomhouse.org/template.cfm?page=15
- *World Values Surveys (R. Inglehart):* http://www.worldvaluessurvey.org
- *Human Relations Area Files:* http://www.yale.edu/hraf

Predominantly psychological sources:

- *World Database of Happiness (R. Veenhoven):* http://www1.eur.nl/fsw/happiness
- *Values (S. H. Schwartz):* http://isdc.huji.ac.il/ehold10.shtml#E2

FOR FURTHER READING

Gupta, V., Sully de Luque, M., & House, R.J. (2004). Multisource construct validity of GLOBE scales. In R. J. House, P. J. Hanges, M. Javidan, P. W. Dorfman, & V. Gupta (Eds.), *Culture, leadership, and organizations: The GLOBE study of 62 societies* (pp. 152–177). Thousand Oaks, CA: Sage.

Van de Vliert, E. (2009). *Climate, affluence, and culture.* New York, NY: Cambridge University Press.

REFERENCES

Bandura, A. (1997). *Self-efficacy: The exercise of control.* New York, NY: Freeman Press.

Buss, D.M. (2004). *Evolutionary psychology: The new science of the mind* (2nd ed.). Boston, MA: Allyn & Bacon.

Dawkins, R. (1989). *The selfish gene* (2nd ed.). New York, NY: Oxford University Press.

Diamond, J. (2005). *Collapse: How societies choose to fail or survive.* New York, NY: Penguin.

Gupta, V., Sully de Luque, M., & House, R.J. (2004). Multisource construct validity of GLOBE scales. In R. J. House, P. J. Hanges, M. Javidan, P. W. Dorfman, & V. Gupta (Eds.), *Culture, leadership, and organizations: The GLOBE study of 62 societies* (pp. 152–177). Thousand Oaks, CA: Sage.

Hanges, P. J., & Dickson, M. W. (2004). The development and validation of the GLOBE culture and leadership scales. In R. J. House, P. J. Hanges, M. Javidan, P. W. Dorfman, & V. Gupta (Eds.), *Culture, leadership, and organizations: The GLOBE study of 62 societies* (pp. 122–151). Thousand Oaks, CA: Sage.

Hofstede, G. (2001). *Culture's consequences: Comparing values, behaviors, institutions, and organizations across nations.* London, England: Sage.

House, R. J., & Hanges, P. J. (2004). Research design. In R. J. House, P. J. Hanges, M. Javidan, P. W. Dorfman, & V. Gupta (Eds.), *Culture, leadership, and organizations: The GLOBE study of 62 societies* (pp. 95–101). Thousand Oaks, CA: Sage.

House, R. J., Hanges, P. J., Javidan, M., Dorfman, P. W., & Gupta, V. (Eds.). (2004). *Culture, leadership, and organizations: The GLOBE study of 62 societies.* Thousand Oaks, CA: Sage.

Inglehart, R., & Baker, W.E. (2000). Modernization, cultural change, and the persistence of traditional values. *American Sociological Review, 65*, 19–51. doi:10.2307/2657288

Inglehart, R., Basáñez, M., Díez-Medrano, J., Halman, L., & Luijkx, R. (Eds.). (2004). *Human beliefs and values: A cross-cultural sourcebook based on the 1999–2002 values surveys.* Mexico City, Mexico: Siglo XXI Editores. Also available from http://www.worldvaluessurvey.org

Kanazawa, S. (2006). Where do cultures come from? *Cross-Cultural Research, 40*, 152–176.

Karasek, R. A. (1979). Job demands, job decision latitude, and mental strain: Implications for job redesign. *Administrative Science Quarterly, 24*, 285–308.

Kemmelmeier, M., Jambor, E. J., & Letner, J. (2006). Individualism and collectivism: Cultural variation in giving and volunteering across the United States. *Journal of Cross-Cultural Psychology, 37*, 327–344.

Knight, C. (1991). *Blood relations: Menstruation and the origins of culture.* New Haven, CT: Yale University Press.

Lazarus, R. S., & Folkman, S. (1984). *Stress, appraisal, and coping.* New York, NY: Springer.

McClelland, D. C. (1961). *The achieving society.* Princeton, NJ: Van Nostrand.

Nolan, P., & Lenski, G. (1999). *Human societies: An introduction to macrosociology* (8th ed.). New York, NY: McGraw-Hill.

Parker, P. M. (1997). *National cultures of the world: A statistical reference.* Westport, CT: Greenwood Press.

Ross, M. H. (1993). *The culture of conflict.* New Haven, CT: Yale University Press.

Schwartz, S. H. (2004). Mapping and interpreting cultural differences around the world. In H. Vinken, J. Soeters, & P. Ester (Eds.), *Comparing cultures: Dimensions of culture in a comparative perspective* (pp. 43–73). Leiden, The Netherlands: Brill.

Smith, P.B., Bond, M.H., & Kağitçibaşi, C. (2006). *Understanding social psychology across cultures*. Thousand Oaks, CA: Sage.

Sorokin, P.A. (1928). *Contemporary sociological theories*. New York, NY: Harper.

United Nations Development Programme. (1998). *Human development report*. New York, NY: Oxford University Press.

Vandello, J. A., & Cohen, D. (1999). Patterns of individualism and collectivism across the United States. *Journal of Personality and Social Psychology, 77*, 279–292.

Van de Vijver, F., & Leung, K. (1997). *Methods and data analysis for cross-cultural research*. Thousand Oaks, CA: Sage.

Van de Vliert, E. (2007a). Climates create cultures. *Social and Personality Psychology Compass, 1*, 53–67.

Van de Vliert, E. (2007b). Climato-economic roots of survival versus self-expression cultures. *Journal of Cross-Cultural Psychology, 38*, 156–172.

Van de Vliert, E. (in press). Climato-economic origins of variation in ingroup favoritism. *Journal of Cross-Cultural Psychology*.

Van de Vliert, E. (2009). *Climate, affluence, and culture*. New York, NY: Cambridge University Press.

Van de Vliert, E., Huang, X., & Levine, R.V. (2004). National wealth and thermal climate as predictors of motives for volunteer work. *Journal of Cross-Cultural Psychology, 35*, 62–73.

Van de Vliert, E., & Janssen O. (2002) "Better than" performance motives as roots of satisfaction across more and less developed countries. *Journal of Cross-Cultural Psychology, 33*, 380–397.

12

USING THE AMERICAN NATIONAL ELECTION STUDY SURVEYS TO TEST SOCIAL PSYCHOLOGICAL HYPOTHESES

DANIEL SCHNEIDER, MATTHEW DeBELL, AND JON A. KROSNICK

Since 1948, the American National Election Study (ANES) has been collecting huge data sets, allowing social scientists to study the psychology of voting behavior, political attitudes and beliefs, stereotyping, political social-ization, the effects of social networks, the impact of the news media on the political process, and much more. Every 2 years, representative samples of more than 1,000 Americans have been interviewed in-depth after the national elections. In presidential election years, these respondents have been inter-viewed in-depth before the election as well. Panel studies have been con-ducted to track changes in people's attitudes, beliefs, and behavior, and pilot studies have been conducted to develop new measurements to be used later in the interviews.

The ANES was conceived at the University of Michigan's Institute for Social Research by Angus Campbell, Philip Converse, Warren Miller, and Donald Stokes. Some of the most widely cited books on the psychology of voting were written by these scholars using ANES data (e.g., Campbell, Converse, Miller, & Stokes, 1960; Converse, 1964; Miller, 1974), and the data have been used by numerous other researchers to test hypotheses and produce thousands of books and articles. In 1977, the National Science

Foundation (NSF) established the ANES as a national research resource for use by scholars around the world, and the NSF has provided funding with long-term grants for the project ever since. The most recent grant, for 2006–2009, marks the first time that the University of Michigan has collaborated with another university (Stanford University) to run the project jointly. In addition to traditional preelection and postelection in-depth interviews and pilot studies, this cycle marked implementation of an ambitious panel study to track large representative national samples of citizens monthly from January 2008 through May 2009. In addition, the ANES is collaborating with the National Longitudinal Survey of Youth to include political questions in their ongoing long-term panel studies tracking huge representative samples of cohorts of Americans.

The ANES is a common and collaborative research instrument of the scientific community. The data are offered publicly and for free shortly after the data collection concludes, and the principal investigators, board of overseers, and staff are barred from making personal use of the data before the data are publicly released. Conducting nationally representative, face-to-face interviews is expensive and is essentially impossible for individual researchers with conventionally available funding. The ANES provides many opportunities for researchers in social psychology, personality psychology, cognitive psychology, and other subdisciplines who wish to investigate the psychology of political thinking and action using nationally representative data.

In this chapter, we offer an overview of the ANES and describe the sorts of measurements that have been made in the surveys, how to obtain the data, and how to conduct analysis of the data using common statistical software. We also briefly describe some other large-scale data sources that might be of value to psychologists.

THE VALUE OF SURVEY DATA TO PSYCHOLOGISTS

From its inception, social psychology has been especially focused on experimental methods for theory testing. Laboratory experimentation has enabled researchers to isolate causal effects and claim strong internal validity by controlling confounding factors. But the generalizability of laboratory-based findings is limited. Replicating findings using the same methodology over time enhances confidence in their reality but leaves uncertain the extent to which the phenomena are relevant to explaining events outside the lab.

Therefore, in the spirit of methodological pluralism, the value of evidence from experiments can be enhanced by coordinated investigation of the same phenomena through survey data (Kinder & Palfrey, 1993). Surveys allow tracking changes in attitudes, beliefs, and behavior over time, either in individual respondents or in the aggregate of the general population. Such data allow for sophisticated statistical analyses to bolster confidence in the directions of causal relations (Finkel, 1995), and researchers can embed experiments in surveys to simultaneously enhance internal and external validity (Piazza & Sniderman, 1998; Visser, Krosnick, & Lavrakas, 2000). Doing so with general population samples allows researchers to explore the impact of a wide array of possible individual difference moderators of effects, when such investigation is more difficult with more homogeneous conventional lab studies with college student participants (Sears, 1986).

SURVEY METHODOLOGY

The core of survey methodology is probability sampling. In probability sampling, all elements of the population have a known probability of being selected. By using scientific sampling approaches and appropriate statistical methods, researchers can produce results that describe the population with a great deal of confidence. In contrast, conducting a study with a so-called convenience sample, whereby large parts of the population have no chance of participation and other probabilities of selection are unknown, a researcher can know only that some effect occurs but not with what prevalence and magnitude in the population.

The most common survey modes used today are face-to-face interviewing, telephone interviewing, mailed self-administered questionnaires, and questionnaires administered on computers through the Internet. Each of these modes has advantages and disadvantages. Face-to-face interviewing yields high response rates and accurate reporting (Holbrook, Green, & Krosnick, 2003), and sensitive questions can be asked by having an interviewer give his or her laptop computer to the respondent, who puts on headphones, listens to questions being read aloud to him or her, and answers the questions privately by typing answers directly into the computer. Interviewers' laptops can implement complex experimental designs embedded within the questionnaires as well. However, face-to-face interviewing is time-consuming and therefore expensive, because interviewers often have to spend much time traveling to contact the respondents and conduct interviews.

Telephone interviewing has been a major source of data collection in recent decades, and telephone methods such as random digit dialing make it relatively straightforward to draw and contact a probability sample of a population by telephone. As with face-to-face interviewing, telephone interviewers use computers that guide them through a questionnaire and implement experimental manipulations in a survey when desired.

Self-administered paper-and-pencil questionnaires, often mailed to respondents, have been used for large-scale survey operations but yield low response rates in general population surveys unless particular methods are used to enhance response rates (Dillman, 2000). Paper-and-pencil questionnaires are not well suited to complex skip patterns, whereby answers to early questions determine which later questions a person should answer. Some studies have shown that telephone interviewing can produce more accurate results than self-administered paper-and-pencil questionnaires (Silver & Krosnick, 2001), but there have also been cases in which mail surveys provided excellent results (Visser, Krosnick, Marquette, & Kurtin, 1996).

Self-administered questionnaires can also be completed through computers and the Internet, and this methodology is now increasingly popular. Internet surveys combine many of the positive features of other survey modes: No interviewers are needed, which saves money; complex filtering and experimental manipulations can be implemented; visual presentation of response options is routine, perhaps reducing respondent burden; and audio and video material can be practically presented. However, Internet access is not universal among the general population (DeBell & Chapman, 2006), which presents challenges in the use of web-based surveys. Some commercial firms in the United States and other countries have recruited representative samples of adults and given computer equipment and Internet access to households without it, thus yielding accurate data through this mode (Chang & Krosnick, 2001a, 2001b).

Regardless of the mode selected, respondent recruitment procedures should be designed to minimize nonresponse bias and maximize the response rate. *Nonresponse bias* occurs when a sample is systematically different from the population. *Response rates*—defined as the percentage of eligible sample members who complete a survey (American Association for Public Opinion Research, 2006)—are of interest to survey researchers because they indicate the degree of risk that a survey sample might be unrepresentative. If nearly all sampled individuals complete a survey, and if the survey is designed and implemented optimally, then the potential for nonresponse bias is low. Conversely, if the response rate is low, there is increased potential for nonresponse bias to affect estimates. However, low response rates per se are not evidence of nonresponse bias; they merely indicate the possibility of bias, and an accumulating body of studies indicates that if a probability sample is drawn from a population and serious efforts are made to collect data from as many sampled individuals as possible, results appear to be minimally affected by response rates (Curtin, Presser, & Singer, 2002; Holbrook, Krosnick, & Pfent, 2008; Keeter et al., 2000).

COMPONENTS OF THE AMERICAN
NATIONAL ELECTION STUDY

The ANES consists of three major components: pre- and postelection surveys, panel studies, and pilot studies. We discuss each of these components in the following subsections.

Pre- and Postelection Surveys

These surveys provide long-term time-series measures. In every presidential election year since 1948, the ANES has interviewed a representative sample of American adult citizens before Election Day and has reinterviewed most of the preelection participants after Election Day. In years of congressional elections through 1998, the survey implemented only postelection interviews; in 2002, pre- and postelection interviews were conducted. Respondents were usually interviewed face-to-face in their homes, although some telephone interviewing was done to test the viability of that method. Preelection interviewing usually started right after Labor Day, and postelection interviewing was usually initiated right after the election and continued in December and January. The pre- and postelection interviews yield the core of the ANES, and many questions have been asked repeatedly in many or every election year to generate a long time-series of measurements of Americans' attitudes on many issues; party identifications; political efficacy; trust in government and the political system; political participation; mass media use; ideology; evaluations of parties, candidates, and the president; and much more.

Such data have allowed psychologists to test a wide range of theory-driven hypotheses. For example, Krosnick and Kinder (1990) studied news media priming using the ANES by focusing on the Iran/Contra scandal. On November 25, 1986, the American public learned that members of the National Security Council had been funneling funds (earned through arms sales to Iran) to the Contras fighting to overthrow the Sandinista government in Nicaragua. Although there had been almost no national news media attention to Nicaragua and the Contras previously, this revelation led to a dramatic increase in the salience of that country in the American press during the following weeks. Krosnick and Kinder suspected that this coverage might have primed Americans' attitudes toward U.S. involvement in Nicaragua and thereby increased the impact of these attitudes on evaluations of President Ronald Reagan's job performance.

To test this hypothesis, Krosnick and Kinder (1990) took advantage of the fact that data collection for the survey conducted after the 1986 election was underway before November 25 and continued after that date. They split the survey sample into one group of respondents who had been interviewed before November 25 and others who had been interviewed afterward. As expected, overall assessments of presidential job performance were based much more strongly on attitudes toward U.S. involvement in Nicaragua in the second group than in the first group.

Abelson, Kinder, Peters, and Fiske (1982) used ANES data collected in 1980 to investigate the affective component of political candidate evaluation. Respondents were asked to say whether various specific politicians had ever made them feel a certain emotion (e.g., being afraid, angry, sad, proud, hopeful). An exploratory factor analysis revealed that negative and positive emotions loaded on two distinct factors, and the impact of these underlying emotional dimensions on candidate evaluations and preferences was investigated. Evaluations of candidates have been measured in the ANES with so-called feeling thermometers, which ask the respondents to indicate how "warm or favorable" or "cold or unfavorable" they feel toward particular politicians on a scale ranging from 0 to 100. Using these measures, Abelson et al. found that both dimensions contributed to overall evaluations of and preferences among politicians, thus enhancing confidence in the notion that positive and negative reactions to people can have partially independent impact on attitudes.

Holbrook, Krosnick, Visser, Gardner, and Cacioppo (2001) used another set of questions in the ANES to investigate how perceived positive and negative features of candidates contribute to overall evaluations. The ANES surveys have often asked respondents to list attributes of the major parties' candidates running for president that might make the respondent want to vote for or against each person. Holbrook et al. (2001) analyzed these data from all presidential elections between 1972 and 1996 to compare two models of the process by which people use candidate attributes to yield overall evaluations. The symmetric linear model (SLM) posits that the difference between the number of positive and negative attributes a candidate is perceived to possess directly predicts overall evaluations. In contrast, the asymmetric, nonlinear model (ANM) proposes a more complex reasoning process, whereby positive and negative attributes contribute differently to the overall evaluation, with negative attributes having more impact and each additional belief having a decreasing marginal effect. The ANM was found to be superior to the simpler SLM.

Panel Surveys

Panel surveys interview the same respondents two or more times to investigate individual-level change over time.[1] Analyses of panel data have often investigated stability of attitudes and beliefs and how they develop.

---

[1] Although the preelection and postelection waves of the face-to-face ANES studies constitute two-wave panels, few questions have been asked identically in both interviews, thus limiting the study's ability to track changes over time in individuals.

Some ANES panel studies have tracked respondents over longer time periods spanning several elections (1956–1958–1960, 1972–1974–1976, 2000–2002–2004). Other ANES panels have tracked changes over 1-year periods, such as from 1990 to 1991 to 1992, or changes during a single election campaign season, such as in 1980, when data were collected in January, June, September, and November–December.

A study by Bannon, Krosnick, and Brannon (2006) used the specific structure of the ANES Panel Study of 1990–1992–1994 to address the occurrence of media priming in election campaigns. It also tested an alternative explanation for the priming effect of media coverage on how issues are used by citizens in their overall evaluations of political candidates. Media priming theories postulate that citizens form the evaluations on the level of issues and then combine those into an overall candidate evaluation. However, past research has shown that sometimes respondents engage in *rationalization strategies* (Rahn, Krosnick, & Breuning, 1994), that is, forming an overall evaluation and then inferring the lower level issue evaluations from that overall evaluation. During the 1990–1992–1994 election cycle, the researchers used the change in public attention from the Gulf War to the state of the economy to check how individuals in the panel study changed their evaluation of the economic policies of the president and how those evaluations translated into changes of the overall evaluation. Using structural equation modeling, the researchers used the panel data to isolate the direction of causality. They found that although both rationalization and traditional media priming do occur, priming has a much stronger effect. In fact, previous studies might have underestimated the media priming effect because it was counterbalanced by the presence of unmodeled rationalization effects.

Pilot Studies and Other Special Studies

ANES pilot studies have been conducted to test new measurement methods or to evaluate the effectiveness of questions used in the past. Some of these have focused on methodological research questions. For example, in 1982, a special study was conducted to compare face-to-face interviewing with telephone interviewing and to evaluate whether a switch to telephone interviewing would allow for continued high quality data collection at a reduced price (Shanks, Sanchez, & Morton, 1983). Others have focused more specifically on matters of traditional interest to psychologists.

The 1998 pilot study included questions investigating two personality attributes: need for cognition and need to evaluate. Bizer and colleagues (Bizer et al., 2004; Bizer, Krosnick, Petty, Rucker, & Wheeler, 2000) found that need for cognition and need to evaluate helped in many ways to illuminate processes of political cognition and action. Respondents high in need for cognition and need to evaluate were more interested in politics and more engaged in the campaign. Those high in need to evaluate had more extreme attitudes, and those high in need for cognition were less likely to be dissatisfied with the experience of taking the survey. Although need for cognition has usually been measured with 18 questionnaire items (Cacioppo, Petty, & Kao, 1984) and need to evaluate has been measured with 16 (Jarvis & Petty, 1996), the ANES implemented two optimally formatted questions measuring need for cognition and three optimally formatted questions measuring need to evaluate, which yielded remarkably effective measurements.

The 2006 pilot study addressed many topics of interest to psychologists: character judgments, defensive confidence, need for closure, belief in a just world, self monitoring, interpersonal trust, basic values, optimism–pessimism, social networks, tolerance, and many others. More than 20 initial reports on many of these topics can be seen on the ANES website (http://www.election studies.org). This is more than for any prior pilot study, but much work remains to be done with the 2006 data set.

USING THE DATA FROM THE AMERICAN NATIONAL ELECTION STUDIES

All ANES data sets are available through the Internet at no cost from the ANES website. Each data file is accompanied by documentation of the study's design. Many ANES data files provide information about the interviewers and their assessments of the respondents and the interview situations, which can be used to investigate methodological issues. The website also provides a great deal of other information about the ANES and maintains a bibliography that documents many of the thousands of articles, books, and papers that have used its data.

Of course, the ANES is only beneficial to the researcher provided the questions he or she is interested in were actually asked in the surveys. There is a bit of a chicken-and-egg problem here: A researcher does not know whether the ANES offers measures suitable to address his or her hypotheses until he or she learns what measures are available, but the task of learning about all available measures administered during many hours of interviewing over many years seems daunting if he or she does not know in advance that suitable measures will be found there. An efficient solution to this problem is for researchers to get familiar with one of the traditional preelection–postelection survey questionnaire pairs. Many of the same sorts of items are asked across many years, so becoming familiar with one questionnaire is a good first step toward becoming familiar with many.

All ANES measures are documented in the codebooks and questionnaires available for each data set (go to http://www.electionstudies.org). The questionnaires list all the questions asked, often also documenting instructions given to the interviewers about how to ask the questions. The codebooks list every variable in each data set, showing the responses to the questions and also many additional variables about the interview process, the interviewer, and the respondent. The documentation also includes descriptions of sample designs, experiments embedded in the surveys, and information on the data collection modes. Researchers should bear in mind that coding approaches may differ across variables, waves, or years of data collection, so it is important to carefully read the codebook description of every variable one works with.

Constructs and Measures

The ANES has measured a wide variety of constructs known or hypothesized to be associated with voter turnout or vote choice and has repeated many such measurements over time. These constructs include the following:

- *Identification with political parties and attitudes toward political parties*. Identification with a political party is one of the strongest predictors of voting decisions, so it is among the most widely used variables in public opinion research.[2] Other questions about partisanship and attitudes toward parties include thermometers measuring warm–cold feelings toward parties, open-ended questions asking what the respondent likes and dislikes about each party, and whether the respondent perceives any differences between the parties in terms of what they stand for.
- *Candidate and incumbent evaluations*. Opinions of candidates and incumbent presidents are measured with feeling thermometers and with questions about perceptions of the candidates' personality traits, approval ratings of politicians' job performance, and questions asking whether the candidate has elicited various emotions from the respondent, including anger, hope, fear, and pride.
- *Issues*. People's attitudes toward various different policy options have been measured in domains such as the economy, the envi-

[2]ANES measures party identification with a branching question that begins, "Generally speaking, do you think of yourself as a Republican, a Democrat, an independent, or what?" If the respondent answers "Republican" or "Democrat," a follow-up question asks, "Would you call yourself a strong [Republican/ Democrat] or a not very strong [Republican/Democrat]?" If the respondent does not answer "Republican" or "Democrat," a follow-up question asks, "Do you think of yourself as closer to the Republican Party or to the Democratic Party?" Responses to these questions can be combined to yield a 7-point summary scale: *strong Democrat, not very strong Democrat, independent closer to the Democratic Party, independent, independent closer to the Republican Party, not very strong Republican, strong Republican*. However, some research indicates that this 7-point scale is not monotonically related to other variables, so analysts should check for monotonicity before computing statistics with it.

ronment, federal spending, foreign relations, racial relations, abortion, gun control, space exploration, capital punishment, social welfare, and much more. Respondents have also been asked open-ended questions about what they view as the country's most important problems.

- *Ideology and values.* Religious values, moral traditionalism, attitudes regarding equality, social trust and altruism, cognitive style, and other values and dispositions have been measured in various years.

- *System support.* ANES surveys have included many batteries of questions about trust in government, political efficacy, government power, patriotism, and other indicators of general attitudes toward the political system, the nation, or the government.

- *Political participation and mobilization.* The ANES has asked people to predict whether they will vote, has measured whether they voted via self-reports, and has in some years validated the turnout measures by checking to see whether official government records indicate that each respondent did or did not vote. In addition to questions about voting behavior, the ANES has regularly asked about political interest, frequency of discussing politics with others, and participation in the election campaigns.

- *Expertise.* The ANES has measured political expertise using quiz questions that asked respondents to identify the jobs or offices held by particular political actors or to answer factual questions (e.g., which political party has the majority of the seats in Congress).

- *Media.* Use of the news media has been measured by asking people how often they have watched television news, read newspapers and magazines, and listened to the radio. Respondents have also been asked how closely they have paid attention to political information in the news.

- *Social groups.* Feeling thermometer questions and other questions have been asked to measure attitudes toward social groups and political institutions, such as Blacks, Whites, Jews, Catholics, farmers, big business, and many others.

- *Personal and demographic data.* An extensive array of background variables is provided with most ANES studies, including age, sex, race, ethnicity, educational attainment, income, employment status, marital status, home ownership status, geographic area of residence, social class, and more.

Weighting and Variance Estimation in the ANES

The ANES does not use simple random samples, so statistical procedures that assume simple random sampling are generally inappropriate for the analysis of ANES data. The extent to which the study design differs from a simple random sample and the extent to which documentation and data files support design-consistent statistical procedures have varied over the decades. In general, specialized statistical steps should be taken when analyzing ANES data. These steps are unfamiliar to most researchers who have not been trained in survey methodology, but they are fairly easy to implement correctly. There are two steps: weight the data and compute design-consistent estimates of variance (including standard errors).

Weights

If an ANES data set includes an analysis weight variable, researchers should use it if they wish to project their results to the population of American adult citizens. It is important to use the weights, because weights adjust the data for unequal probabilities of selection and correct for nonresponse bias, making estimates such as percentages, means, and regression coefficients more accurate as parameter estimates for the entire population. In statistical software such as Stata, SAS, and SPSS, researchers can implement simple instructions to tell the software to use a weight. For example, in SPSS, once the 2006 Pilot Study data set has been opened, implementing the syntax command "weight by v06p002" tells SPSS to run subsequent analyses using the pilot study's weight variable, V06P002. The name of the weight variable(s) for each study can be found in the study's codebook.

Design-Consistent Estimates

Running analyses with the weights is sufficient to obtain correct point estimates such as percentages and regression coefficients for the population. However, by default, most statistical software will calculate sampling errors and statistical significance using procedures designed for simple random samples (SRS). The complex sample designs used in most ANES studies differ in important ways from simple random sampling, so standard errors, confidence intervals, and levels of statistical significance reported using SRS assumptions for ANES data are incorrect. Normally, the use of SRS significance statistics will lead to Type I errors (i.e., false rejection of the null, or making differences look significant when they are not).

To avoid these errors, data analysts should always use design-consistent statistical procedures when the data support them. Recent ANES data sets support Taylor series methods (Kish, 1965; Lee & Forthofer, 2006) to estimate standard errors, and many statistical programs, including Stata (http://www.stata.com),

SAS (http://www.sas.com), SUDAAN (http://www.rti.org), SPSS with the Complex Samples option (http://www.spss.com/complex_samples), and AM (http://am.air.org), implement these estimation procedures. To use these procedures, the user must specify a stratum variable and a cluster (or primary sampling unit or standard error computation unit) variable in much the same way that analysis weights are defined prior to analysis. For further information about design-consistent estimation, see the software manuals, Lee and Forthofer (2006), and ANES documentation (DeBell et al., 2009).

CODA

As we hope is clear, the ANES offers wonderful opportunities for psychologists to test a wide range of hypotheses using best practices survey methodology and to yield findings of much value to the discipline. We look forward to much more such work in the future.

RECOMMENDED DATA SETS

- *American National Election Study (ANES)*. See http://www.electionstudies.org.
- *Comparative Study of Electoral Systems (CSES)*. Election studies from around the world include a common module of survey questions that are merged into a single, free data set. See http://www.umich.edu/~cses.
- *European Social Survey (ESS)*. ESS is conducted in more than 30 countries and includes questions on topics including values; political engagement; well-being; health; security; and national, ethnic, and religious identity. See http:// www.europeansocial survey.org.
- *General Social Survey (GSS)*. GSS has administered demographic, behavioral, and attitudinal questions in the United States on a recurring basis since 1972. See http://www.norc.org/GSS+Website.
- *International Social Survey Programme (ISSP)*. ISSP consolidates and coordinates survey data from numerous countries on many topics including social inequality, the role of government, gender roles, religion, and national identity. See http://www.issp.org.
- *Interuniversity Consortium for Political and Social Research (ICPSR)*. ICPSR archives contain numerous data sets of interest for psychological research. See http://www.icpsr.umich.edu.

- *National Annenberg Election Studies (NAES)*. NAES has used very large samples to track changes in public opinion during campaigns, with particular emphasis on media and political communication. See http://www.annenbergpublicpolicycenter.org.
- *Roper Center*. The Public Opinion Archives at the Roper Center contain numerous data sets of interest for psychological research. See http://www.ropercenter.uconn.edu.
- *World Values Survey (WVS)*. WVS surveys have focused on politics, religion, economic and social life, happiness, and other areas of concern. See http://www.worldvaluessurvey.org.

FOR FURTHER READING

Robinson, J. P., Shaver, P. R., & Wrightsman, L. S. (Eds.). (1991). *Measures of personality and social psychological attitudes*. San Diego, CA: Academic Press.

Contains the exact wording of numerous sets of questions used to measure dimensions of personality and other psychological constructs.

Robinson, J. P., Shaver, P. R., & Wrightsman, L. S. (Eds.). (1999). *Measures of political attitudes*. San Diego, CA: Academic Press.

Contains the exact wording of numerous sets of questions used to measure political attitudes, as well as essays on conceptualization and measurement issues in political survey research.

REFERENCES

Abelson, R. P., Kinder, D. R., Peters, M. D., & Fiske, S. T. (1982). Affective and semantic components in political person perception. *Journal of Personality and Social Psychology, 42*, 619–630. doi:10.1037/0022-3514.42.4.619

American Association for Public Opinion Research. (2006). *Standard definitions: Final dispositions of case codes and outcome rates for surveys* (4th ed.). Lenexa, KS: Author.

Bannon, B., Krosnick, J. A., & Brannon, L. (2006, August/September). *News media priming: Derivation or rationalization?* Paper presented at the annual meeting of the American Political Science Association, Philadelphia, PA.

Bizer, G. Y., Krosnick, J. A., Holbrook, A. L., Wheeler, S. C., Rucker, D. D., & Petty, R. E. (2004). The impact of personality on cognitive, behavioral, and affective political processes: The effects of need to evaluate. *Journal of Personality, 72*, 995–1027. doi:10.1111/j.0022-3506.2004.00288.x

Bizer, G. Y., Krosnick, J. A., Petty, R. E., Rucker, D. D., & Wheeler, S. C. (2000). *Need for cognition and need to evaluate in the 1998 National Election Survey Pilot Study*.

Retrieved from ftp://ftp.nes.isr.umich.edu/ftp/resourcs/psreport/98pilot/bizer98.pdf, 01/27/2008

Cacioppo, J. T., Petty, R. E., & Kao, C. F. (1984). The efficient assessment of need for cognition. *Journal of Personality Assessment, 48,* 306–307. doi:10.1207/s15327752jpa4803_13

Campbell, A., Converse, P. E., Miller, W. E., & Stokes, D. (1960). *The American voter.* New York, NY: Wiley.

Chang, L., & Krosnick, J. A. (2001a, May). *The accuracy of self-reports: Comparisons of an RDD telephone survey with Internet Surveys by Harris Interactive and Knowledge Networks.* Paper presented at the annual meeting of the American Association for Public Opinion Research, Montreal, Canada.

Chang, L., & Krosnick, J. A. (2001b, May). *The representativeness of national samples: Comparisons of an RDD telephone survey with matched Internet surveys by Harris Interactive and Knowledge Networks.* Paper presented at the annual meeting of the American Association for Public Opinion Research, Montreal, Canada.

Converse, P. E. (1964). The nature of belief systems in mass publics. In D. E. Apter (Ed.), *Ideology and discontent* (pp. 206–261). New York, NY: Free Press.

Curtin, R., Presser, S., & Singer, E. (2000). The effects of response rate changes on the index of consumer sentiment. *Public Opinion Quarterly, 64,* 413–428. doi:10.1086/318638

DeBell, M., & Chapman, C. (2006). *Computer and Internet use by students in 2003* (NCES 2006-065). Washington, DC: U.S. Department of Education, National Center for Education Statistics.

DeBell, M., Howell, D., Krosnick, J. A., Lupia, A., & Luevano, P. (2009). *Methodology Report for the 2006 ANES Pilot Study.* Palo Alto, CA, and Ann Arbor, MI: Stanford University and the University of Michigan.

Dillman, D. A. (2000). *Mail and Internet surveys: The tailored design method* (2nd ed.). New York, NY: Wiley.

Finkel, S. E. (1995). *Causal analysis with panel data.* Thousand Oaks, CA: Sage.

Holbrook, A. L., Green, M. C., & Krosnick, J. A. (2003). Telephone versus face-to-face interviewing of national probability samples with long questionnaires. *Public Opinion Quarterly, 67,* 79–125. doi:10.1086/346010

Holbrook, A. L., Krosnick, J. A., & Pfent, A. (2008). The causes and consequences of response rates in surveys by the news media and government contractor survey research firms. In J. Lepkowski, C. Tucker, J. M. Brick, E. D. De Leeuw, L. Japec, P. J. Lavrakas, et al. (Eds.), *Advances in telephone survey methodology* (pp. 499–528). New York, NY: Wiley.

Holbrook, A. L., Krosnick, J. A., Visser, P. S., Gardner, W. L., & Cacioppo, J. T. (2001). Attitudes toward presidential candidates and political parties: Initial optimism, inertial first impressions, and a focus on flaws. *American Journal of Political Science, 45,* 930–950. doi:10.2307/2669333

Jarvis, W. B. G., & R. E. Petty. (1996). The need to evaluate. *Journal of Personality and Social Psychology, 70*, 172–194. doi:10.1037/0022-3514.70.1.172

Keeter, S., Miller, C., Kohut, A., Groves, R. M., & Presser, S. (2000). Consequences of reducing nonresponse in a national telephone survey. *Public Opinion Quarterly, 64*, 125–148. doi:10.1086/317759

Kinder, D. R., & Palfrey, T. R. (1993). On behalf of an experimental political science. In D. R. Kinder & T. R. Palfrey (Eds.), *Experimental foundations of political science* (pp. 1–39). Ann Arbor, MI: The University of Michigan Press.

Kish, L. (1965). *Survey sampling*. New York, NY: Wiley.

Krosnick, J. A., & Kinder, D. R. (1990). Altering popular support for the president through priming: The Iran-Contra affair. *The American Political Science Review, 84*, 497–512. doi:10.2307/1963531

Lee, E. S., & Forthofer, R. N. (2006). *Analyzing complex survey data*. Thousand Oaks, CA: Sage.

Miller, A. H. (1974). Political issues and trust in government: 1964–1970. *The American Political Science Review, 68*, 951–972. doi:10.2307/1959140

Piazza, T., & Sniderman, P. M. (1998). Incorporating experiments into computer assisted surveys. In M. P. Couper, R. P. Baker, J. Bethlehem, C. Z. F. Clark, J. Martin, W. L., Nicholls, & J. M. O'Reilly (Eds.), *Computer assisted survey information collection* (pp. 167–184). New York, NY: Wiley.

Rahn, W. M., Krosnick, J. A., & Breuning, M. (1994). Rationalization and derivation processes in survey studies of political candidate evaluation. *American Journal of Political Science, 38*, 582–600. doi:10.2307/2111598

Sears, D. O. (1986). College sophomores in the laboratory: Influences of a narrow data base on social psychology's view of human nature. *Journal of Personality and Social Psychology, 51*, 515–530. doi:10.1037/0022-3514.51.3.515

Shanks, J. M., Sanchez, M., & Morton, B. (1983). *Alternative approaches to survey data collection for the National Election Studies* (ANES Technical Report No. nes010120). Ann Arbor, MI: University of Michigan.

Silver, M. D., & Krosnick, J. A. (2001, May). *An experimental comparison of the quality of data obtained in telephone and self-administered mailed surveys with a listed sample*. Paper presented at the annual meeting of the American Association for Public Opinion Research, Montreal, Canada.

Visser, P. S., Krosnick, J. A., & Lavrakas, P. J. (2000). Survey research. In H. T. Reis & C. M. Judd (Eds.), *Handbook of research methods in social and personality psychology* (pp. 223–252). Cambridge, England: Cambridge University Press.

Visser, P. S., Krosnick, J. A., Marquette, J., & Kurtin, M. (1996). Mail surveys for election forecasting? An evaluation of the Columbus Dispatch Poll. *Public Opinion Quarterly, 60*, 181–227. doi:10.1086/297748

13

FAMILY-LEVEL VARIANCE IN VERBAL ABILITY CHANGE IN THE INTERGENERATIONAL STUDIES

KEVIN J. GRIMM, JOHN J. McARDLE, AND KEITH F. WIDAMAN

The Intergenerational Studies (IGS)[1] are a collection of three longitudinal studies—the Berkeley Growth Study (BGS), the Guidance Study (GS), and the Oakland Growth Study (OGS)—that began at the Institute of Human Development at the University of California, Berkeley, in the late 1920s and early 1930s. The participants in these studies have been repeatedly measured as children and adults, with the most recent measurements occurring in the 1990s for the GS and OGS, and in 2008 for the BGS. The three studies were initiated for different reasons, but they all include detailed repeated assessments of cognitive abilities, personality, social well-being, health, and socioeconomic status throughout the life span, as well as information on parenting, marriage, employment, and military service in adulthood. Additionally, information is available from and about their parents (Generation 1), their spouses, and their children (Generation 3). Taken together, the IGS is one of the most, if not the most, comprehensive life-span longitudinal study in the world.

---

[1]Data from the IGS are currently not publicly available. However, efforts are currently being made to make IGS data available to the research community. Interested researchers should contact the first author.

The IGS have provided results that established fundamental findings in the study of cognitive development across the life span. Bayley and Jones (1937) intensely studied the development of cognitive and motor skills during the first few years of life. Bayley (1955, 1957) continued to measure and track changes in cognitive abilities through adolescence and into adulthood, dealing with measurement issues as different cognitive tests were administered at different phases of development. Moreover, Bayley (e.g., 1964, 1968) was among the first to document continued growth in intellectual abilities during middle adulthood. Following Bayley's lead, Sands, Terry, and Meredith (1989) documented changes in item performance on the Wechsler intelligence tests (Wechsler–Bellevue Intelligence Scale [Wechsler, 1946], Wechsler Adult Intelligence Scale [WAIS; Wechsler, 1955], Wechsler Intelligence Scale for Children [Wechsler, 1949], and the Wechsler Adult Intelligence Scale—Revised [WAIS–R; Wechsler, 1981]) through adulthood. Sands, Terry, and Meredith reported positive changes (i.e., improvement) between ages 18 and 54 in the performance on items from verbal subtests (e.g., Information, Comprehension, and Vocabulary) but negative changes (i.e., decline) in answering difficult items from performance subtests (e.g., Picture Completion and Block Design). More recently, McArdle, Grimm, Hamagami, Bowles, and Meredith (2009) investigated the development of verbal ability and short-term memory from early childhood (age 4) to late adulthood (age 72) with data from the IGS archive. Overall, McArdle et al. (2009) found sharp increases in verbal ability and short-term memory through childhood and adolescence. However, the two cognitive constructs diverged in adulthood, as verbal ability was more or less maintained into late adulthood, whereas short-term memory peaked in the mid-20s and declined through adulthood into late adulthood.

In this chapter, we extend the work of McArdle et al. (2009) by describing the extent to which verbal ability and changes in verbal ability have a familial component. This work has been undertaken to add to the relatively small amount of genetic and family research that has focused on changes in cognitive ability. Family studies (e.g., twin, adoption, sibling, parents, and children studies) represent a unique data collection and analysis tool enabling researchers to estimate the level of familial transmission (e.g., genetic or family environment) and specific, nontransmissible environmental influences (Vogler & DeFries, 1985) in behavioral outcomes. Family studies can take many forms, some of which provide specific information regarding the magnitude of genetic and both shared and unshared environmental effects (i.e., twin and adoption studies). In terms of existing data, family data are part of several publicly available secondary data sets, including the National Longitudinal Survey of Youth (NLSY; e.g., Rodgers, Rowe, & Li, 1994) and the National Longitudinal Study of Adolescent Heath (e.g., Cleveland, 2003; Harris, Halpern, Smolen, & Haberstick, 2006).

FAMILIAL RESEMBLANCE IN COGNITIVE ABILITIES

The amount of familial similarity in cognitive abilities has been extensively studied, and previous studies have shown substantial amounts of genetic contribution in virtually all cognitive abilities and relatively small amounts of shared environmental variation. Familial resemblance or similarity represents an upper limit on the amount of genetic variation because familial resemblance is the sum of genetic and shared environmental variances. Estimating the amount of familial or genetic variation is a first step in the study of genetic influences.

Estimates of the genetic contribution to mental or cognitive abilities tend to vary depending on the aspect of cognition studied (e.g., see Finkel, Reynolds, McArdle, & Pedersen, 2005) and the ages at which participants were measured (e.g., see Bartels, Rietveld, Van Baal, & Boomsma, 2002). For example, estimates of the percentage of variance in cognitive abilities due to genetic sources have varied widely, with estimates ranging from 20% to 80%. Additionally, the combination of genetic and shared environment variation (which can be estimated using the IGS family data) has produced estimates upward of 85% (e.g., see McArdle & Goldsmith, 1990; Rietveld, Dolan, Van Baal, & Boomsma, 2003). However, traditional family studies tend to produce more modest estimates of familial resemblance than do twin studies, as midparent–offspring correlations (*midparent* is the average of the parents' scores) for cognitive abilities have ranged from .19 to .76 (see DeFries et al., 1979; Nagoshi & Johnson, 1993; Spuhler & Vandenberg, 1980).

Longitudinal family studies enable researchers to investigate the amount of familial resemblance in change (i.e., McArdle, 1986), as well as how the relative size of familial variance changes across time. Researchers often find that the amount of genetic contribution (familial variance) changes with age (i.e., depends on the age of participants; see McArdle, Prescott, Hamagami, & Horn, 1998) and that the familial (or combined genetic and shared environment) component of cognitive change is smaller than the familial component at any given occasion (or age).

Relatively few published studies have used longitudinal family data to examine the amount of genetic variation in cognitive change. McArdle, Prescott, Hamagami, and Horn (1998) fit longitudinal growth models to fluid (i.e., Block Design) and crystallized measures (i.e., Vocabulary) of cognition to twin data collected as part of the New York Twin Study. In the univariate growth models (with an intercept, linear slope, and a practice component), 33% of the variance in the linear slope for the crystallized measure was estimated to be genetically based, whereas 70% of the variance in the linear slope for the fluid measure was estimated to be genetic. In both variables, no contribution from shared environment was found.

More recently, Finkel, Reynolds, McArdle, and Pedersen (2005) fit longitudinal growth models to twin data from the Swedish Adoption Twin Study of Aging. A quadratic growth model was fit for verbal ability, and the genetic contributions to the intercept, linear slope, and quadratic slope were examined. Finkel et al. reported a large (79%) genetic contribution to the intercept (centered at age 65), a small (13%) and nonsignificant genetic contribution to the linear slope, and no genetic contribution to the quadratic slope. In their study of four cognitive abilities (verbal, spatial, memory, and speed), they found that the only significant genetic contribution to the linear slope was found for the speed factor (32%); however, larger genetic contributions were found for the quadratic slopes for certain abilities. Additionally, nonsignificant amounts of common environment variation were found in the intercepts and in the linear and quadratic slopes for all cognitive variables, suggesting that the development of these abilities arises from a combination of genetic and unshared environmental contributions.

USING EXISTING DATA TO STUDY DEVELOPMENTAL CHANGES

Existing data, public (e.g., Early Childhood Longitudinal Study—Kindergarten Cohort [ECLS–K; National Center for Education Statistics, 2001], NLSY) or private, are an extremely valuable, yet often underused, resource in psychological research, especially for studying developmental change. Several advantages of using existing data can be identified. Existing data, especially public-use data, are often either representative or contain sampling weights to obtain appropriate estimates when groups are oversampled, have measures of many constructs, and use a longitudinal measurement design, enabling researchers to examine change and lead-lag relationships. Additionally, many existing data sets include measurements of family or school units that enable researchers to account for the dependencies and cluster-level effects, making parameter estimates more precise. Finally, existing data are often freely obtainable, providing a very cost-effective way to conduct research.

However, existing data sets may not include data on the specific construct that the researcher is interested in, and the extensive data can lead researchers to more exploratory sorts of analysis as opposed to hypothesis-driven and more confirmatory analyses. That is, researchers may be tempted to search for interesting relations among variables in the database as opposed to formulating a research question and using existing data to help answer the research question. Additionally, many secondary data sets may lack extensive measurements of any particular construct because so many constructs are measured. In many cases, fewer items from a given measure are administered, leading to less reliable measures and making it difficult to compare scores (and parameter estimates) obtained from the secondary data set with scores obtained from other studies that used more complete or comprehensive measurements. For example, in the NLSY–Children and Young Adults, a measure of children's behavior—the Behavior Problems Index (Zill & Peterson, 1986)—has much in common with the Child Behavior Checklist (Achenbach & Edelbrock, 1983), a popular measure of children's behavior problems. However, direct comparison of these scores is not appropriate. A second example comes from the ECLS–K, in which the academic achievement measures (reading, mathematics, and general knowledge) were obtained using adaptive testing formats. That is, each participant was administered a set of items targeted toward his or her ability level. Even though participants were asked different sets of questions, their scores were comparable because the items have been linked using item response theory techniques. However, the ECLS–K cognitive ability scores are not comparable with commonly used cognitive ability measures (e.g., Woodcock–Johnson Tests of Achievement; Woodcock & Johnson, 1989) collected in other studies.

The foregoing considerations regarding the lack of comparability of scores across studies underscore the importance of the presence of item-level data. Item responses represent the most basic unit of data, and with item-level data, comparable scores can be created using linking techniques from item response theory if some items are shared by the measures used in the secondary and ancillary data sets, as long as differential item functioning is not present. Item-level data have been necessary to examine change in the IGS, as different measures of the same construct (e.g., verbal ability) have been administered throughout the course of the study.

METHOD

Intergenerational Studies

Berkeley Growth Study

The BGS was initiated in 1928 by Nancy Bayley (1932, 1943, 1949) to trace early mental, motor, and physical development during the first 2 years of life. Sixty-one infants born between September 15, 1928, and May 15, 1929, were enrolled into the study. An additional 14 infants were enrolled within the first 3 years of the study to replace infants who had moved, bringing the final sample size to 75.

The BGS was the most intensive study in the IGS. Data collection began shortly after the child's birth, as anthropometric and physiological measurements were made in the hospital by a pediatrician within 4 days of an infant's birth. The infants were assessed every month from 1 to 15 months, every 3 months from 18 through 36 months, and annually from 4 to 18 years of age. In adulthood, BGS participants were assessed at ages 21, 26, 36, 52, 66, and 72.[2]

Data from the BGS participants include measures of maternity and prenatal health, cognition, motor skills, personality, social behavior, anthropomorphic characteristics, psychological health, military service, marriage, alcohol, smoking, and physical examinations. Cognitive data come from the California First-Year Mental Scale (Bayley, 1933), California Preschool Mental Scale (Jaffa, 1934), Stanford–Binet (Terman, 1916), Wechsler–Bellevue, and WAIS.

Many children of the BGS participants ($N = 149$) were also repeatedly measured through childhood and adolescence with many of the same mental tests (e.g., California Preschool Mental Scale, Stanford–Binet, WAIS) administered to the original participants. The children of the BGS participants were assessed up to 17 times during childhood, adolescence, and early adulthood. Additionally, personality and mental test performance data are available from the parents (in 1968) and spouses of BGS participants (in 1980, 1994, and 2000).

Guidance Study

The GS was initiated in 1928 by Jean Macfarlane (1939). The 248 participants were drawn from a survey of every third birth in Berkeley, California, for the 18-month period starting January 1, 1928. Home visits began when infants were 3 months of age and continued through 18 months. Infants and parents were interviewed and tested every 6 months from 2 through 4 years and then annually from 5 to 18 years of age. In adulthood, the GS participants were assessed at 40 and 52 years of age. Measurements in the GS included medical examinations, health histories, anthropometric assessments, intelligence tests, socioeconomic and home variables, and personality characteristics.

As in the BGS, data from the children of the GS participants ($N = 424$) are available and include cognitive and personality assessments. These measurements were conducted in 1960 and 1970. Personality measures and mental tests were also administered to the parents (Generation 1) in 1970, and spouses of GS participants were assessed in 1970 and 1980.

Oakland Growth Study

The OGS began in 1931 under the guidance of Harold Jones, Mary Jones, and Herbert Stolz (Jones, 1938, 1939a, 1939b). A total of 212 students in 5th or 6th grade in elementary schools in Oakland were recruited to study

---

[2]McArdle et al. completed interviews with BGS participants and spouses in 2008 (age 80).

physical and physiological maturation and peer relationships through adolescence. Initial measurements were taken in 1932, when the participants ranged in age from 10 to 12 years.

OGS participants were assessed semiannually during the 6 years of junior and senior high school. Participants completed inventories of adjustment, interests and attitudes, and vocational preferences, as well as a series of intelligence and achievement tests. Additional information was obtained from parents, including measures of child health, personality, friendships, and interests, as well as parents' attitudes and behaviors toward child rearing. All OGS members had medical examinations, health histories, strength tests, and anthropometric measurements on a semiannual basis. In adulthood, OGS participants were measured at approximately 50 and 60 years of age.

The children of the OGS participants ($N = 334$) were repeatedly assessed through childhood and into adulthood with mental tests and personality measures. As with the GS, the children were assessed in 1960 and 1970. Spouses of OGS participants were also measured at the adult follow-ups. (Additional information regarding the IGS is available at http://psychology.ucdavis.edu/labs/Grimm/personal/IGS.html.)

Intergenerational Studies Data Archive

The IGS data are archived at the Institute of Human Development at the University of California, Berkeley. Original documents of all tests and measures, as well as interesting notes and documented interactions between study members and project leaders, are stored. Electronic data files for many of the major tests and measures were created in the 1970s. In the early 1980s, Jack McArdle and Mark Welge coded the Wechsler intelligence tests (Wechsler–Bellevue, WAIS, and WAIS–R) administered to the original participants in adulthood at the item level. Over the past few years, the first two authors of this chapter made several visits to UC Berkeley to copy and code all Stanford–Binet (1916 Stanford–Binet Forms L and M (Terman & Merrill, 1937), and LM (Terman & Merrill, 1960) and remaining Wechsler intelligence tests at the item level.[3]

Change Information and Measurement Equating

The IGS provides a wealth of data across the life span, but extracting longitudinal change information across this extended time period is not always straightforward. For example, in the work by Block (1971) examining life-span development of personality, Q-sort data had to be constructed because Q-sorts

---

[3]The IGS data archive is now located in the Department of Psychology at the University of California, Davis.

were not administered in adolescence and early adulthood. Q-sort ratings were made by three clinically trained professionals and were based on case material from the relevant life stage (see Huffine & Aerts, 1998).

As previously mentioned, McArdle et al. (2009) investigated life-span development of verbal ability and short-term memory with data from the IGS. In this project, McArdle et al. (2009) attempted to separate changes in participants' ability over the life span from changes in the intelligence tests, collating information from the 16 different intelligence batteries that had been administered over the course of the study. To separate change in ability from change in testing protocols, an outside data set—the Bradway–McArdle Longitudinal Study (Bradway, 1944; McArdle, Hamagami, Meredith, & Bradway, 2000)—was included because these participants took multiple intelligence tests (i.e., WAIS and Stanford–Binet) within a short period of time. Item-level data were analyzed because the revisions of the Stanford–Binet (e.g., 1916 Stanford–Binet Forms L, M, and LM) and Wechsler scales (e.g., WAIS and WAIS–R) shared items even though their scale or raw scores were not comparable because the tests had a different number of items, different standardization samples, and/or do not contain all of the same items. McArdle et al. (2009) fit a combined item response and nonlinear growth model to examine the growth and decline of verbal ability and short-term memory across the life span.

Longitudinal Item-Level Data

Item-level data are available for a select set of intelligence tests that represent the most comprehensive and often administered scales in the IGS. These include the Stanford–Binet (1916 Stanford–Binet, 1937 Revisions, and 1960 Revision) and Wechsler intelligence scales (Wechsler–Bellevue, Wechsler Intelligence Scale for Children, WAIS, and WAIS–R). Table 13.1 contains information on the number of participants in Generations 2 and 3 for which intelligence test data are available. The item-level data from the vocabulary scales, as well as item data from the Information Scale of the Wechsler tests, were combined into a single data file as if the items composed a single test. This longitudinal file contained multiple records per participant to represent the repeated nature of the data. The file contained a total of 231 items and 4,563 records from 1,373 individual participants from 501 families.

Analytic Techniques

Verbal Ability Estimates

Verbal ability was estimated at each measurement occasion using a strategy similar to that applied by McArdle et al. (2009). Under this approach, the

TABLE 13.1
Number of Subjects and Total Data Points Available for Each Intelligence Test Broken Down by Study and Generation

Intelligence test	BGS (G2)	BGS children (G3)	GS (G2)	GS children (G3)	OGS (G2)	OGS children (G3)
1916 Stanford–Binet						
Subjects	58	—	211	—	202	—
Data points	107	—	409	—	203	—
Stanford–Binet Form L						
Subjects	62	139	212	303	—	251
Data points	235	621	634	387	—	309
Stanford–Binet Form M						
Subjects	61	142	199	63	152	—
Data points	171	496	375	63	158	—
Stanford–Binet Form LM						
Subjects	—	—	—	20	—	5
Data points	—	—	—	25	—	5
Wechsler–Bellevue						
Subjects	50	85	157	—	—	—
Data points	151	90	157	—	—	—
Wechsler Intelligence Scale for Children						
Subjects	—	63	—	244	—	65
Data points	—	73	—	245	—	65
Wechsler Adult Intelligence Scale						
Subjects	54	59	156	100	78	158
Data points	54	60	156	100	78	158
Wechsler Adult Intelligence Scale—Revised						
Subjects	42	—	118	—	78	—
Data points	61	—	118	—	78	—

Note. BGS = Berkeley Growth Study; GS = Guidance Study; OGS = Oakland Growth Study; G2 = Generation 2; G3 = Generation 3. A dash indicates patients were not administered the scale.

longitudinal item-level data were stacked such that repeated observations were contained as multiple records (e.g., long file). The partial credit model (PCM; Masters, 1982) was fit to the item-level data, without accounting for the dependency due to the repeated observations, and person–ability estimates were derived from the model for each person at each occasion. The PCM can be written as

$$\ln\left(\frac{PX[t]_{in}}{1 - PX[t]_{in}}\right) = \theta[t]_n - \beta_i, \tag{1}$$

where $PX[t]_{in}$ is the probability the response of person n to item i is in category x, given that the response is either in category x or $x-1$, $\theta[t]_n$ is the ability estimate for person n at time t, and β_i is the item step difficulty (which is assumed to be constant across time). The ability estimates ($\theta[t]_n$) were then used as observed scores in the growth curve analysis to account for the dependency due to participants being repeated testing and coming from the same family.

Family Growth Curve Model

The family growth curve model was fit as a three-level nonlinear multilevel model (Bryk & Raudenbush, 1992), with the repeated assessments nested within participants and participants nested within families. Growth modeling (McArdle, 1986, 1988; Meredith & Tisak, 1990; Rogosa & Willett, 1985) is a contemporary analytic technique for modeling systematic within-person change across a series of repeated measurements and between-persons differences in change. A dual exponential growth curve was found to be an adequate representation of individual changes and individual differences in the growth and decline of verbal ability with the original participants (see McArdle et al., 2009), and this nonlinear curve was fit to the family data. The dual exponential has been found to adequately model changes in life-span cognitive abilities because it allows for growth as well as decline in ability (see McArdle, Ferrer-Caja, Hamagami, & Woodcock, 2002). The family curve with a dual exponential growth pattern can be written as

$$\theta[t]_{nj} = I_{nj} + S_{nj} \cdot \left(\exp(-a_1 \cdot t) - \exp(-a_2 \cdot t)\right) + e[t]_{nj}, \tag{2}$$

where $\theta[t]_{nj}$ is the estimated verbal ability score from the PCM for participant n in family j at age t, I_{nj} is the intercept score for participant n in family j, S_{nj} is the slope score for participant n in family j representing the individual's rate of change, a_1 is the rate of decline (as participants reach older adulthood), a_2 is the rate of growth (as participants increase in age from early childhood through adolescence and into adulthood), and $e[t]_{nj}$ is a time-specific residual score. The individual intercept and slope can be decomposed into family-level scores and individual deviations from the family-level scores such as

$$I_{nj} = \beta_{0j} + u_{0nj}$$
$$S_{nj} = \beta_{1j} + u_{1nj},$$ (3)

where β_{0j} and β_{1j} are the family-level intercept and slope scores for family j and u_{0nj} and u_{1nj} are individual deviations from the family-level scores for participant n in family j. Finally, the family-level intercept and slope scores are composed of sample-level means (γ_{00}, γ_{10}) and family-level deviations (s_{00j}, s_{10j}), such as

$$\beta_{0j} = \gamma_{00} + s_{00j}$$
$$\beta_{1j} = \gamma_{10} + s_{10j}.$$ (4)

The variability of u_{0nj} compared with s_{00j} and u_{1nj} compared with s_{10j} indicates the amount of within-family versus between-families variance in the intercept and slope, and the ratio of between-families variance to total variance for the intercept and slope are estimates of familial resemblance. The family growth curve models were fit using Mplus 4.13 (Muthén & Muthén, 1998-2007). Input and output scripts can be downloaded from http://psychology.ucdavis.edu/labs/Grimm/personal/downloads.html.

RESULTS

Verbal Ability Estimates

The model-based reliability under a partial credit model was .97; however, this estimated reliability was likely to be positively biased because the dependencies among observations that were not modeled with the PCM. On average, individuals were administered 38.6 items (17.9% of the items in which there was variability in the response pattern). The estimated ability scores (i.e., $\theta[t]_n$) are a function of the items administered and the person's pattern of correct and incorrect responses. The scale of the ability estimates, as well as of the item difficulties, is in the logit metric, which is an arbitrary scaling of the scores (i.e., as is the scale of factor scores). The logit metric was scaled such that the mean item difficulty was zero and item discrimination was 1. In this scale, the mean and standard deviation of the person ability was estimated to be −1.38 and 3.72, respectively.

The verbal ability estimates for each person are plotted against the persons' age at testing in Panels A and B of Figure 13.1 for the original subjects (Generation 2) and the children of the original subjects (Generation 3),

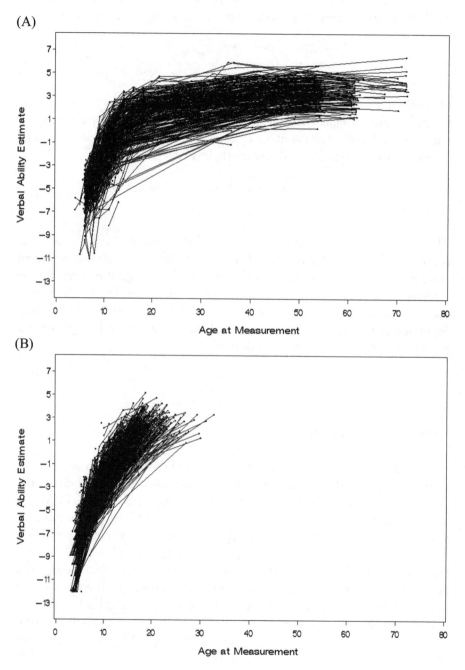

Figure 13.1. Longitudinal plots of verbal ability for (A) Generation 2 and (B) Generation 3 of the Intergenerational Studies.

respectively. The longitudinal trajectories are represented for each person, and the scores have, under the PCM, the same interpretation at ages ranging from 3 to 75. Changes in verbal ability from ages 3 to 75 appear to be rapid through childhood and adolescence, after which there was little or no decline in verbal ability through older adulthood.

Longitudinal Growth and Family Modeling

Parameter estimates and their respective standard errors from the dual exponential family growth curve are contained in Table 13.2. The intercept was centered at age 10 years, making estimates associated with the intercept (i.e., intercept mean, and the family and individual-level intercept deviations) indicative of parameters at age 10. The growth and decline rates control the overall shape of the curve and are important parameters for describing changes in verbal ability across the life span. The growth rate was .126, the decline rate

TABLE 13.2
Parameter Estimates and Standard Errors for the Dual Exponential Family
Growth Curve for Verbal Ability

Parameter	Parameter estimate (standard error)
Fixed effect parameters	
Intercept (γ_{00})	−1.94*
	(.053)
Slope (γ_{10})	6.23*
	(.163)
Decline rate (a_1)	.005*
	(.001)
Growth rate (a_2)	.126*
	(.003)
Random effect parameters	
Family-level intercept deviation (s_{00j})	.78*
	(.109)
Family-level slope deviation (s_{10j})	.32*
	(.126)
Family-level intercept–slope correlation	.08
	(.157)
Individual-level intercept deviation (u_{0ij})	.70*
	(.068)
Individual-level slope deviation (u_{1ij})	.61*
	(.110)
Individual-level intercept–slope correlation	−.63*
	(.091)
Residual deviation ($e[t]_{ij}$)	.82*
	(.050)

* $p < .05$.

was .005, and both were significantly different from zero, suggesting a rapid increase in verbal ability through childhood and a very slight decline in verbal ability into older adulthood. Previous research with IGS and additional life-span data (e.g., McArdle et al., 2009; McArdle, Ferrer-Caja, Hamagami, & Woodcock, 2002) has found similar significant, but relatively small, estimates of decline in verbal ability through older adulthood.

The mean intercept was −1.94, and the mean slope was 6.23. Therefore, performance at age 10 is about .17 deviations less than the average for the sample. The mean intercept represents the expected family score for verbal ability at age 10, and the mean slope represents how rapidly verbal ability was expected to grow for the average family. Significant between-families and within-family variances were obtained for the intercept as well as the slope, indicating that families differed in their verbal ability at age 10 years and in how quickly they change across the life span. Additionally, these estimates captured how family members differed from one another in their level of verbal ability at age 10 and how quickly they changed across the life span. Fifty-five percent of the variation in the intercept was at the family level, whereas 22% of the slope variance was at the family level. These percentages represent how families differ from one another and reveal the extent of familial resemblance in verbal ability and verbal ability change. The mean predicted trajectory of verbal ability is shown in Figure 13.2 surrounded by two times the expected family-level and then two times the expected individual-level standard deviations. This plot gives a visual representation of the relationship of the expected between-families variance compared with the within-family variance at each age across the life span.

DISCUSSION

In this chapter, we presented new analyses of existing IGS data to help understand the development of verbal ability across the life span and to examine familial variation in verbal ability and verbal ability change. Specifically, we examined the extent to which the level (e.g., at age 10 years) and the life-span changes in verbal ability had a family component. Overall, 55% of the true variability at age 10 and 22% of the variance in change was between families, suggesting a sizable amount of between-families differences in the intercept and slope. The relative amount of between-families variances are a measure of familial resemblance, as they represent the extent to which families differ from one another. The greater amount of variance between families is directly related to the magnitudes of the correlations among members within a family. The estimates of between-families variance in the intercept and slope were consistent with estimates from previous family and longitudinal family studies. The

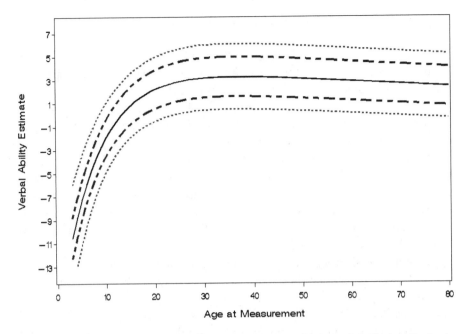

Figure 13.2. Expected life span trajectory for verbal ability based on the longitudinal family models. Solid line is the expected mean trajectory; hard dashed lines are a two standard deviation confidence boundary of the expected between-families variance; soft dashed lines are an additional two standard deviation confidence boundary of the expected within-family variance.

familial component for the intercept was nearly identical to the median value (.53) reported by DeFries et al. (1979) for regressions of midchild (i.e., average of children's scores) on midparent cognitive scores. The size of the between-families variance for the slope was slightly higher than the heritability estimate for the linear slope reported by Finkel et al. (2005) but was lower than estimates for quadratic slope. These discrepancies in the amount of familial resemblance in rates of change were likely to be due to differences across studies in the ages at which participants were assessed, the particular measured variables analyzed, the use of alternative (e.g., twin vs. family) study designs, and the homogeneity of participants in the IGS, among other factors. But differences can also arise because two sources of interindividual differences in change were evaluated in the quadratic growth model fit by Finkel et al. (2005), whereas only one source of interindividual differences in change was included in the exponential model fit in this project. The estimate of familial resemblance was in line with the heritability estimate obtained by McArdle, Prescott, Hamagami, and Horn (1998) for vocabulary ability change (33% genetic; 0% shared environmental), even though the age ranges were distinct across studies.

CONCLUDING REMARKS

The analysis of secondary data is an excellent way to begin or continue a line of research. As a starting point, secondary data analysis can help inform future data collection efforts in terms of the sampling of individuals, measurement occasions, and constructs. Furthermore, recent attention has been placed on the integrative data analysis or the analysis of multiple data sets simultaneously (see Curran & Hussong, 2009; Hofer & Piccinin, 2009; McArdle & Horn, 2002), where the goal is to synthesize research information—much like the goal of meta-analysis. This is an ideal way to continue a line of inquiry, and the use of existing or secondary data is necessary for these purposes, whether the goal is to conduct parallel or coordinated analyses (see Hofer & Piccinin, 2009) or to conduct a mega-analysis (see McArdle & Horn, 2002).

There are always going to be challenges when it comes to conducting research. The biggest challenge of secondary data analysis is usually data access—many researchers are unwilling to share data they spent so long collecting. We hope that the barrier to accessing secondary data will fall and researchers will consider the benefits of having their data conceptualized and analyzed in a different light. Similarly, researchers interested in accessing secondary data will recognize the cost, in terms of money and time, spent to collect the data (especially longitudinal data of the kind considered here). We hope also that consortiums can be created so that the analysis of secondary data can be beneficial to all involved (see Hofer & Piccinin, 2009).

The analysis of existing data sets is likely to become more common in the future as funding agencies advocate their use as a cost-effective means of examining hypotheses in nonexperimental settings before allocating funds for experimental types of research (e.g., Institute for Education Sciences). Additionally, researchers who collect data using funds from granting agencies have been encouraged to make their data available to the research community, and many state departments of education are now making longitudinal student-level data available to the research community. Therefore, secondary data are likely to become more available in the coming years, and researchers should take greater advantage of the opportunities afforded by such data to help answer questions that fall beyond the boundaries of the issues that drove the original investigators to engage in the original data collection. In using such data to answer new questions, current researchers can stand on the shoulders of giants to exploit existing data, collected across long spans of time using painstaking methods, and to answer questions that cannot be answered without such available data. The use of secondary data to answering pressing research questions cannot be understated.

RECOMMENDED DATA SETS

- *National Longitudinal Surveys of Youth:* http://www.bls.gov/nls/
- *National Institute of Child Health and Human Developmen Study of Early Child Care:* http://secc.rti.org/
- *National Longitudinal Study of Adolescent Health:* http://www.nichd.nih.gov/health/topics/add_health_study.cfm
- *Early Childhood Longitudinal Studies:* http://nces.ed.gov/ecls/

FOR FURTHER READING

Block, J. (1971). *Lives through time.* Berkeley, CA: Bancroft Books.

Block's book is about his interesting investigation into stability and change in personality across the life span, using data from the IGS.

Elder, G. H., Jr. (1974). *Children of the great depression: Social change in life experience.* Chicago, IL: University of Chicago Press.

Elder compares how the economic hardships of the Great Depression differentially affected the participants from OGS and GS, as the OGS participants were approximately 12 years older.

McArdle, J. J., Grimm, K. J., Hamagami, F., Bowles, R. P., & Meredith, W. (2009). Modeling life span growth curves of cognition using longitudinal data with multiple samples and changing scales of measurement. *Psychological Methods, 14,* 126–149.

This article includes descriptions and discussions about linking longitudinal data using item response models to examine change. Alternative methods are also discussed and evaluated.

Hofer, S. M., & Piccinin, A. M. (2009). Integrative data analysis through coordination of measurement and analysis protocol across independent longitudinal studies. *Psychological Methods, 14,* 150–164.

This article describes and presents results from the Integrative Analysis of Longitudinal Studies on Aging Project—a project to coordinate analyses on existing longitudinal studies of aging.

REFERENCES

Achenbach, T. M., & Edelbrock, C. (1983). *Manual for the Child Behavior Checklist and Revised Child Behavior Profile.* Burlington, VT: University of Vermont Department of Psychiatry.

Bartels, M., Rietveld, M. J. H., Van Baal, G. C. M., & Boomsma, D. I. (2002). Genetic and environmental influences on the development of intelligence. *Behavior Genetics, 32,* 237–249. doi:10.1023/A:1019772628912

Bayley, N. (1932). A study of the crying of infants during mental and physical tests. *The Journal of Genetic Psychology, 40,* 306–329.

Bayley, N. (1933). *The California First-Year Mental Scale.* Berkeley, CA: University of California Press.

Bayley, N. (1943). Skeletal maturing in adolescence as a basis for determining percentage of completed growth. *Child Development, 14,* 1–46. doi:10.2307/1125612

Bayley, N. (1949). Consistency and variability in the growth of intelligence from birth to eighteen years. *The Journal of Genetic Psychology, 75,* 165–196.

Bayley, N. (1955). On the growth of intelligence. *American Psychologist, 10,* 805–818. doi:10.1037/h0043803

Bayley, N. (1957). Data on the growth of intelligence between 16 and 21 years as measured by the Wechsler–Bellevue Scale. *The Journal of Genetic Psychology, 90,* 3–15.

Bayley, N. (1964). Consistency of maternal and child behaviors in the Berkeley Growth Study. *Vita Humana, 7,* 73–95.

Bayley, N. (1968). Behavioral correlates of mental growth: Birth to thirty-six years. *American Psychologist, 23,* 1–17. doi:10.1037/h0037690

Bayley, N., & Jones, H. E. (1937). Environmental correlates of mental and motor development: A cumulative study from infancy to six years. *Child Development, 8,* 329–341.

Block, J. (1971). *Lives through time.* Berkeley, CA: Bancroft Books.

Bradway, K. P. (1944). IQ constancy on the Revised Stanford–Binet from the preschool to the junior high school level. *The Journal of Genetic Psychology, 65,* 197–217.

Bryk, A. S., & Raudenbush, S. W. (1992). *Hierarchical linear models: Applications and data analysis methods.* Newbury Park, CA: Sage.

Cleveland, H. H. (2003). Disadvantaged neighborhoods and adolescent aggression: Behavioral genetic evidence of contextual effects. *Journal of Research on Adolescence, 13,* 211–238.

Curran, P. J., & Hussong, A. M. (2009). Integrative data analysis: The simultaneous analysis of multiple data sets. *Psychological Methods, 14,* 81–100. doi:10.1037/a0015914

DeFries, J. C., Johnson, R. C., Kuse, A. R., McClearn, G. E., Polovina, J., Vandenberg, S., & Wilson, J. R. (1979). Familial resemblance for specific cognitive abilities. *Behavior Genetics, 9,* 23–43.

Finkel, D., Reynolds, C. A., McArdle, J. J., & Pedersen, N. L. (2005). The longitudinal relationship between processing speed and cognitive ability: Genetic and environmental influences. *Behavior Genetics, 35,* 535–549. doi:10.1007/s10519-005-3281-5

Harris, K. M., Halpern, C. T., Smolen, A., & Haberstick, B. C. (2006). The National Longitudinal Study of Adolescent Health (Add Health) twin data. *Twin Research and Human Genetics, 9*, 988–997. doi:10.1375/twin.9.6.988

Hofer, S. M., & Piccinin, A. M. (2009). Integrative data analysis through coordination of measurement and analysis protocol across independent longitudinal studies. *Psychological Methods, 14*, 150–164. doi:10.1037/a0015566

Huffine, C. L., & Aerts, E. (1998). *The Intergenerational Studies at the Institute of Human Developmental University of California, Berkeley: Longitudinal studies of children and families, 1928–present: A guide to the data archives.* Available from http://ihd.berkeley.edu/igsguide2.pdf

Jaffa, A. S. (1934). *The California Preschool Mental Scale, Form A.* Berkeley, CA: University of California Press.

Jones, H. E. (1938). The California Adolescent Growth Study. *The Journal of Educational Research, 31*, 561–567.

Jones, H. E. (1939a). The Adolescent Growth Study: Principles and methods. *Journal of Consulting Psychology, 3*, 157–159. doi:10.1037/h0050181

Jones, H. E. (1939b). The Adolescent Growth Study: Procedures. *Journal of Consulting Psychology, 3*, 177–180. doi:10.1037/h0060864

Macfarlane, J. W. (1939). The Guidance Study. *Sociometry, 2*, 1–23. doi:10.2307/2785296

Masters, G. N. (1982). A Rasch model for partial credit scoring. *Psychometrika, 47*, 149–174. doi:10.1007/BF02296272

McArdle, J. J. (1986). Latent variable growth within behavior genetic models. *Behavior Genetics, 16*, 163–200. doi:10.1007/BF01065485

McArdle, J. J. (1988). Dynamic but structural equation modeling of repeated measures data. In J. R. Nesselroade & R. B. Cattell (Eds.), *Handbook of multivariate experimental psychology* (2nd ed., pp. 561–614). New York, NY: Plenum Press.

McArdle, J. J., Ferrer-Caja, E., Hamagami, F., & Woodcock, R. W. (2002). Comparative longitudinal structural analyses of the growth and decline of multiple intellectual abilities over the life span. *Developmental Psychology, 38*, 115–142. doi:10.1037/0012-1649.38.1.115

McArdle, J. J., & Goldsmith, H. H. (1990). Alternative common factor models for multivariate biometric analyses. *Behavior Genetics, 20*, 569–608. doi:10.1007/BF01065873

McArdle, J. J., Grimm, K. J., Hamagami, F., Bowles, R. P., & Meredith, W. (2009). Modeling life span growth curves of cognition using longitudinal data with multiple samples and changing scales of measurement. *Psychological Methods, 14*, 126–149. doi:10.1037/a0015857

McArdle, J. J., Hamagami, F., Meredith, W., & Bradway, K. P. (2000). Modeling the dynamic hypotheses of Gf-Gc theory using longitudinal life-span data. *Learning and Individual Differences, 12*, 53–79. doi:10.1016/S1041-6080(00)00036-4

McArdle, J. J., & Horn, J. L. (2002, October). *The benefits and limitations of mega-analysis with illustrations for the WAIS*. Paper presented at the 18th International Conference of Committee on Data for Science and Technology, Montreal, Quebec, Canada.

McArdle, J. J., Prescott, C. A., Hamagami, F., & Horn, J. L. (1998). A contemporary method for developmental–genetic analyses of age changes in intellectual abilities. *Developmental Neuropsychology, 14*, 69–114. doi:10.1080/8756564980954 0701

Meredith, W., & Tisak, J. (1990). Latent curve analysis. *Psychometrika, 55*, 107–122. doi:10.1007/BF02294746

Muthén, L. K., & Muthén, B. O. (1998–2007). *Mplus user's guide* (4th ed.). Los Angeles, CA: Authors.

Nagoshi, C. T., & Johnson, R. C. (1993). Familial transmission of cognitive abilities in offspring tested in adolescence and adulthood: A longitudinal study. *Behavior Genetics, 23*, 279–285. doi:10.1007/BF01082467

National Center for Education Statistics. (2001). *User's manual for the ECLS–K public-use data files and electronic codebook*. Washington, DC: U.S. Department of Education.

Rietveld, M. J. H., Dolan, C. V., Van Baal, G. C. M., & Boomsma, D. I. (2003). A twin study of differentiation of cognitive abilities in childhood. *Behavior Genetics, 33*, 367–381. doi:10.1023/A:1025388908177

Rodgers, J. L., Rowe, D. C., & Li, C. (1994). Beyond nature versus nurture: DF Analysis of nonshared influences on problem behaviors. *Developmental Psychology, 30*, 374–384. doi:10.1037/0012-1649.30.3.374

Rogosa, D. R., & Willett, J. B. (1985). Understanding correlates of change by modeling individual differences in growth. *Psychometrika, 50*, 203–228. doi:10.1007/BF02294247

Sands, L. P., Terry, H., & Meredith, W. (1989). Change and stability in adult intellectual functioning assessed by Wechsler item responses. *Psychology and Aging, 4*, 79–87. doi:10.1037/0882-7974.4.1.79

Spuhler, K. P., & Vandenberg, S. G. (1980). Comparison of parent–offspring resemblance for specific cognitive abilities. *Behavior Genetics, 10*, 413–418. doi:10.1007/BF01065603

Terman, L. M. (1916). *The measurement of intelligence*. Boston, MA: Houghton Mifflin.

Terman, L. M. & Merrill, M. A. (1937). *Measuring intelligence*. Boston, MA: Houghton Mifflin.

Terman, L. M. & Merrill, M. A. (1960). *Measuring intelligence*. Cambridge, MA: Houghton Mifflin.

Vogler, G. P., & DeFries, J. C. (1985). Bivariate path analysis of familial resemblance for reading ability and symbol processing speed. *Behavior Genetics, 15*, 111–121. doi:10.1007/BF01065892

Wechsler, D. (1946). *The Wechsler–Bellevue Intelligence Scale*. New York, NY: Psychological Corporation.

Wechsler, D. (1949). *Wechsler Intelligence Scale for Children*. New York, NY: Psychological Corporation.

Wechsler, D. (1955). *Manual for the Wechsler Adult Intelligence Scale*. New York, NY: Psychological Corporation.

Wechsler, D. (1981). *WAIS–R manual*. New York, NY: Psychological Corporation.

Woodcock, R. W. & Johnson, M. B. (1989). *Woodcock–Johnson Psycho-Educational Battery—Revised*. Allen, TX: DLM Teaching Resources.

Zill, N., & Peterson, J. L. (1986). *Behavior Problems Index*. Washington, DC: Child Trends.

INDEX

BHPS. *See* British Household
    Panel Survey
Bias
    confirmation, 50
    nonresponse, 196
    sampling weights for, 95
    from statistical perspective, 65n3
Biased mean, 68
Bibliography of Data-Related Literature,
    22
Big Five dimensions of personality, 54,
    109
Big Five Inventory (BFI), 109
Biomarkers, 114
Biomedical studies, 124
Bizer, G. Y., 199
Block, J., 215
Blozis, S. A., 166
Bowles, R. P., 210
Brannon, L., 199
British Household Panel Survey
    (BHPS), 105–106, 109, 115–116

Cacioppo, J. T., 198
Calhoun, C., 166
California Health Kids Survey, 166
Campbell, Angus, 193
Campbell, D., 50, 85
Canadian Research Institute for Social
    Policy at the University of New
    Brunswick (UNB-CRISP), 27
Candidate evaluation, 198, 201
CAP (Colorado Adoption Project),
    134–135
CAPI (computer-assisted personal
    interviewing techniques),
    112–113
Causal generalizations, 85
Centre for Longitudinal Studies in the
    Institution of Education at the
    University of London, 172
Change(s)
    in ability vs. in testing protocols, 216
    developmental. *See* Developmental
        changes
    in diagnostic criteria, 153–154
    long-term, 123–124
    over time, 198–199
    in verbal ability. *See* Verbal ability
        and verbal ability change

Children of the Great Depression (G. H.
    Elder, Jr.), 164
Chin, N., 34
Cholesky model, 142–143
Clark, L. A., 46
Climate, culture and, 182–183
Climatic demands, 183–184, 186–188
Climato-economic niches, 183–184, 188
Cluster effect, 67
Cluster sampling, 71–72
Codebook(s)
    for ANES measures, 200–201
    as documentation, 17
    public access, 75n9
    quality of information in, 33–35
Coding, 159
Coefficient alpha, 41–42, 44–45, 54
Coefficient omega, 43–45, 54
Cognitive abilities, 113, 211–212
Cognitive development, 210
Cognitive testing, 112–114
Cohen, D., 178
Cohort and cell diagram, 33, 34
Collection methods, 109–115
Collective income, 186
Collectivistic cultures, 178–179
College students, 14, 29
Colorado Adoption Project (CAP),
    134–135
Comorbidity, of mental disorders,
    150–151
Comparative studies, 179
Comparative Study of Electoral Systems
    (CSES), 204
Comparisons, cultural, 179
Complex variables, 31–32
Computer-assisted personal interview-
    ing techniques (CAPI), 112–113
    audio computer-assisted self-
        interview, 169
    self-administered questionnaires, 196
Confidentiality, 23, 75
Confirmation bias, 50
Conflict, culture-based, 177–178
Conger, K. J., 166
Consequences (culture), 177–179
Constructs
    in American National Election
        Study, 201–202
    in data collections, 19

ABOUT THE EDITORS

Kali H. Trzesniewski, PhD, is an assistant professor of developmental psychology at the University of Western Ontario. Dr. Trzesniewski's research interests are at the intersections of developmental psychology, personality psychology, and social psychology. Her current research focuses on biological and social-cultural influences on the development of the self and self-related processes. To address her research questions, she uses secondary data sets, along with primary data.

M. Brent Donnellan, PhD, is an associate professor of social and personality psychology at Michigan State University. He is currently an associate editor of the *Journal of Research in Personality*. Dr. Donnellan's research interests are at the intersections of personality psychology, developmental psychology, and psychological assessment, and he has analyzed secondary data in several of his publications. His current efforts focus on personality development and the role of individual differences in interpersonal relationships.

Richard E. Lucas, PhD, is an associate professor of psychology at Michigan State University. His research focuses on the factors that contribute to stability and change in subjective well-being. He has served as an associate editor for the *Journal of Personality and Social Psychology* and is currently editor-in-chief of the *Journal of Research in Personality*. He is a coauthor of the book *Well-Being and Public Policy*, which examines the role that well-being measures can play in informing public policy decisions.